The Chicken Runs at Midnight is a beau[...] [...].
Tom Friend does a wonderful job of w[...] d
telling you a story that will give you the chills. You will cry; you will laugh; and
you will tell the story over and over again—just as I have.

Craig Counsell, manager of the Milwaukee Brewers

How do you begin to describe a story that defies description? Well, Tom
Friend has done it, masterfully. He has captured the essence of what made Rich
Donnelly one of the most respected men in baseball without sugar-coating his
personal trials. And he leaves us wishing we had been lucky enough to have met
Rich's daughter, Amy. It is the fascinating story of a girl with a vision and a man
after God's own heart.

Ernie Johnson Jr., TBS/TNT sportscaster, author of
the *New York Times* bestseller *Unscripted*

The Chicken Runs at Midnight is the kind of heartwarming story *all* of us need,
not just baseball fans. In our loud, busy world, it's a poignant reminder of what
is truly important.

Tom Verducci, bestselling author of *The Yankee Years* and *The Cubs Way*

In *The Chicken Runs at Midnight*, Tom Friend does a masterful job of depicting
how the tragic death of Rich Donnelly's daughter, Amy, resulted in the ultimate
victory of the human spirit. Through it all, it's clear to see that Rich was not
only a great baseball man in his day. He's also an outstanding human being.

Congressman Pete King, 2nd District, New York

I enjoy everything Tom Friend writes, and the story of Rich Donnelly and his
dying daughter's encouragement is one of the most compelling I've heard in more
than three decades of covering baseball. This book is sure to be a must-read.

Ken Rosenthal, The Athletic/Fox Sports/MLB Network

Rich Donnelly is one of the funniest people I've ever met—in baseball and in
life. But more important, he's one of the most amazing human beings I've ever
met. So I'm so glad he and Tom Friend have collaborated on this incredible book.

You'll laugh. You'll cry. But when you're through, you'll know the real, beautiful Rich Donnelly his friends know. And you'll be glad you do.

Jayson Stark, senior baseball writer, *The Athletic*

The Chicken Runs at Midnight moved me from the minute I began reading it. Having grown up as a Braves fan in the 1990s when Sid Bream slid in safely at home and having watched the '97 World Series, I was mesmerized. But also getting to spend some time with Rich Donnelly at the 2017 World Baseball Classic made this book even more special to read. I admire Rich for putting himself out there with total transparency, and Tom Friend for telling the story with passion. I'm sure this book will help many people in more ways than one!

Buster Posey, San Francisco Giants catcher, five-time All-Star selection, and 2012 National League MVP

Tom Friend has written a sweet book that tells the story of family, faith, death, and redemption. What lives beyond the pages is the indomitable spirit of an unforgettable young woman.

Gary Pomerantz, author of *The Last Pass: Cousy, Russell, the Celtics, and What Matters in the End*

Our daughter, Babe, died of brain tumors in 2005. When I saw the video of Rich's story, I cried. I picked up the phone and called Rich. For the next two hours, we bonded like we had been friends for years. I told him about the Canuso Foundation and our "Babe's Kids" program. I invited him to come to New Jersey and tell the story of Amy and "the chicken runs at midnight" for a group of high schools in our region. Wherever Rich spoke, the audience was overwhelmed and in tears. Rich's story is some sort of miracle, and it motivates people who hear it. He is a good man and a great father with an incredible story.

John Canuso, founder and president of the Canuso Foundation

Tom Friend's *The Chicken Runs at Midnight* is an incredible story beautifully told. It's much more than a sports book; it's a wonderful gift to our culture.

Christine Brennan, USA Today sports columnist; CNN, ABC News, and *PBS NewsHour* commentator; bestselling author of *Inside Edge*

The Chicken Runs at Midnight

*A Daughter's Message from Heaven That
Changed a Father's Heart and Won a World Series*

TOM FRIEND

ZONDERVAN
BOOKS

ZONDERVAN BOOKS

The Chicken Runs at Midnight
Copyright © 2018 by Tom Friend

Published in Grand Rapids, Michigan, by Zondervan. Zondervan is a registered trademark of The Zondervan Corporation, L.L.C., a wholly owned subsidiary of HarperCollins Christian Publishing, Inc.

Requests for information should be addressed to customercare@harpercollins.com.

Zondervan titles may be purchased in bulk for educational, business, fundraising, or sales promotional use. For information, please email SpecialMarkets@Zondervan.com.

ISBN 978-0-310-37048-2 (softcover)
ISBN 978-0-310-35208-2 (audio)

Library of Congress Cataloging-in-Publication Data

Names: Friend, Tom, author.
Title: The chicken runs at midnight : a daughter's message from heaven that changed a father's heart and won a World Series / Tom Friend.
Description: Grand Rapids, Michigan : Zondervan, [2018]
Identifiers: LCCN 2018006831| ISBN 9780310352068 (hardcover) | ISBN 9780310352075 (ebook)
Subjects: LCSH: Donnelly, Rich, 1946- | Baseball coaches--United States--Biography. | Fathers and daughters.
Classification: LCC GV865.D59 F75 2018 | DDC 796.357092 [B] --dc23 LC record available at https://lccn.loc.gov/2018006831

Published in association with Blauner Books Literary Agency.

Cover design: Faceout Studio
Cover photos: Shutterstock
Interior design: Kait Lamphere

To the best word
in the English language—
family.

Contents

Foreword by Tim Kurkjian 9
Introduction: I Am Third 13

FIRST BASE

Chapter 1: Free to Be Me 19
Chapter 2: Father and Sons 29
Chapter 3: Bubble Wrap 42
Chapter 4: Peggy 54
Chapter 5: Love and Baseball—Not Necessarily in That Order 64
Chapter 6: Minor Leagues, Major Issues 72
Chapter 7: Boys Will Generally Be Boys 82

SECOND BASE

Chapter 8: Queen Elizabeth 95
Chapter 9: Family, God, and Baseball—Definitely Not in
    That Order 106
Chapter 10: Convenient Catholic 114
Chapter 11: Infidelity 127
Chapter 12: A Daughter Scorned 135
Chapter 13: "Amy, What Do You Want to Do?" 144
Chapter 14: Amy Wants to Rage 156
Chapter 15: Amy Wants to Win 164

THIRD BASE

Chapter 16: "Dad, I'm Sorry"..................................... 179
Chapter 17: "What Is He Cupping His Hands and
    Telling Them?"..................................... 193
Chapter 18: The Ninth Month.............................. 216
Chapter 19: "Half of Me Is Gone"......................... 230
Chapter 20: Chicken Man 239
Chapter 21: World Series................................. 250

HOME

Chapter 22: Did God Run the Bases? 261
Chapter 23: Spreading the Gospel 269
Chapter 24: How to Live and How to Die 276
Afterword... 282

Acknowledgments... 287

Foreword

Baseball writers are not supposed to become friends with the people they cover. It is a conflict of interest, a rule I diligently followed in my forty years in the game with one exception: my friend, Rich Donnelly.

No one has ever made me laugh like he has—or at the same time made me cry. We've had beers together and attended funerals together. One day, he threw me batting practice at Fenway Park. Another year, he coached our winter league basketball team and still brags about how we erased a twenty-eight-point halftime deficit to win the championship game. No one tells a story better than Rich Donnelly, and now he has told, with the help of another friend, the brilliant Tom Friend, the greatest baseball story of all time—*The Chicken Runs at Midnight*.

The best stories in sports come from baseball, given its rich tradition, deliberate pace, and wonderful unpredictability. Yet some baseball stories, including portions of the 1919 Black Sox Scandal, Babe Ruth's famous called shot in the 1932 World Series, and nearly any story about Rickey Henderson, are apocryphal or embellished. But my favorite baseball story ever—the one told in this book—is all true. And it has every element of a transcendent story—tragedy and triumph, tears and cheers, regret and redemption. It will make you smile; it will make you weep; it will inspire you and make you a better person for having read it, as it did Rich Donnelly for having lived it. This book is his life prophecy come true.

It is a baseball story, but like so many baseball stories, it's about something more crucial: family. Baseball is a marvelous sport, a beautiful sport, but it can turn cruel. It can tear apart a family because the season is so long, the grind so rigorous and the game so difficult to play. Or as Rich says, "If you don't smoke, the game will make you smoke. If you smoke, it will make you stop."

Yet so many great people were part of the Donnelly baseball family, led by his first wife, Peggy and, now, beautiful Roberta. There is no overstating what the game can put a family through and what it can do to a man, and maybe it's that sort of searing heartache that helped Rich become the man he is today.

He has always been a good man, everyone's friend. It's impossible to know Rich Donnelly and not like him. I've known him for thirty-six years. We've talked a lot about basketball and Big Red high school football and, of course, baseball. I've written three books and have quoted Rich more than anyone because of his knowledge, perspective, and wry sense of humor.

When asked about the great work ethic of the Pittsburgh Pirates hitters, Rich said, "We've spent more time in the cage than Gunther Gebel-Williams." About a Pirates team that was so young, he said, "We have a shoe contract with Buster Brown." On six-time All-Star Prince Fielder's strength, he said, "He has the biggest biceps in baseball. You could put a tattoo of the United States on one bicep and still have room for Argentina." Rich's love for the game never was clearer than when Brewers general manager Doug Melvin said the highlight of the 2003 season was the smile he received from Rich when he hired Rich to be their third base coach.

But Rich's biggest smiles have always come when he talks about children. He still references my daughter Kelly's 96.4 percent free throw shooting her senior year in high school ten years ago. He knows that family is at the core of all of us. His oldest son, Bubba, was an aspiring basketball player—so, growing up, every Tuesday at the Donnellys was Left-Handed Tuesday. Bubba had to eat and write and do everything left-handed to improve his dexterity with his off hand, and it worked. Bubba played four years at Robert Morris University. We talked about Mike, the tough little kicker from Cumberland College. We talked about Timmy and the most amazing Donnelly, Amy. When we spoke, there was such pride, along with deep regret that the game cost Rich so much time with his kids, time he'd never get back. But the time that baseball took away only made their times together, especially those at the ballpark, that much sweeter.

I've written about *The Chicken Runs at Midnight* story myself; I remember wiping away tears as I wrote. I wish I would have written this book, but I'm thrilled it has been beautifully written by Tom Friend, who knows sports and knows people and is a master at getting to the heart of deeply emotional stories. I've known Tom for nearly forty years. We grew up in the same county in Maryland, covered high school sports together, and share similar interests, including a love/hate relationship with the Redskins. And now, through this book, we have another shared experience—a love and respect for Rich Donnelly and his family.

A Friend writing a book about a friend. Perfect. You'll laugh. You'll cry. You will be moved.

Tim Kurkjian,
ESPN writer (espn.com) and analyst,
June 2018

Introduction

I Am Third

No one has ever made it home safely without touching third base. It's one of life's absolute certainties. Third base, in the purest sense, is the final pit stop on a glorious and treacherous journey. You may be passing through at warp speed or parking there out of complete necessity, but third base is your ultimate reminder that something grand is near.

The anticipation and anxiety at third are palpable. You are so close to home, and yet so incalculably far away. You don't want to end up stranded there, which is why you are tempted, at times, to make a run for it. Yet, if you leave hastily or haphazardly, without great thought, you're *outta there*—a victim, a goat, a bum.

Third base, on its best day, is the gateway to victory, to euphoria, to understanding, to heaven. But third base will also break your spirit if you let it. People have died there—not in the literal sense, of course. But they've died there just the same, whether they are baserunners in extra innings or middle-aged men who have been stopped short of finding peace.

So that's where it helps to have a third base coach—a partner in crime, a wingman, a sage counselor, an adviser—whose sole purpose is to wave you on home as soon as it is safe or apropos. In other words, a life coach.

This third base coach can give you wings or bad advice. His is a hazardous, thankless, behind-the-scenes existence. No one knows his name or asks for his autograph. His uniform number is irrelevant, and he'll never gain entry to the Hall of Fame. He doesn't have a baseball card or even a union card. His only statistic of relevance is how many times he's let you down. To the general public, he's a lucky fool when you're safe and a blind fool when you're out. Otherwise, they see him for what he is: perfectly invisible.

Once every blue or blood moon, he may earn a pat on the back, usually from the one who hired him: his manager. But when he gets you thrown out, gunned, hosed, or eviscerated at home plate—and trust me, he will—he's more of a wanted man than you are. You can escape to the dugout, or to your house or car. You can slip a hood over your head and slink away. But a third base coach must stand there without a shield and without earplugs, fair game to be heckled. Fair game to be strung up.

You can bet the third base coach knows his lot in life, knows what's at stake, knows how consequential it is that you're standing next to him. Whether you are on third base in the ninth inning or on the third base of life, you are precious cargo, and he is your eyes, ears, and limbs. His job requires the frantic use of his arms (for waving) and of his larynx (for last-ditch verbal instructions). He will assuredly flash you secret signs or coded hand signals at vital moments. He may even go old school, cup his hands, and yell something out to you across the diamond. It's all for the greater good.

Whatever it takes to guide you home, to deliver you to your safe, tranquil place, the third base coach is all-in. But not many people can handle the stress of the job. It takes cold blood, a sense of time and distance, an expertise in geometry, and an innate sense of how to boss people around. You must be verbose, and you must be subtle. You must be able to operate ten seconds ahead of everyone else on the field, the better to visualize the inevitable play at home plate. You must be able to live with failure and without ego. You must be prepared to be fired.

It is no one's dream scenario. No one grows up wishing to coach third base; they grow up hoping to round third base and score. Better yet, they hope to score the winning run in the seventh game of the World Series. They want to make it home so they can be mobbed, hugged, forgiven, loved, parented. They want to come home again and again and again.

Of course, there are always exceptions to the rule. There are always a few unique people who are well suited for the position, who genuinely thrive on the opportunity, pressure, intensity, and anonymity that come with coaching third base. There's even one man who stuttered through a rosary once, praying for the chance to stand on that island, hoping to lose his voice on a nightly basis, just so he could set up shop on the periphery of the playing field—or, more accurately, the periphery of life. Just so he could make a difference in the game and on this planet somehow, in some unexpected way.

That rare third base coach's name is Rich Donnelly, and heaven knows—*heaven definitely knows*—he ended up making a difference, ended up introducing his daughter Amy to the world, ended up saving lives, ended up sending someone near and dear to his heart home.

Letter from Amy

Dad,

I want to thank you for flying me in for the playoff game the other night. My ears are still ringing from the crowd noise. Mom says having ringing in my ears isn't such good news, but she just worries about me, you know? I can tell you I'm fine. Don't you give it a second thought.

Did you see the seats I had—the fifth row!! I had a perfect view of all those runners you waved home. You are really fantastic at your job. Third base coaching is, shall we say, a little busy. Boy, you were yelling a lot! Like I mentioned in the car ride home, I saw you crouching down and cupping your hands over your mouth so the baserunners at second base could hear all of your shouting. That's why I made the joke I made. Hahaha.

Anyway, I'm writing you this note—even if you don't receive it in time—to let you know that I'm rooting for you guys with all my heart the rest of these playoffs. You deserve a World Series more than anybody I know, bar none. I don't know what's going to happen—to me, to you—but what an amazing journey we're all on. Like you always tell me, life is like a trip around the bases. Part of our life takes place on first base; the next part of our life takes place on second; and the next part of our life takes place on third. I believe that now. So how about you guys have a lot of trips around the bases in your next game. That would be perfect, right?

The Chicken Runs at Midnight!

Love,

Amy

FIRST BASE

FIRST BASE

One

Free to Be Me

O ne of Rich Donnelly's first playgrounds was a cemetery. He didn't
    have to stray far to find it either, because the graveyard was the
first thing he laid eyes on every morning straight outside his childhood
bedroom window. Rich vividly recalls playing army and tag amid the
tumbled marble tombstones as a five-year-old. Out of respect, he just
made sure to sidestep the mausoleums.

Otherwise, little about Union Cemetery in Steubenville, Ohio,
made Rich squeamish. He used to brag about living only a stone's throw
from a couple hundred dead people, and, Lord knows, young Rich did
throw stones from there. He tossed them at cars and windows, and he
also tossed them up in the air and hit them with his wooden baseball
bat. Where those stones would land, nobody knew—much less Rich.
Hopefully not in somebody's living room. But it was 1950, and in a town
of gamblers and goodfellas, no one was going to turn a five-year-old ruf-
fian in to the police. As he likes to say, he was "free to be me."

Rich had quite the setup. Other than the cemetery, which was
catty-corner to his home on 127 Langley Avenue, he had a back alley for
stickball games and a high school football field to run rampant in just
over a flimsy chicken wire fence. In his mind, within a 100-foot radius
of his kitchen, he had everything he'd pretty much ever heard about
in church: death (i.e., the graveyard) and heaven (i.e., the wide-open
football field).

He'd also heard about angels in church, and as far as he was concerned, his mother, Helen Donnelly, was one of them. She had grown up in Monongahela, Pennsylvania, of Slavic descent, and her entire life was predicated on kindness, order, unpretentiousness, and bare-knuckled hard work. Every morning, breakfast was on the table at 7 a.m. sharp, always hot and fresh, including the coffee, bacon, and biscuits. She was a nurse in her spare time, and her bedside manner was helpful when it came to her youngest of three children, Rich. Because if anyone needed soothing tones in his life, it was wild Rich.

At Christmas, New Year's, and Easter—or whenever his extended family gathered—the conversation always turned to the unorthodox adventures of Rich Donnelly. He was a wunderkind if you ever saw one, as early as preschool. Except Rich didn't attend preschool. Rather, he attached himself to his mother's hip every morning until the town clock struck 10:20. Then he'd amble down the alley to nearby Harding Elementary School—to crash recess.

As the local first, second, and third graders skipped and dashed onto the playground, there standing on the fringe of it all was five-year-old Rich, just biding his time. It would happen this way nearly every recess. The kids would start a game of kickball or softball and pick teams. Almost regularly, a team would be short a player, and a teacher would see Rich conspicuously leaning against a fence post. "You want to play?" they'd ask. Of course he did. Before long, the teachers and the nine-year-olds knew his name by heart. By the time he legitimately attended kindergarten there a year later, he considered himself "a six-year letterman."

Either way, it was all part of the rugged life of Rich. Once those recesses ended, he would hightail it down to the Steubenville High School football field to report for work. This was the field just south of his living room window, and the maintenance men there had no problem assigning five-year-old Rich hard labor. He would help the men cut grass or pluck weeds or harpoon lampoon trash with a steel pick. His mother, knowing her son's rituals, would pack him a salami sandwich to take with him. That way, preschool-age Rich would be able to sit down and take a lunch break with the grownups.

In a town of roughnecks, Rich was—pound for pound—among the roughest. When he was still five, his mother took him to the family pediatrician, Dr. Jack Kohen, for a checkup. When the doctor told Rich to pull down his pants for a booster shot, Rich hauled off and punched the doc in the mouth. "Decked him," Rich says.

It is Donnelly family lore that the doctor was knocked ten feet back into a plaster wall, and that tyke-sized Rich then ran after the stumbling man to get some more. Every time Dr. Kohen would see Rich in the street after that, he'd turn and head the other way. But that's how reputations were made in Steubenville, Ohio.

Another day, Rich was sitting on a porch with a pal named Brucie Boggs. Brucie started pretending he was fishing on a lake. So Rich, playing along, shoved Brucie off the porch into the pretend water, which was hilarious—until Brucie wound up cracking his head wide open on the concrete landing below. Rich's mom sent him to Brucie's home that night—ten houses up Langley Avenue—to hand Brucie a Hershey's chocolate bar as a peace offering. Problem was, Rich ate half the Hershey's bar on the way there.

What goes around comes around, of course, and one day, the neighborhood boys got back at Rich by depantsing him. Somebody grabbed his right arm and somebody else grabbed his left (maybe Brucie), and they yanked his trousers straight off. They tied his pants to the cemetery flagpole. Rich had no choice but to run home half naked, whereupon his mother chuckled and decided not to ask for an explanation.

But don't confuse Helen Donnelly's compassion for weakness. When Rich was a rambunctious toddler with a tendency to run out into the street nude, she would tie him to a pole in the basement while she was ironing so he wouldn't streak out there again. Later, if Rich was ever profane, she would wash his mouth out with brown Fels-Naptha soap, which tasted far worse—more bitter, anyway—than regular bath soap. Or if Rich ever complained about sharing a bathroom with his older sister, Patti, his mom would remind him that when she grew up in Monongahela, her family was so poor that their version of toilet paper was four pages of the Sears catalog.

Helen knew how to negotiate with Rich. You had to tug at his heartstrings (à la the toilet paper story) or, as a last resort, flat-out bribe him. Not long after he punched Dr. Kohen in the jaw, Rich found out he needed his tonsils out. As far as Helen was concerned, this could be catastrophic. If her son had already assaulted a doctor over a simple booster shot, imagine what he would do when the next one showed up with a scalpel. Her strategy was simple: promise him new baseball catching gear if he kept his fists to himself.

Five-year-old Rich fell for it immediately. Baseball was his first love, and catching was the quintessential position for a roughneck like him. His idol, his inspiration, and his reason for being was his older brother, Jerome Jr., otherwise known as Romey, who just so happened to be the best pitcher in Steubenville. Romey may have been fourteen years older than Rich, and a freshman on the University of Notre Dame baseball team, but Rich's dream was to catch fastballs from his brother someday—some magical day way off in the future.

His mother's catcher's gear bribe was a win-win for everyone. The doctor who removed his tonsils lived to tell about it; Helen kept her sanity; and Rich soon had the shiniest red chest protector, red shin guards, and red catcher's mask in town. This changed his morning routine entirely. Instead of hightailing it to the graveyard first thing every morning, Rich would slip on his catcher's gear and, in full red regalia, walk down the middle of Langley Avenue to his buddy Dewey Guida's house. All the passersby would honk their horns at the little big man in the catcher's mask, his fierce eyes peering out defiantly. Little Rich Donnelly wore his game face 24/7.

This kid was made for that city. Steubenville, circa 1950, was a booming coal and steel mill town with the type of underground entertainment only a wise guy could love. In fact, residents there say that whenever

Al Capone was feeling the heat from the feds in Chicago, he'd hide away in Steubenville. The place became ultimately known as "Little Chicago," and it actually may have had more per-capita bookies and brothels than the Windy City. The cigar shops on Main Street doubled as betting parlors, and according to old-timers, the mob supposedly controlled the mayor, the police chief, and the ladies of the night.

In an odd and perverse sort of way, the local Mafia seemed to keep the town safe and invigorated. The crime families, headed up by Jimmy Tripodi and Cosmo Quattrone, wanted Steubenville to be a tri-state mecca—because, let's face it, the more money coming in, the more money they could launder. So the goodfellas ended up being good fellows and policed the town themselves. Violence was passé—that is, unless you crossed them. In other words, if you messed with the town, Jimmy and Cosmo messed with you. But otherwise, you could roam the streets of Steubenville at 4 a.m. without a care, and by the late 1950s, Steubenville's population had soared to a bustling forty thousand. Mob money had helped build shiny new schools, hospitals, and restaurants. Everybody knew it; everybody accepted it.

You could tell the city had personality by all the nicknames. This was a town that, at one time, had a police chief named Runt Mavromatis. But that was nothing. There was Ape-Head Torcasio and Tootsie Mieczkowski and Teeth Mancini and Tennis Shoe Ernie. Little Rich—who would later be known as "Diamond Duke Donnelly," or "Duke," for short—even hung with a pair of brothers named Mousie and Ratsy Gaylord.

But the undisputed face of the city was Dino Crocetti, more commonly known as the singer/actor/comedian Dean Martin. Dino grew up on 9th Street, right in the sternum of Steubenville, and he was as sly as all the other scoundrels in town. He was a croupier at a backroom gambling parlor, and it's well documented that he would purposely flip chips into his oversized loafers when no one was looking. That way, he'd leave the casino with twenty-five extra bucks and also with a slick story to tell the goodfellas and girls.

If he hadn't had such a dreamy singing voice, Dino might have ended up like many of the other poor suckers in town—working at the mill or moving to Las Vegas to become a card shark. But Dino fortuitously hit the mother lode as Dean Martin—crooning and doing slapstick with Jerry Lewis all over the world. After that, all that remained of him in Steubenville was his aura, which was more than enough. Every kid wanted to be the reincarnation of Dino, wanted to be cool, wanted to walk around with a cigarette dangling from his lips.

Down the alley from where Dino grew up, on South 6th and Slack Streets, was another Steubenville treasure, if you want to call him that— Jimmy Synodinos. Jimmy wasn't cool, handsome, or a ladies' man. But word among the locals is that Jimmy took advantage of a slow clock at a local bookie joint and laid bets there on horse races that were already completed. In other words, he had the answers, or winners, ahead of time and became a prognosticating legend. He shortened his name to Jimmy Snyder and ultimately became known as "Jimmy the Greek," the Nostradamus of CBS's *NFL Today* in the 1970s and '80s. If Dino had been the face of the city, Jimmy the Greek, like it or not, was the potbelly. But he would also make a lasting impact. Before long, you could bet on anything in that town, including the over-under on how many drunks would die on the local highway over Memorial Day weekend. That was Steubenville—everybody wanted to be a moneybags; everybody had an angle.

Young Rich Donnelly's angle, as he grew older, was to become a catcher someday for the Pittsburgh Pirates, some thirty miles down the road at Forbes Field. Every afternoon, after pegging his buddies with apples in the cemetery or sprucing up the high school stadium, he'd head for his basement for a game of Pirates baseball. And it wasn't to watch the game on the family's black-and-white TV; it was to re-create the game with a rubber ball. He'd announce the name of each hitter and then throw the ball flush against a basement wall. If it caromed and hit a pole, it was a single. If it sailed beyond the pole, it was an automatic double. And so on and so forth. His mom would climb down the basement stairs to do laundry, and he'd shoo her away. He was determined to complete nine Pirates innings each afternoon.

His other routine was to *slide* into his house from the backyard instead of walking in. It took some ingenuity, but this was his way of practicing stealing second base. He would take eight or nine packages of Jell-O powder and dump them all over his linoleum kitchen floor. Then, from the backyard, he'd sprint, shove open the screen door, and slide toward the refrigerator. If he reached the fridge before the screen door slammed shut, he was safe. If the screen door closed first, he was out. But the genius was the Jell-O powder—as he slid, it would rise up like infield dust.

He was borderline obsessed. When Rich's Little League took field trips to Pirates games, Rich—fidgety Rich—was the only one who would sit still and watch the entire game. All the other kids would be darting in and out of their seats, hoarding cotton candy and frankfurters. But Rich would be studying the way shortstop Dick Groat pounded his glove or how hard catcher Jack Shepard threw balls back to the pitcher. In fact, since this was Steubenville, people would've been wise to enter Dixie Cigar Store and lay down a twenty-five-dollar bet that Rich would someday end up being a Bucco himself. Either that or a priest.

Rich had long been fascinated by church—which to him was just one step below Forbes Field on the totem pole. His mother was a devout Catholic who considered the family church, Holy Name Cathedral, their home away from home. Every Sunday morning, Rich would shine his black shoes, wet his hair, comb it straight, wipe the breakfast crumbs from his face, button his dress shirt, and follow Helen and his sister to the cathedral's front door.

Before long, his goal was to be an altar boy, and once he could recite a sufficient number of prayers in Latin, he was in. This was cause for celebration. Status wise, being an altar boy in Steubenville was the equivalent of being a first-string jock. There were fourteen Catholic churches in town—thirty-nine churches in all—and you essentially picked one based on your nationality. St. Peter was for the Irish, St. Anthony's for the Italians, and Saint Stanislaus for the Polish. Holy Name Cathedral was more of a mix, and it was majestic at that. As an altar boy, Rich got to wear white gloves with red buckled slippers—almost better than a baseball uniform—and because he was also Master of Ceremonies, he got to shadow the priest as he handled the incense. "I was the *man*," Rich says.

All the altar boys also wore flattop haircuts, so Rich—even with his egg-shaped head—asked his Uncle Pete, an expert barber, to carve a flattop on him too. The result was a "roundtop," but the message was clear: Rich worshiped the baseball gods and cathedral gods, equally. If his family drove by any church at all, he thought it was a mortal sin if he didn't stop and enter. He began to attend Holy Communion every day before his Catholic school began, the fringe benefit being that all kids in attendance received powdered donuts and hot chocolate at the start of first period. Since first period was math, it meant Rich didn't have to answer any questions—because his mouth was full. "I told myself, 'If I eat the donut real slow, I'll never have to answer a question again,'" Rich says. "I didn't miss Communion for the next six years. I was always looking for an angle."

Catholic school wasn't always the best fit, though, not for a boy of Rich's fury. He was generally a conscientious student, but one day in the third grade, he was seated between two of his more garrulous classmates, Eddie Joe Chanoski and Vinnie Trivoli. Eddie Joe and Vinnie began debating who could burp louder, and Sister Eusebius overheard. She chastised the boys, including Rich, who'd been caught in their crossfire and hadn't said a word. Rich, fuming at what he considered an injustice, began giving the nun his best stink eye. He stared and glared at her for several days, to the point that Sister Eusebius had no choice but to call his home.

Rich's mom heard about her son's insubordination and dealt with it how she always did—with a soft voice and a subtle nod toward the Fels-Naptha in the laundry room. Helen knew just how to handle him, and it wasn't long until the nuns were back in Rich's good graces. Another day in third grade, a sister caught Rich in class with a betting sheet of college football games. He'd been playing parlays since he was five—"That's how I learned to count," he says—and on this day, he was trying to decide who to pick in the annual Ohio State-Michigan game.

"Mr. Donnelly!" the nun snapped. "What do you have there?"

"Sister, well, it's a thing," he stammered.

"What do you do with it?" she asked, remembering who she was dealing with.

"Well," the eight-year-old answered, "you pick three teams and then you give five bucks to a bookie and you play a three-team parlay."

"Let me see that," the nun said. She paused, circled a trio of teams, and later slipped him five dollars to lay down a bet with.

It just confirmed what young Rich "Duke" Donnelly always suspected: Steubenville was the finest, most exquisite place on earth, where even nuns played parlays. People kept telling him he had an attitude problem, but his patented response became, "This *whole town* has an attitude problem."

The city even had its own personal scent, the sour smell of sulfur from the coal mines and steel mills. Every morning, the smokestacks left soot caked on the sidewalk and automobiles. Mixed with the odor of cigars, the place needed a giant stick of deodorant. But Rich was in love with Steubenville, not to mention baseball; religion; Dean Martin; his brother, Romey; his mother, Helen; and the cemetery in his backyard. It was the cheeriest time of his life. To him, every day was Christmas.

That is, until five o'clock in the afternoon, when his father came home.

Letter from Amy

Dad,

    I wait up every night for you when you have a home game. But you're almost never home before I fall asleep. What time do these games end? Midnight? After midnight?

    I guess that's the one thing about baseball. It's the only sport I can think of that doesn't have a clock. Sometimes I'm listening to the game on the radio and you're one strike away from winning—and then, boom, somebody hits a home run and it goes into extra innings! How do you handle that?

    You've always told me it's the baseball gods who determine this, but is it also the real God too? All I know is the sooner you're home the better. Anyway, I'm writing this note to you while you're gone at a really long game again.

    Hurry back.

Love,

Amy

Two

Father and Sons

Rich basically had two separate lives. One was the time spent with his mother by day; the other was the time spent with a madman by night. Weekends were potluck.

Jerome Donnelly Sr. worked tirelessly at the steel mill as a superintendent and also doubled as a mediator for nearby Wheeling Steel. By all appearances, he was a well-kept, congenial, competent man who was lauded by management for his negotiating skills. He traveled as far away as Switzerland and Rome to broker delicate deals—and he also arbitrated complex corporate disagreements in Chicago. He was always impeccably dressed in a dark suit, skinny tie, and starched white shirt, which went perfectly with his Brylcreemed, gray-speckled hair. His word was as solid as Steubenville steel. He could enter any bank in town and walk out with a jumbo loan in twenty-some-odd minutes. But the way he harassed his youngest son was unforgivable.

Rich just assumed this was the way of the world, that every kid on the block had a father who couldn't be satisfied, a father who whipped him with a belt for striking out in Little League. For that naive reason, Rich was still able to remain in love with his Steubenville childhood. But down the road, this would end up giving him a nervous twitch.

It's not that Jerome Donnelly was a heavy drinker; he'd only have an Iron City when he ate spaghetti. He wasn't a gambler either, although he did play the college football parlays on Saturday—like the nuns.

He didn't have a colorful nickname; nobody called him Bugsy. He attended church, espoused the importance of school, and didn't yell at Helen. Still, something was amiss about him, and all three of his children recognized it.

Probably, in psychological terms, it was a deep-seated insecurity. But in practical terms, it played out as an obsession to get both of his two sons to the big leagues.

The oldest boy, his namesake Jerome Jr.—Romey—looked like he had the goods. Romey was a six-foot-two, 205-pound right-handed flamethrower who had scouts driving in to see his fastball hum. At that point, Jerome Sr. licked his lips and decided Junior was not going to screw this opportunity up, not over his dead body.

He made sure everything was at Romey's disposal—pitching coaches, twenty-five-pound dumbbells, a pull-up bar, a queen-sized bed, and as many hotcakes as he could eat. Romey was the chosen one, the golden boy, the Catholic school whiz kid. He was the smartest one in the family, eventually his high school's class president. Jerome let him stay out late into the Steubenville night, knowing the mob would protect him. If Romey drank too much—and he would occasionally toss back a few Iron Citys himself—Jerome turned the other way. Rich thinks Jerome was hesitant to lay a hand on Romey because broad-shouldered Romey "would've kicked his butt all over the house." And if Jerome ever did yell at him the tiniest bit, Romey would simply give him an eye roll.

Romey just seemed to have that Steubenville Dean Martin gene working for him—good looks and the innate ability to wink and stay cool. The ladies swooned over Romey, and his girlfriend happened to be the gorgeous to-die-for majorette of the marching band, Marlene Salata. He had blond hair, blue eyes, played the accordion, and had a curled-up lip, à la Elvis. He wore a leather jacket and diligently shined his shoes for hours on end. He was the opposite of his grungy, hot-headed younger brother, Rich, which served Romey well when it came to dealing with their overbearing father. Rich would've done anything to be as suave as

Romey, and he followed him around endlessly, hoping it would happen by osmosis.

Romey let Rich ride on his coattails too. When Romey's American Legion team made the state championship game up in Columbus, Romey invited five-year-old Rich to be the batboy. Rich thanked him eight times a day. When Romey's team lost, Rich cried a river, while Romey chatted up the Columbus girls in the stands and called a bookie to make a bet on the Pirates-Reds game.

If anyone would've taken a step back and analyzed it all, there was no way Romey had the fire, the gumption, and the mean streak to reach the big leagues. He was a shy, sensitive, thoughtful, provocative pretty boy with an above-average fastball and a father breathing down his neck. Romey was playing ball for the wrong reasons, playing to keep his father at bay. From the outside looking in, it was only a matter of time until he called it a day.

He ended up enrolling at the pantheon of Catholic colleges, the University of Notre Dame. No one was prouder than Jerome and Helen Donnelly, particularly the ultra-religious Helen. To graduate from the Golden Dome would mean Romey was equally spiritual and wise; it was her wish come true. No one in their family had ever finished college. Jerome had dropped out of Ohio State to work in the mill, and Helen's family had been too poor to even contemplate higher education. Romey would be breaking new ground—until the day he called home his sophomore year to say he'd been kicked out of school.

"What happened?" Helen asked with a moan.

"I flunked a class," Romey said.

"Which one?"'

"Religion."

The horrific sound on the other end of the line was Helen, who shrieked, caught herself, and went to sob privately in her room. It wasn't her way to show emotion publicly or create a scene. But make no mistake, she'd have done anything to have him fail Physics or English Lit—anything but *Religion*.

A perturbed Jerome grabbed the phone from her. There wasn't a worse scenario for him as a father. Baseball and school had been Romey's ticket, and now the kid had neither. He'd known for a while that Romey's grades weren't stellar, and earlier in the year, he and Helen asked Marlene to drive up to South Bend with them to give Romey a pep talk. But Romey had just yessed them and then pulled Marlene aside to say how "lovesick" he was for her. Flunking Religion was perhaps his way of rebelling against baseball, against his old man. Or having his girl back full-time.

Either way, Jerome's temper emerged that day at nuclear level for all to see and hear. Although he was probably tempted to chew Romey out or dole out a whipping, Jerome instead hung up the phone on his son. Then he proceeded to dial the distinguished president of Notre Dame, Father Theodore Hesburgh.

He demanded to speak to Hesburgh, pronto, and threatened to call every five minutes if they didn't patch him through. Every vein in his forehead was oversized and crimson, and since somebody had to pay, it might as well be the No. 1 person on campus. Once Father Hesburgh picked up the line, Jerome yelled out the question, "How can a smart boy who spent twelve years in Catholic school flunk *RELIGION?* That class must be too tough! What kind of curriculum are you running there?" Father Hesburgh had no definitive answer for him, of course, but the language from Jerome just got saltier and louder.

Rich overheard it; all of Langley Avenue must've overheard it. Somehow, some way, Rich knew he was going to pay for this as well. He wasn't sure how, but his sense was there would be enough of his father's venom to infect all of them secondhand.

The first thing Jerome did was find a college baseball program that would take on Romey and his F in Religion. Romey had no say in the matter. The place ended up being Mount St. Mary's University in Emmitsburg, Maryland, where the eventual Hall of Fame basketball coach Jim Phelan also happened to be the temporary baseball coach. Phelan knew enough about baseball to pitch Romey as much as possible.

But Phelan also knew enough about people to sense Romey wasn't the most grounded and serious ballplayer on campus. Romey had already gotten in some hot water at Notre Dame for playing summer semipro ball for twenty bucks a game—violating amateur rules. There was chatter that it may have contributed to Father Hesburgh's final decision to boot the kid out. And now Phelan was seeing for himself that Romey didn't exactly eat and sleep the sport. In particular, he noticed that after Saturday games, Romey would make a beeline for the Pimlico Race Course in Baltimore, where he'd bet to his heart's desire. You could take the kid out of Steubenville, but you couldn't take the Steubenville out of the kid.

Whenever Romey came home from school for a visit, though, it was an instant holiday for Rich. If Romey was arriving at night, Rich would hide under his brother's bed—ready to burst out with a surprise welcome. But as was Romey's custom, he'd usually arrive around midnight, Marlene's lipstick on his collar. It didn't matter to Rich; he would wait up regardless. He'd watch Romey shine his wing-tip shoes, slick back his hair, play his accordion, and riff about striking out some lame hitter with his heater. Before long it was 2 a.m. But this was Rich's hero, and nothing as inconsequential as sleep would disrupt their time together.

Little did Rich know he was about to be Romey, take 2. Although Jerome's aspiration was to still see Romey reach the big leagues, he began to see as much potential in his mercurial youngest son. Romey would often pull his father aside and explain that Rich was rugged enough to be a professional catcher someday, that he had a certain spark in him that all the neighborhood kids were chirping about.

Whereas Romey was a subtle mix of Dino Crocetti, Elvis, and James Dean, prepubescent Rich seemed as wicked as Ty Cobb, as farcical as Yogi Berra, and as conniving as Leo Durocher. At least that's what began to dance around in Jerome's head.

The eye-opener for Jerome was the day Rich, all of age seven, had just finished playing tackle football with the neighborhood high school kids. Nobody could see how Rich had survived the game, much less how he gained entry. But Rich figured if he could handle his father's fury, he could certainly handle being tackled around the neck by boys eight and nine years his senior. Rich was just macho at a ridiculously young age. He had already been belt-whipped multiple times by his dad—after he coldcocked Dr. Kohen and after he cheap-shotted Brucie Boggs, to name two. And these weren't amateur spankings; these were high-intensity, grown-man whippings that got fiercer with each slap. The whippings left half-dollar-sized welts on his rear end and would sting for hours. Compared to that, tackle football was a day at the park.

Anyway, Rich was hanging out with these older boys in his back alley after the game when one of the teens, Raymond Payne, found some clinkers on the ground—burned-out coals from the Donnelly family furnace. Payne smirked and whipped a couple at Rich, peppering him in the foot. So Rich grabbed one himself and from thirty feet away impersonated Bob Feller as best he could, nailing Payne in the center of his forehead.

All the other boys scattered, half laughing, half afraid of the bodily harm Payne would inflict on Rich. But Payne was down for the count or, as Rich describes it, "down like a buffalo." When Payne finally stood up, he had what appeared to be a three-inch knot on his head and stumbled over his own two feet. Rich figured that when Jerome got wind of this at 5 p.m., he'd be on the receiving end of another beastly beating.

But interestingly, Jerome hardly batted an eye. His measured response was, "Gee, that's too bad; you shouldn't have done that." That was the extent of it. Rich had been so sure his father was going to brandish a belt that he'd already half dropped his trousers. It was an unexpected reprieve, but the truth was, Jerome's wheels were turning. His seven-year-old son was not only manly enough to play football with teenagers, but he had a rifle for an arm. The notion that Rich could be a big league catcher was cemented that very day.

After the clinker incident, Rich was no longer a seven- or eight-year-old in his father's eyes. Jerome promptly enrolled Rich to play Little League, which meant he'd be competing against twelve-year-olds—kids twice as big. The standards had been raised for Rich—and raised high, to the point that Jerome came home at five o'clock one day to say they were moving to a brand-new home in suburbia, several miles down the road in West Steubenville. Partly because of Rich's baseball.

Not that the women in the house knew any of that. To Helen and Patti, the move to suburbia was an exquisite step up. Helen would have a larger kitchen, a fancier refrigerator, and no cemetery outside her back window. Patti would have her own spacious room—after sharing one for years with Rich—and a wondrous view of oak trees.

But the real reason Jerome wanted this house was the custom backyard that came along with it. Jerome had negotiated to have the house built on a double lot, meaning the home would have twice the space in the back. Envisioning a Whiffle ball field, he had the contractors level the ground as flatly as possible. Better yet, he made sure the backyard was precisely 120 feet, 6 inches—the exact length of a catcher's throw from home plate to second.

The house that Jerome built was essentially an ode to his youngest son—the inference being that Rich was going to train the next eight or so years to be a major league catcher, or else. And the *or else* part was compounded by even more incredulous news: Romey was quitting baseball.

To anyone who'd been paying attention all this time, Romey's retirement was inevitable. But in the moment, it was stunning to say the least. After graduating from Mount Saint Mary's, Romey had gotten married to his majorette sweetheart, Marlene, and then signed with the Kansas City Athletics of the American League. Talk about redeeming yourself, talk about overcoming your F in Religion. He'd been discovered by two ornery scouts, Spook Jacobs, a former second baseman for the A's, and Burleigh Grimes, a Hall of Famer who was the last big league pitcher to throw a legal spitball. Those two men had been bullish on Romey, and even though Romey was assigned to the Abilene Blue Sox of the Class B Big State League (the equivalent of low A ball), he'd achieved his lifetime goal. All of Jerome's blood, sweat, and dysfunction had finally produced a professional contract.

At first, after having only marginal success in spring training, Romey appeared to be sticking it out. He and Marlene had just had their first of four sons by then, and, if nothing else, he needed the nest egg. But after a rough stretch in Abilene, including getting drilled in the head by a line drive, he was released in late June 1956. He had a cup of coffee with the 1957 Savannah Red Legs, a Cincinnati Reds affiliate, and then a one-day tryout with the North Platte (Nebraska) Indians. The Indians passed.

After the two arduous years of playing in obscure outposts with limited results, both Romey and his bride, Marlene, were burned out. The way Marlene describes it, Romey was "depleted and exhausted." The minor leagues were a grind, from the bus trips through overheated Texas to the roach-infested apartments. It was no place to raise a family unless you were in absolute love with the game, and Romey absolutely was not. He'd have rather bet on a game than play in one.

So that's why he called it quits. Marlene didn't exactly try talking him out of it either. She was pregnant again with their second son, and she was just as ready as he was to exit the sport. As was Romey's way, he shrugged, winked, and packed up his baseball equipment for the last time. Maybe Rich would want his bat, glove, and stirrups. His only remorse was that he'd be letting Jerome down. And his only fear was letting Jerome know.

He called his father on the phone that summer of 1957, telling him he'd be back in Steubenville in a couple of days. He didn't tell Jerome why. Forty-eight hours later, he pulled into the driveway at 156 Brockton Road in his Ford Fairlane, a wedding gift he'd received from his father a year earlier. Eleven-year-old Rich was playing in an oak tree above the driveway, and at the sight of the familiar Fairlane, he let out a whoop and jumped twelve feet straight to the ground to hug his big brother.

"What are you doing here?" Rich asked. "Aren't you supposed to be playing ball?"

"I got some news," Romey answered. 'But let's talk about it at five when Dad comes."

Marlene had accompanied Romey for moral support, and they all sat pensively among themselves, waiting for Jerome to arrive home from the mill. The greeting between Romey and his father was brief, awkward, and measured. Jerome had never hugged any of his children—not as toddlers, not ever—and he wasn't about to start now. He had the convenient generational excuse: dads from the 1950s and early '60s just weren't comfortable physically embracing their children. Besides, Romey was supposed to be on a field in Savannah or Augusta or Charlotte somewhere. So something must have been patently wrong. To Jerome, the mere sight of Romey in midsummer was no occasion for a bear hug.

When Romey broke the news of his voluntary retirement, he made it clear it was his decision, and his alone. The last thing he was ever going to do was point the finger at Marlene, even though he knew his father was going to blame her. Romey was an honorable man, twenty-four-years-old at this point, and he told himself he was going to take the hit from his father—even if it meant a literal whipping. He simply told his dad he'd lost his fire for the game (a true statement) and that his arm hurt (false statement). But Jerome simply stared at the ground before finally giving Marlene a piercing glance. For whatever reason, Jerome instinctively believed it was this woman who caused Romey to flunk baseball. And just like Father Hesburgh, Marlene became the scapegoat.

The retirement was heartbreaking to Rich, as well. Romey was the epitome of a baseball player to him—strapping and unflappable. The thought of him going to work for their dad in the mill, which was what ended up happening, was absurd to him. Either way, Romey's retirement was about to have a domino effect, because the baseball baton had officially been passed to Rich.

In the days to follow, Rich could feel the pressure shift, could feel his father turning up the heat on "Project Rich." Jerome soon drew up a set of rules for his youngest son, or edicts, so to speak. They weren't well received at all by Rich, but Jerome made it quite clear what was and wasn't permitted for his son during Little League:

- No striking out allowed
- No swimming allowed on game days
- No leaving the front porch on game days
- No watching TV on game days
- No movies at the theatre house for the foreseeable future, if ever

It was a grand plan to keep Rich's body healthy, his eyes clear, and his mind sharp. If he violated any of those laws, he'd be whipped with a thin leather belt. In return, Rich gave his father his first nicknames: "the General," "the Warden," and "Boss of the World." Behind his back, of course.

It was the opposite of how his father had handled Romey. Jerome was mostly hands-off during Romey's rise and fall. But with Rich, he was going to flip the script and be hands-on, or hands clenched, as the case may be.

For instance, Rich asked to have a basketball hoop installed in their front driveway on Brockton Road, and Jerome refused. Basketball was taboo. It was baseball or bust. Rich was suddenly more than a son; he was a prop, a mission statement.

No one wanted to wear a big league uniform someday more than Rich. But Rich couldn't help but push back. He would hit a pair of home runs in a Little League game, and there wouldn't be a hug, a handshake, or even a nod from his old man. Home runs and extra base hits were expected. Jerome's only comment would be, "You might've had three or four home runs if you didn't take those first-pitch fastballs for strikes." Eleven-year-old Rich thought that was just rude and mean.

On days like that—if his father was out or at work—Rich would release his pent-up anger by removing every canned good out of Helen's kitchen cabinets, slamming them on the counter, and then reinserting them before Jerome came home. It became his nervous habit. If he talked back to Jerome or Helen, Jerome would force him to swallow castor oil. If Rich didn't eat his peas at dinner, Jerome would shove a banana down the toilet and make Rich dig it out. When Rich swatted an annoying girl at school, Jerome made him eat an entire bowl of sugar, which can make you sweat profusely and gag. "I almost thought he wanted to kill me," Rich says.

Jerome was so intent on reining Rich in that he asked Romey for help. "Talk to that boy for me," Jerome would tell Romey. The sight of his big brother would lift Rich's spirits. They'd escape to Rich's room and talk baseball or Dean Martin or the weekend's college football odds. Romey ended up teaching Rich how to nod to and ignore his father at the same time. It was an art. Romey had dealt with this fanaticism long before Rich had, and he promised his kid brother he would teach him everything he could about catching, hitting, and tuning out the monster.

Every morning, weather permitting, Romey would drive Rich over to the practice field at Steubenville High and teach him something novel about baseball. He even let Rich try catching his fastball. It was Rich's pipe dream come to life; he was actually catching his hero, a former pro. Romey didn't hold anything back and threw his eighty-five-mile-an-hour four-seamer, which had a natural sink to it. Rich swears the first time he caught one, he nearly broke his left thumb. Romey could see his kid brother grimacing, so he taught him how to soften his hand as he received the pitch. It was the kind of advice Rich would never forget, and there were no more near-broken thumbs after that.

Here he was, twelve years old, handling a former professional pitcher. Afterward, they'd hop in the Ford Fairlane and head over to Spahn's Dairy, where Romey would buy him a milkshake for twenty-two cents. Those were the days Rich wished would go on forever.

"He knew he didn't make it in baseball, and by God, he wanted to make sure his little brother did," Rich says.

By the time Rich was thirteen, Romey had become the coach of his Babe Ruth League team, which brought the two even closer, if that was possible. Now they had both a brother and coach-catcher relationship. Romey taught Rich how to call a game intelligently, how to frame a pitch, how to hustle to back up first base on ground balls. They were together at the field without fail—until Romey began to miss practices for doctor appointments.

It turned out that Romey had noticed a lump in his neck area and needed to have multiple blood tests run at the Cleveland Clinic. A few years earlier, during his senior year at Mount St. Mary's, he had noticed a similar lump, and a country doctor in Maryland diagnosed him with mononucleosis. But, this time, the lump had returned in precisely the same spot. Romey, twenty-eight, was diagnosed with Hodgkin's disease.

Since this was 1960, the prognosis wasn't promising. Romey would spend weeks on end at a Pittsburgh hospital, and the prolonged absences unnerved his little brother. Rich asked to visit him once, and Romey acted as if he had only a head cold or something. Romey made sure to only talk baseball, and then he'd send Rich back to Steubenville with a practice plan for his Babe Ruth League team.

But with every hospital stay in Pittsburgh, where Romey was being treated with blood transfusions and an early version of chemotherapy called nitrogen mustard, the news became more dire. Romey's cancer was terminal.

In Romey's final days, ninth-grader Rich was asked to come to the hospital to say good-bye. In fact, those were the exact words his parents used: *Tell him good-bye.* How do you tell your idol good-bye? Fourteen-year-old Rich was shaking when he entered to see Romey one last time.

"Hey, Richie, how are you?" Romey asked.

"Good, Rome, good."

"Listen, I feel sorry for you," Romey went on.

"What do you mean?"

"All the mistakes I made—Dad's not gonna allow you to do nothing. I mean, *nothing.*"

"What?"

"Listen, all I can tell you is practice hard, work hard. Dad is going to be terrible on you because of me. Because he thinks a girl caused me to quit. All those things. Like I said, work hard. Outhustle the world. Prepare yourself. Practice hard."

The conversation didn't carry on much further than that, other than Romey advising Rich not to flunk Religion. It was their final light moment, their last laugh. But truth be told, Rich was about to have his own test in Religion—not a final exam, because he was just fourteen, but an assessment just the same. And the questions he felt needed answers were, "What do I make of this cruel, confusing move by God? What do I do with death?"

Letter from Amy

Dad,

I heard you used to play in a graveyard growing up. I don't know if you know it or not, but I go to graveyards too.

The other day, Bubba had a Little League game, and there was a cemetery right by the field. I walked around in there and saw some tombstones with pictures of little girls on them. I feel so badly for those girls. How could they die so young?

I'm going to go back during Bubba's next game. I'm going to see them again.

Love,

Amy

Three

Bubble Wrap

———————

R omey's funeral was the first time Rich was ever leery of a cemetery. All those mornings he frolicked in the graveyard off Langley Avenue, he never stopped to look at the names, the epitaphs, or the ages of the dead. But this time, it was personal. This time, he would be stepping around the body of his brother. It was about to change his life.

Whatever Rich loved about his Steubenville childhood—the nuns' gambling, crashing recess, his bright red catching equipment—was history now. July 7, 1961, was the end of his innocence. Whereas Rich was once happy-go-lucky, creating infield dirt in his kitchen with Jell-O powder, he was suddenly a pensive loner, with no older brother to confide in.

His sister, Patti, six years older, remembers trying to hug him the day of the funeral—and Rich yanking himself away from her. There was almost a hollow, blank look on his face, a look of denial and defeat. At the cemetery, he particularly wrestled with the finality of Romey's death. During the burial, the priest kept using words such as *eternity* and *final resting place*, causing tears to leak down Rich's face. It just hammered home that he would never see Romey again, catch his fastball, or share a milkshake with him at Spahn's.

His solace, of all places, was his bedroom at home, where he could lock the door and turn on his radio. That radio had rescued him the night Romey died. He was watching the Pirates game on the living room TV when his parents called from the hospital. They informed his babysitter—his cousin Donna Jean—that Romey was gone. Donna Jean wailed at first and then told Rich he had better turn off the game, that there was awful, horrible news.

Once Rich heard, he sat stoically in a chair by the window and then got up and headed for his room. He didn't throw himself on his bed or scream into the night. Instead, he found the Pirates game on his radio and immersed himself in the familiar cadence of Pirates broadcaster Bob Prince. If not for the game, he may still be mad at the world, at God. But the Pirates were playing the Milwaukee Braves that night of July 7, and when Dick Groat homered and Bill Virdon doubled—leading the Buccos to a 6–5 victory—Rich found himself at peace. The game of baseball had done what it had always done: it had been his trustworthy friend.

After the last out, he got on his knees and whispered the Serenity Prayer four times straight: *God, grant me the serenity to accept the things I cannot change, courage to change the things I can, and wisdom to know the difference.* It dawned on him then that he was more somber than mad, more in control than even he imagined he'd be. His mother tapped on his door later that night, afraid he'd need comforting, and he calmly told her he would see her in the morning.

All those trips to Holy Communion before school, all those Easter Sundays as an altar boy, all those Saturday mornings at confession, all the times he had stopped at a random church and introduced himself to the priest—it was equity he had built up for just this kind of tenuous moment.

If this was his test in Religion, he had earned an A, not an F. He wasn't furious with God; instead, he wanted to be there for Romey's four boys, wanted to be the hero to them that their father had been to him. He dedicated whatever career he'd have in baseball to Romey. His obsession was to get where Romey couldn't get: Forbes Field.

Unfortunately, Romey's deathbed warning to Rich had turned out to be prophetic. If Jerome was fanatical about baseball before, now he had gone over the top. In Jerome's opinion, Romey had failed because of Marlene and a severe lack of focus. So as Rich entered high school, Jerome's list of edicts grew:

- No looking at girls.
- No talking to girls.
- No ogling girls.
- No driver's license—because that might impress a girl, not to mention he could get in a car wreck and ruin his baseball career.
- No working at the mill—because that might impress a girl, not to mention he could injure himself handling the machinery and ruin his baseball career.
- A mandatory curfew between 9:30 and 10:30—which would definitely not impress a girl.
- Definitely no girls.

This list was not to be negotiated, and when Rich dared to ask for clarification on the girls part, Jerome sternly obliged. Under no circumstances would Rich be permitted to go out on dates, attend dances, or even contemplate having a girlfriend. He was not even to be seen with a girl in public.

More or less, this had everything to do with Marlene. When Marlene first laid eyes on Romey, for instance, she virtually stalked him, sitting behind the backstop at his baseball games, wishing she could pass him notes between innings. At least that's what Jerome heard. With that in mind, Jerome mandated that Rich go straight to the field on game days and then straight home afterward. No mingling with or making eyes at the opposite sex.

That was easier said than done, especially now that girls were starting to wink at him. One of his so-called admirers was his classmate Marlene Swan, who personally invited him to her eighth-grade dance party. Rich knew Jerome would have disapproved, loudly, so he assured young Ms. Swan that he would do his best to sneak his way there. It was a Sunday afternoon affair, and when Rich clandestinely arrived, he saw kids shimmying and, even more scandalously, kissing. Now he knew what he was missing. But it wasn't long before the phone rang at the Swan household. It was for Rich.

"For me?" Rich asked. "Who the heck knows I'm here?"

"Some man."

When Rich grabbed the phone to say hello, the voice on the other end of the line was the madman.

"What are you doing?" Jerome spouted. "Look across the street at Hutter Meat Market."

Rich groaned, looked across the boulevard, and saw who else but his father inside the Hutter Meat Market phone booth. Either his dad had followed him or had been shopping for brisket. But the day wasn't going to end well.

"Get your little butt over here," Jerome said, which meant Rich was about to get a whipping at home.

From then on, Rich knew he would have to get creative. For instance, Jerome would allow him to attend high school basketball games, as long as he was home twenty minutes after the final buzzer. Rich would bury a box of dress clothes in his mother's garden and leave his house in jeans and a T-shirt—pretending he was headed to the game. On his way out, he'd scoop up the box and hitch a ride to a girl's house with his high school buddy Danny Abramowicz (the future New Orleans Saints receiver). After changing clothes in the passenger seat, Rich would flirt with the girl for two hours while making sure to listen to the game on the radio. Right after the final buzzer, he'd change back into his jeans and have Abramowicz chauffer him home. It went like clockwork.

"How did the team look?" Jerome would ask.

Rich—aware that Jerome listened to all the games—spiced up much of what he'd heard on the radio broadcast and got away with it every time. If it was up to Jerome, he would've kept Rich in Bubble wrap. One day, Jerome read about Curt Simmons, the Phillies star pitcher who in 1953 lost part of his toe in a lawnmower incident. So from then on, when Rich cut the grass, he was required to wear his father's steel-tipped shoes.

Rich despised all of this babying. He wanted to come and go as he pleased; he wanted a summer job as a gas station attendant. He used to admire how the attendants sprinted out to pump the gasoline, their hands spattered with motor oil, small towels tucked into their back pocket. Now *that* was a uniform. But again, Jerome wouldn't permit it. The only place Rich was allowed to get down and dirty was the baseball diamond.

On the field, Rich could hear Romey's voice in his head: *work harder, work harder, work harder.* One of Rich's most impressive moments in high school was the time, from his catcher position, he hustled down the first base line on a ground ball and caught an overthrown ball by his shortstop—in the air. Fortuitously, a couple of scouts were in the stands.

As usual, Jerome offered no compliment. But rest assured, he'd seen the play. He'd seen them all. He would drive up to each game in his bleach white Dodge DeSoto, a boat of a car that had fins on the side of the trunk. Rich would keep an eye out for him; he couldn't have missed that monstrosity of a car if he tried.

Helen would step out of the vehicle first, carrying her rosary beads, praying Rich stayed injury-free. Then Jerome would emerge and stand hands on hips in that parking lot, eyeballing his boy's every move. Rich could see him clearly from his spot behind home plate, this lone figure pacing back and forth between parked cars. Jerome never yelled anything Rich's way; he'd save his critiques for the tense car rides home.

Rich remembers thinking he could just never please his dad. One of his teachers sent a note home from school one day, explaining that Rich couldn't see the blackboard clearly and needed glasses.

"You're faking," Jerome shouted at Rich. "You just want to wear glasses."

"I can't see!" Rich replied.

But reality was irrelevant to Jerome. He'd never heard of a big league catcher wearing glasses, and his son wasn't about to be the first. "He about whipped me," Rich says. "He was furious that my eyes were bad. *Furious.*"

It was reprehensible parenting, but Rich's sister, Patti, believes that Romey's death had hardened Jerome beyond repair. In fact, Patti wonders whether the loss led her dad to a nervous breakdown. Jerome, in the months and years to follow, was chronically sullen, often mumbling profanity to himself. He would take off on winding, solitary car rides. He would be gone for hours, just cruising from Ohio to West Virginia to Pennsylvania and back again, a lonely excursion to nowhere. He would also leave on one-man vacations, gone for days with little to no communication. Upon his return, no one had the guts to ask him where he'd been.

When they did take family trips, they would visit Buffalo; Jamestown, New York; and Palatka, Florida—all minor league baseball cities. They wouldn't know a soul in town. But these weren't vacations as much as scouting trips. The idea was to familiarize Rich with the life Romey was supposed to have. Romey had been ill-prepared for the minor league grind, so Jerome was simulating the minors as best he could for Rich. If that meant two days at a Holiday Inn to cheer on the Lancaster (PA) Red Roses, so be it.

Rich enjoyed these minor league glimpses, though his mother was another story. Helen had tried to return to normalcy after Romey passed away, but traveling to these ball fields only caused her to miss him more. Patti would spy her crying a lot, especially at Christmas and Easter, and when Patti would try to comfort her, Helen would say, "When you lose a child, half of you is just gone."

Sometimes it felt like three-quarters of Helen was gone, especially when family members would hear her saying, "Romey, Romey, Romey" to no one in particular. There was honestly nothing anyone could say at times like that.

Add up all this dysfunction, and it's no wonder that Rich—at age fifteen, sixteen, and seventeen—began to stutter. It was basically a nervous twitch of his voice; his words just wouldn't come out with his normal cadence. He was overcome with embarrassment the first time it happened in public. He became antisocial and would avoid wandering into crowded rooms. "I was afraid I'd get pointed at—'There's Rich; he stutters,'" he says. "I'd turn purple. I was afraid and so shy. I was nervous about everything I did."

Here he was, the best baseball player Steubenville had to offer. But Romey's death, coupled with Jerome's odd behavior and Helen's depression, turned Rich into a recluse. Conscious of his speech impediment and growing tired of Jerome's wrath, Rich eventually stopped trying to sneak out to meet girls. His last couple of years of high school were spent mostly in his room on Brockton Road, door locked and radio blaring.

That room had everything he needed, starting with that Motorola radio. Every night during the baseball season, he would tune in to the Pirates games on KDKA, the AM radio station out of Pittsburgh. He would meticulously keep score. If the Pirates lost, he would pout and not even say good night to his parents. But if they won, he'd race into their bedroom reciting the final score and the stars of the game.

His whole evening depended on the Pirates; after losses, he'd need to say the Serenity Prayer to calm himself. The better the team got, the more invested he became. In 1960—the year before Romey passed away—the Buccos had, in fact, provided Rich with the seminal moment of his life. They had reached the World Series against Mickey Mantle's Yankees that year and forced a winner-take-all seventh game at Forbes Field. Game time was 1 p.m. on Thursday afternoon, October 13, and Rich was dying to be there in person. Jerome got tickets through his job at Wheeling Steel, ten rows behind the Yankees dugout. But he went with his bosses, leaving Rich behind, salivating.

The whole tri-state area was shut down that day, so the principal at Rich's Catholic school, Monseigneur Cornelius, sent everyone home early. Rich watched the game exactly two inches from his black-and-white television screen, while Helen boiled spaghetti. In the bottom of the ninth, the score was 9–9, with No. 9—Pirates second baseman Bill Mazeroski—coming to the plate. Nines were wild. Mazeroski was a local kid who had played semipro ball with Romey in the Ohio Valley League—so *that* had Rich moving one inch closer to the TV. And then, boom!

Mazeroski blasted a 1–0 pitch into the trees behind the left field wall, the first walk-off Game 7 home run ever. At Forbes Field, grown men and teenage boys chased after Mazeroski as he rounded third base, several of them trying to hop on his shoulders as he pranced toward home plate. Back at Brockman Road, Rich was with them in spirit; he'd have done anything to run alongside Maz. As the ball sailed over the wall, Helen threw her plate of spaghetti into the air, whereupon Rich says the two of them "danced around the kitchen like two wild animals." They then hurried back to the TV to see whether they could find Jerome on camera.

It gave Rich something to shoot for, although what were the odds of a Game 7 walk-off ever happening to him? He'd have to visit a Steubenville cigar shop to find that one out, but he allowed himself to dream it at least.

That Mazeroski moment was indelibly etched in his mind, and winning his own World Series—even better with a Game 7 walk-off—became his personal obsession. He wanted his name up in lights like Maz. He would drive to games at Forbes Field to see how far, talent-wise, he was from the Majors. He'd sit by himself in the upper-deck cheap seats, using his binoculars to see what brand of gloves the catchers were wearing. "My friends didn't understand that," Rich remembers. "Especially any girls who liked me. I remember one girl saying, 'You're impossible to like. You're impossible. All you want to do is go to those baseball games.'"

His love life even became a topic of conversation at his high school, Steubenville Catholic Central.

"You dating somebody, Rich?"

"Yeah."

"What's her name?"

"Baseball."

Still, on those excursions to Forbes Field, he'd notice how enormous and skilled the players were. Roberto Clemente, he thought, was out of this universe. These were the times Rich wondered whether reaching the major leagues was just a ridiculous pipe dream. On one of his more insecure days, he drew up a backup plan: perhaps he could get to the Pirates as a third base coach . . . and *wave in* a World Series Game 7 winning run instead.

One night in his senior year, he kneeled at his bed, fingered his rosary beads, and prayed to reach a World Series in any capacity. "Third base coach," he told God, "would be absolutely fine."

Sometimes he'd wonder if God was really listening. He was convinced no kid in salty Steubenville prayed more than him, but what did he have to show for it yet? Certainly not a big league contract.

With all that time alone in his room, Rich spent 75 percent of it pressing his hands together in prayer. He would say morning prayers, night prayers, Serenity prayers, Christmas prayers, Easter prayers, spur-of-the-moment prayers. Every spring, he'd build a May altar by his bedroom window, complete with a blessed Virgin Mary, candles, and a Bible. But still, no big league scouts were knocking on his door.

Impatient, he began to pray to St. Jude, the patron saint of lost causes. That's how Rich saw himself by now—a gangly, bespectacled, shy, abused, stuttering lost cause. A desperate case if you ever saw one.

He stuck it out with God though. He would go into his basement and hold his own private Mass, using some of Helen's homemade Italian bread. At church, he had been recruited to be a pontifical server, shadowing the bishop, helping create the incense, traveling with the bishop to bless cattle at local farms. He considered the red silk cassock and the red buckled suede shoes to be as sacred as a baseball uniform, and certainly on a par with a gas station attendant's oily shirt and slacks. For two full years, every place the bishop went, Rich went.

Since the major league scouts still weren't coming around, he thought maybe he should just be a priest. One day, through his church, he and about twenty teens visited a seminary, and that's what planted the idea in his head. No one would dare make fun of his stuttering if he were a priest. Priests were just as popular as Mazeroski. But Rich noticed there was no seminary baseball team. That presented a problem.

He began leaning toward the priesthood when his grades started to go south in his senior year of high school. The seminary became his escape plan. It was decided then. All he had to do was tell Jerome he was quitting baseball to be a priest.

That next evening, his father was sitting quietly in the living room reading the newspaper. That was Jerome's after-dinner ritual, and Rich knew better than to disturb him. But this was big news.

"Dad, I want to be a priest," Rich pronounced.

At that very second, the newspaper came down and came down hard. Rich knew from experience he was about to get a whipping.

"No! Now get out of here and go to your room," Jerome said.

Rich had no choice but to abandon the seminary idea—he admits he may not have gone through with it anyway—but he was also ready to abandon Jerome. Because not long after that, Jerome forced Rich to turn down the New York Mets.

This was 1964, one year before the first ever Major League Baseball draft. A Mets scout had been wandering through Steubenville from time to time and had seen the play where Rich hustled from his catcher spot to catch the errant throw from the shortstop. The scout was sold then and sold even more after he'd seen Rich bat roughly .375 in American Legion ball the summer after his junior year. So even though Rich missed a portion of his senior season with mononucleosis, the Mets were prepared to sign him after graduation.

The scout invited Jerome and Rich to a hotel in nearby Weirton, West Virginia, and offered a $5,000 signing bonus and a brand-new Buick Electra if Rich signed. Who cared if Rich didn't have his driver's license yet? Rich's pro dream—and perhaps his World Series dream—was coming to fruition. The Mets were in the same division as the Pirates; if he reached the big leagues, he'd get to play against Mazeroski at Forbes Field and get to invite half of Steubenville to come watch it.

The words "Yes, sir, I'll take it" were just about out of Rich's mouth when Jerome said, "No, thank you, he'll be going to college." It was a stunner, and hypocritical. Rich had endured eighteen years of his father's edicts and prohibitions and curfews and stalkings. He'd stayed away from girls just for this big league moment. And now Jerome was calling off the whole thing?

On the ride back to Steubenville that night, Jerome explained that $5,000 was a relative pittance, that college would best prepare him for the future in case Rich failed like Romey. Matter of fact, Jerome had even devised Rich's backup plan: he would be a doctor if baseball didn't work out.

His father was dictating Rich's entire life with little or no feedback from his son. A doctor? Rich hated the sight of blood. The kid had had enough. Steubenville was Rich's home, his favorite place on earth. Everything from the cigar shops to Spahn's Dairy to Brucie Boggs's porch to Bill Mazeroski's blast was indelibly etched in his mind. But it was time to get out, get away from Jerome, go to Xavier University, and play in front of even more professional scouts.

He knew one thing for certain: he'd keep praying. He was convinced that God, St. Jude, the Serenity Prayer, the May altar—not necessarily in that order—had all played a part in the Mets offer. The heavens had been paying attention. Come to think of it, he felt his faith had also gotten him through Romey's death as well. He was a believer. He was ready for everything life had to offer, ready for the next stage of his journey, ready to leave home . . . and start heading toward first base.

Letter from Amy

Dad,

I know this sounds a little dark, but if I happen to die young, I don't want anything corny or flowery on my tombstone.

I don't know why I'm telling you this. But I went back to the cemetery next to Bubba's Little League field, and you should've seen some of the things written on the headstones. On a little girl's tomb, it said, "Sleep, my little one, sleep." That just really bugged me to no end. So if something happens to me, don't write something like that. Just put my name on there. That's more than enough.

Okay, back to happier thoughts. Win your game tonight!

Love,

Amy

Four

Peggy

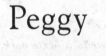

T he first semester of his freshman year, it showed up on his class
schedule: *Religion I.*

Being that Xavier was a Catholic university, similar to Notre Dame,
the course was bound to be in the basic curriculum. But it scared the
living daylights out of young Rich Donnelly.

He was a free man in terms of being on his own, living in a dorm and
not having Jerome breathing down his neck. But his father was still in the
air. Even though Xavier was in Cincinnati, four and a half hours down I-70
and I-71 from Steubenville, Jerome Donnelly was proving to be omnipresent.

All Rich thought about as his grade in Religion dipped was how his
father was going to murder him if he flunked it. He thought college was
going to be a rite of passage and he was going to become his own man.
But the fear of Jerome, along with the stuttering, had gone down the
Interstate with him.

Part of the pressure was that his older sister, Patti, had flunked out of
Ohio State a few years prior. And considering Rich was supposed to be
the weakest student of the three kids, odds were there would be a repeat
performance. Perhaps the Steubenville cigar shops should have set the
over-under on Rich's college stay at three months. But one thing about
Rich and the Religion class: he was going to compete.

Rich had assumed that learning Latin and making incense in church
would prepare him for the course. But he says it was more like taking

advanced history, with names he couldn't pronounce. He earned a D by the skin of his teeth, and he's certain the only reason he passed Religion was his expert praying.

To be eligible for baseball that spring, Rich needed an overall 1.75 grade point average, and his mind kept visualizing a 1.25 or worse. His grades finally arrived right after New Year's Day 1965. He ripped open the envelope, said the Serenity Prayer, and looked down to find a . . . 1.76. By a hundredth of a percentage point, he was a college baseball player. The "Peace On Earth" sign on the Donnelly's front door was never a truer statement. No whippings were imminent.

By his sophomore year, he appeared to be a new man. He began to attend the daily Mass at noon without fail. His morning courses would wrap up by 11:30 a.m., which meant he had the next ninety minutes to spend in the nearby church before baseball practice. The priest, Father McElroy, knew Rich from the weekly Sunday Mass he conducted in the dorms. But now that Rich had become a regular in his local Catholic church, the Father invited Rich to become a lector and read the Scriptures out loud each day.

Rich agreed because he couldn't bear to disappoint a priest. Public speaking was torture to him, of course, but a most peculiar thing happened every time Rich read the Epistle or anything else: he didn't stutter.

"It was like magic," he told Helen on the phone.

"Amazing," Helen said.

"It's a miracle from God, Mom. I've never believed in miracles. But this is a miracle. I still stutter every place else I know."

Rich started getting brave. His first year in college he had barely left his dorm, other than maybe to grab a pepperoni pizza. He certainly didn't venture out on any dates. He was a relative hermit, a carryover from high school and Jerome's edict to avoid the opposite sex. But his sophomore roommate Tim Gorman—a defensive back on the football team—practically ordered him to test out college night life. Gorman said the girl he was dating had a cute friend and that it was now-or-never to go on a double date. "Just one time," Gorman said. "One time."

That night, Rich took one swift look at Peggy Haines—blonde and athletic, a Julie Christie look-alike—and melted. Not only was she attractive, but she knew all about Oscar Robertson and laughed at all of the Steubenville nicknames, particularly Mousie and Ratsy Gaylord. They were headed to a campus mixer, but the only mixing Rich did was with Peggy.

It was December 17, 1965, a day he would never forget. He wouldn't take his eyes off her all night. They danced, even though he had two left feet and wore a borrowed suit three sizes too small. At the end of the evening, she gave him her precious phone number.

He was dying to call her as soon as he got back to the dorm that evening. But he waited until the following night, when he knew the only telephone close by—the pay phone in the front lobby of Brockman Hall—would be available. Almost all of the students were exiting campus for Christmas break, so he figured the phone would be all his. He couldn't have been more right.

He put his dimes in the pay phone at eight o'clock on the night of December 18 and didn't hang up until noon on the 19th. That's a grand total of sixteen hours. He and Peggy talked about her life, his life, Cincinnati, Steubenville, church, gambling, Romey, her mother, his mother, her father . . . not his father. There were several long, pregnant pauses, but she thought he was funny and charming, and he thought she was the only girl on earth.

Jerome had ripped Rich away from every female he'd ever met—and he half expected Jerome to burst into Brockman Hall, the same way he'd barged into Marlene Swan's party. But that's why Rich would have kept talking for another sixteen hours, another thirty-two. "I didn't want to lose her," he says. "I just didn't want to lose her."

He had finally seen how the other half lives, and there was no turning back. Jerome's rule was to never fraternize with girls in public, but now he was going to be arm in arm with Peggy Haines in broad daylight or bright moonlight for the foreseeable future.

Now on cloud nine, he decided he was staying on campus over

Christmas break. Peggy would pick him up in her Corvair convertible—top down, heat on—because he still hadn't learned to drive. When she asked him why, he mumbled something about his old man, but not even that was going to put him in a sour mood. They would then grab something to eat, park the Corvair, and make out. Rich considered all of this "being in love."

It was the time of his life, and college baseball season hadn't even started yet. Over Christmas break, he began to spend time in the Xavier gymnasium playing basketball—the sport Jerome had forbidden him to play. He was long and lanky, with a knack for rebounding, defending, and passing to the open man. He made his teammates better, even in random pickup games, and one day, he happened to be on the same team as Xavier freshman point guard Joe Pangrazio.

He and Pangrazio were a picturesque duo—one pass kept getting sweeter than the next—and the head basketball coach, Don Ruberg, was an eyewitness. After the game, Ruberg asked Pangrazio, "Who's that guy playing with you?"

"That's Rich Donnelly. He's on the baseball team."

"Well, now he's on the basketball team," Ruberg said.

Ruberg approached Rich. "You like basketball? Here's what we can do. You haven't played a varsity sport yet, have you?"

"No, sir."

"How about this: you play on the freshman team the rest of this year, and next year, we'll put you on scholarship?"

"Sounds like a deal," Rich said.

Rich was now just days into 1966—and completely out of his shell. He had a new girl, a new sport, and a newfound courage. To prove it, he even called home in February to tell Helen about Peggy.

"Mom, I met this girl," he said. "I want you to meet her."

Jerome, though, was hovering, trying to listen in over Helen's shoulder. When he saw Helen's eyebrows raised, he knew there was news. So Jerome did what came natural: he hijacked the telephone.

"I hear you met a girl," Jerome blurted. "I've got a business trip to

Cincinnati next week. Let's see—the basketball team has a home game Wednesday night against Marquette. We can all go to the game."

Rich swallowed hard. He then told Jerome to meet a Julie Christie look-alike named Peggy outside Xavier's Schmidt Field House three hours before game time. "I'll meet up with you two closer to tip-off," Rich told him, "because I've got to do something."

What he had to *do* that day was play his freshman game against Kentucky at the same arena, hours before the varsity game. Rich figured this was the most efficient way to break his basketball news to Jerome—by showing his dad, firsthand, how intense he was in the sport. Hopefully, Jerome wouldn't sprint on the court to strangle him.

So on that Wednesday, February 16, 1966, Jerome laid eyes on his son's first official girlfriend. He shook her hand, and then she led him by his into the arena.

"What are we doing at the freshman game? The varsity game against Marquette doesn't start till seven," Jerome protested.

"Well, they're playing Kentucky, and I love basketball," Peggy said. "Is it okay if we stay?"

"Where's Rich?"

"He'll be here pretty soon," Peggy deadpanned.

A minute later, there was Rich, rushing out of the tunnel and into the layup line in a Xavier uniform.

Jerome did a quadruple take and cleaned up his next comment because he was in mixed company. "What's going on?" he stewed.

But Jerome also wouldn't dare leave his seat—because Rich was playing a beautiful game. He had six points, three look-away assists, five steals, and six rebounds off the bench in a Xavier victory. One of those artistic assists, a no-look feed to future NBA player Luther Rackley for a dunk, had set the home crowd on fire, and Peggy thinks she saw Jerome clap. But when Rich showered and met Peggy outside afterward, she was in tears.

"What's wrong, Peg?"

"Your dad is gone."

"What do you mean gone?"

"He went back to Steubenville."

Rich, who had a love affair to get back to himself, didn't bat an eye. He and Peggy would study together every night at her nursing school library—until the day she excused herself to go to the ladies' room and he saw her through a window, puffing on a cigarette.

Appalled that she was a smoker and hurt that she'd hidden it from him, he bolted. That's how straitlaced he was—and also how perfect and pristine he expected her to be. He called her from the same Brockman Hall pay phone and told her it was all over. The breakup lasted all of an hour. He called back to apologize, and, after making him sweat for a minute, she accepted his mea culpa.

If love was new and strange, so was college baseball. His sophomore year was his first varsity season, and he hit a walk-off inside-the-park home run in his debut game versus Kentucky. His teammates thought he was nuts—because he even hustled to get a drink of water. He was the catcher, the leader, and the most likely to reach the big leagues. The Yankees were already scouting him.

With the big leagues on his mind, Rich took a drive with Danny Abramowicz to see a Pirates-Reds game on a frigid Cincinnati night in 1966. Their seats were directly behind the Pirates radio booth, and they kept whistling toward Bucs radio announcer Bob Prince. Prince's broadcasts had helped keep Rich sane after Romey's death, so just the sight of the dapper announcer had Rich beaming. He just *had* to meet him. Between one of the innings, they rapped on the door of the booth, and Rich asked Prince if he'd "tell Steubenville that the boys from Xavier say hello." Prince not only complied, but he also let Rich—who was shivering in the forty-degree temperatures—borrow his jacket. It made Rich aspire to be a Bucco even more.

On evenings like that, Rich missed home terribly. He still had Steubenville on the brain, and always would. Another night in his dorm room, he was preparing to deliver a lecture in his Speech 101 class, a course no stutterer should probably take. Abramowicz had convinced Rich it was an easy class—give four speeches a semester and you'd have an A—but Rich was worried he'd lose points for stumbling over his words. He asked his roommates if he could rehearse in front of them and joked that he never used to stutter in front of the nuns back home. Next thing they knew, he was riffing about Tennis Shoe Ernie, who would ride a scooter up and down Main Street in Steubenville as he cleaned the storefront windows. He began reminiscing about Barking Barry and Bible Bill—and all the other Steubenville characters.

One of his roommates made an observation. "Richie, you didn't stutter one time when you were telling us about all those wack-jobs," he said.

"Really?"

"That's what you should give your speech on—Steubenville."

So Rich switched gears and delivered a speech on the Steubenville mob, Steubenville nuns, Steubenville nicknames, and Dino Crocetti—all without a single stutter. He earned an A. "From then on, I was good," he remembers. It only proved that "The Ville"—even the town had a nickname—would always be Rich's happiest place on earth.

He was twenty years old and just experiencing a lot of firsts. First time driving . . . first time meeting a girlfriend's parents . . . first time sneaking off to a hotel to be alone with Peggy.

He says he and Peg were both virgins and that the relationship had escalated to the point she wanted to sleep with him, and vice versa. He saw Peggy as his future wife, so it seemed like less of a sin to him. They drove her Corvair to a hotel and checked in as Mr. and Mrs. Donaldson. The time to consummate their love affair was now . . . until it wasn't.

Rich got cold feet. After they kissed for a spell on the bed, he abruptly pulled away and asked if they could wait until after they were married. She thanked him profusely and said she felt the same way.

So Mr. and Mrs. (wink, wink) Donaldson were in that hotel room for a grand total of thirty minutes. They checked out and took the Corvair straight to the cathedral—so Rich could go to confession.

He had been adamant that they stop there on the way back to her dorm. She remained in the Corvair while he entered the church. His conversation with the priest was an awkward one.

"Father, I didn't have sex today, but I would've."

According to Rich, the priest began to chuckle.

"Wait a minute. You're here, but you didn't have sex?" the priest asked.

"No, Father, I didn't," Rich continued. "We went to a hotel to have sex and we both changed our minds and left. But I felt like that was a sin."

"Oh, I see."

There was silence for twenty seconds, thirty seconds, forty-five seconds—which Rich took to mean the priest was at a loss. Rich exited sheepishly.

From then on, he thought it was best to focus on baseball. Although he'd been selected by the New York Yankees in the fifteenth round of the 1966 June Major League draft, Jerome considered that an insult and instructed his son to return to school. Rich, he contended, was too good for the fifteenth round. So Rich's junior season of 1967 became his one last year to impress the major league scouts—not that there was any pressure.

Rich stepped up. His batting average hovered around .350 all season, and considering he'd been known more for his glove than his bat, his stock was rising. From a team standpoint, it was also Xavier's greatest baseball season ever. The Musketeers received their first-ever NCAA bid, and Rich had set the tone all year with his energy and camaraderie with the pitching staff. His forte was calling pitches from behind the plate, and he felt they could do some damage as a team in the tournament.

But Xavier's administration nixed it all. The tournament's opening round was taking place during final exams, so the school's priests declined the NCAA bid for academic reasons. Rich was so perturbed that he refused to go to church for two weeks. He wanted out of college baseball, and his best-case scenario was getting drafted by a major league club—preferably the Pirates—that June.

Two months before the draft, the phone rang in the hallway at Brockman Hall. The caller had a raspy voice and asked to speak with Rich. Summoned to the pay phone—that near and dear Brockman pay phone—Rich wasn't sure who it could be, other than Peggy, Helen, or Jerome.

"Is this Rich Donnelly?"

"Yes."

"This is Pat Patterson of the New York Yankees."

Rich thought it was Danny Abramowicz pulling his leg.

"Cut it out," Rich moaned.

"No, really, this is Pat Patterson of the Yankees, and we want to know if you'd be interested in signing with us this time if we draft you."

"Yes, sir, I would," Rich answered in a nanosecond.

The next sixty days dragged on and on. But finally in the ninth round of the secondary phase of the June 1967 Major League baseball draft, the New York Yankees—*the New York Yankees, the team Bill Mazeroski slayed seven years before*—selected the left-handed hitting catcher out of Xavier, Rich Donnelly.

Rich never called Jerome to let him know. Instead, his dad had to hear it from the local Steubenville newspaper. It could have been the ultimate father-son moment. All those edicts and whippings and stale-mates and insensitive car rides home could have all been forgotten. After twenty-one years of bullying, the slate could have been wiped clean. The domineering dad and the repressed son could have finally met in the middle. Rich was a Major League draft pick.

But when Jerome finally reached his son on the phone to tell him the news, to tell him he'd be playing for the team that gave the world Babe Ruth, Lou Gehrig, Joe DiMaggio, and Mickey Mantle, Rich's cold and calculated response was, "Yeah, I already know."

He didn't stutter.

Letter from Amy

Dad,

    I saw what you did to Bubba the other night. Mom and I both saw the marks on his body.

    Did you whip him or just plain hit him?

    If you did, I'm really, really mad at you. I mean, why would you do something like that? Are you angry about something? Is there something from your past that would cause you to do that?

    I still love you though.

Amy

Five

Love and Baseball—
Not Necessarily
in That Order

R ich was thrilled to be drafted by the Yankees, the team that Bill
Mazeroski beat seven years earlier. But it didn't seem real until
he received a letter from the Yankees front office a week later via certi-
fied mail.

Rich ripped open the envelope, hoping they would be offering him
five figures to sign on the dotted line. Instead, it was a personal note
written by team president Dan Topping:

> Rich, the scout who recommended we draft you,
> Pat Patterson, thought very highly of you. He compared
> you as a catcher to Tim McCarver—and we relied on his
> word. But there's a problem. Pat is dead. He died on
> April 24. So just to be sure, we'd like you to try out
> for a contract.

Talk about rotten luck. It was a sad ending for the sixty-nine-year-old Patterson and an inauspicious beginning for Rich. The rest of Topping's note explained that Rich would play in the Central Illinois League in the summer of 1967, and, if the Yankees declined to extend an offer within sixty days, he'd become a free agent.

There was no underestimating the stress Rich was about to be under. His entire baseball future boiled down to one summer. By August, he'd either belong to New York or nobody at all. He could always return to Xavier for his senior year, but he was still ticked off over the school's decision to turn down the previous year's NCAA bid. So it was now or never, now or move back to Steubenville to work in the mill. Now or move to Vegas and become a card shark.

It turned out to be none of the above. With Yankees scout Lou Maguolo watching, Rich barely hit his weight (.180), and Maguolo said thanks but no thanks at the end of July. The Yankees were out. Rich had no choice but to rethink his future. By day, he worked as a groundskeeper at a ball field in Bloomington, Illinois, mowing the outfield grass—without steel-tipped shoes, of course—and grooming the infield dirt. By night, he played for a summer collegiate team, the Bloomington Bobcats. Between the humidity, the mosquitoes, and the gnats, it all felt like hard labor. But it also had him reminiscing about his days as a five-year-old sprucing up the field behind his house at Steubenville High. It became clear to him right then: home was the ticket.

He called in some favors and landed two jobs back in Steubenville—one as a high school assistant football coach (even though he'd never played football) and one as a high school history teacher (even though he hated history). He was about to break the news to Peggy when a man showed up at the field and tapped him on the shoulder.

"Excuse me, I'm looking for Rich Donnelly," the man said.

"Yeah, that's me," Rich said.

"Well, my name is Bill Messman, and I'm a scout for the Minnesota Twins. We're prepared to make you an offer to sign with us because you're a free agent now."

In a flash, Rich was back in the baseball business. Having seen him catch for the Bobcats, Messman offered an $8,000 signing bonus, plus $2,000 toward his tuition for the upcoming coming school year at Xavier. The last time he'd received an offer—back in high school from the Mets—Jerome had stepped in and rejected it. But in Rich's mind, there was no nixing this one. He called Jerome with the news out of courtesy, but now Rich was going to be "the General," "the Warden," and "Boss of the World" all wrapped up into one.

Predictably, Jerome thought something was fishy. He wondered why the Yankees would pass on him while the Twins were offering cash and tuition. Jerome's comment to Rich was, "What? They're going to pay for your schooling? No, they would never do that." After the Yankees' rejection, Jerome had essentially made up his mind that Rich's baseball quest was done. He assumed anyone who hit .180 for a summer was a non-prospect and considered the Twins offer a hoax. "He trusted nobody," Rich says.

Jerome had one request for his son: hand over Bill Messman's phone number. So much for Rich being "Boss of the World"—he acquiesced. Jerome must have called Messman ten times, and when he finally caught the scout at home, he delivered an ultimatum.

"My son will not sign until you wire us the money immediately via Western Union," Jerome pronounced.

Jerome was certain the Twins would show their true colors and back out. But little did Jerome know that the three Bobcats games Messman had scouted were fortuitously Rich's three best offensive games of the summer. So Messman's response to Jerome was, "Where do I send the money?"

The cash came in handy because Rich had a wedding ring to buy. He and Peggy had managed to remain a couple all this time, though not for a lack of drama. During September of his senior year, after Rich continued to complain about her smoking, she dumped him for the punter on the Xavier football team. Rich was soon lovesick, and after not speaking with her for two weeks, he bared his soul to Joey Pangrazio.

Joey was perhaps the Don Juan of campus, his dorm room equipped with blue lights, strobe lights, shag carpet, and an 8-track tape of The Temptations looping nonstop on his stereo. His buddies called him "the white James Brown"; Joey just had a way with the ladies. But Pangrazio was also a fireball whose nickname was "Crazy Joe," and when he heard Rich's tale of woe, he snapped. "I'm tired of this %$#^. Give me her phone number."

Pangrazio then headed for the Brockman Hall pay phone, the same one Rich had used for his and Peggy's sixteen-hour marathon. This call lasted only twenty minutes, and it was Pangrazio who did nearly all of the talking. His opening comment to Peggy was, "I'm going to tell you something right now, you ungrateful . . ."—and it was all downhill from there. He went on to holler, "You gotta a guy over here who will do anything for you, who loves you. And you treat him like dirt. You should have your rear end kicked. You're going with that no-good punter, and you've got the best guy in the world right here."

A dozen guys at Brockman Hall crowded close to hear the high-octave tirade, which Pangrazio concluded by slamming down the phone's receiver. This whole time, Rich had sat with his head in his hands, certain that Peggy was gone forever. But an hour later, the phone rang. Peggy was begging him to take her back.

She had done a complete 180 and was now pining to marry him. Her mind was made up, though she was convinced he'd never propose unless she converted to Catholicism. She'd been raised a Presbyterian, but she would do anything under the sun to land her man. After visiting with a priest and taking the requisite steps, she pronounced to Rich that she was Catholic. He decided to pop the question.

Because Rich tended to go by the book, he wanted to ask Peggy's father for her hand in marriage. It was a conversation he dreaded because Gene Haines was Jerome's twin, just as strict and ornery as his old man. "I think that's why Peggy and I were a match," Rich says.

Rich envisioned asking Gene for permission and hearing Gene tell him to get lost. It wasn't out of the realm of possibility. But Rich had just turned twenty-one, and, in his mind, if he waited until he was twenty-three or twenty-four to get engaged, he'd be considered old and "no girl would want me." Just like his baseball career, it was now or never.

He went to the Haines's trilevel home in the picturesque Kenwood section of Cincinnati on a night Peggy was working a late nursing shift. It was the Christmas season 1967, and Rich was greeted gleefully at the door by Peggy's mother, Ruth. They were already well acquainted because the Haineses had often invited Rich and Peggy—and sometimes Rich alone—to Cincinnati Royals NBA basketball games. Ruth and Rich would typically talk about the Royals' previous game or about their favorite players, Oscar Robertson and Connie Dierking. But on this night, an uptight Rich was stuttering again—and asked if he could relieve himself in the upstairs bathroom.

He sat on the toilet seat, drenched in nervous sweat. When he flushed, the toilet overflowed. He had inserted too much toilet paper into the bowl, and soon the bathroom was an inch deep in soiled water. Rich could literally hear it seeping through the drywall and didn't know whether to sound an alarm or escape out a back window. His feet were splashing around in muck; he was legitimately afraid to come out. Finally, he whipped open the door to call for Ruth.

"I need towels up here, Mrs. Haines," he said. "I'm sorry. The toilet overflowed."

"I know," Ruth said with a moan. "It's dripping into the downstairs rec room right in front of Gene's chair."

Rich hightailed it down two sets of stairs to the basement, hoping for minimal damage. But he entered the room only to find Gene on his hands and knees, mopping up the sewage and cussing.

The toilet water had leaked into the rec room through a light fixture—not a good way for Rich to join the family. But he had driven to Kenwood that night for a reason, and even though Gene was fuming, Rich sat in a chair beside him.

"Gene," he said, "before I leave, I'd like your permission to marry Peggy."

"Yeah, go ahead," Gene grumbled.

The sun came up the next morning, and Rich marched straight to his local bank. He withdrew some of his bonus money and bought a $325 diamond engagement ring for Peggy. The only downside was he'd have to return to the Haines's house.

He knocked inconspicuously on the door, his head low. He certainly wasn't going to ask to use the restroom. But it hardly mattered, because Ruth Haines was his ally on this. With Peggy upstairs in her room getting dressed, Ruth and Rich drew up a proposal plan. Ruth would make her delicious potato salad and cover the bowl with a plastic wrap. Rich would then put the ring box on top of the plastic. Come dinnertime, Ruth would ask Peggy to bring out the potato salad. Hopefully, she wouldn't drop it once she saw the surprise.

It worked the way they drew it up. Peggy gave Rich a hearty yes, while Gene rolled his eyes and retreated to his freshly mopped rec room. Rich would've preferred to get married the next day—before Gene Haines had a chance to change his mind. But the Haineses wanted the wedding held at the enormous Saint Peter in Chains Cathedral, one of the most gothic and picturesque churches in the Midwest. The wedding would have to wait six months; the wedding date was set for June 1, 1968.

Once the day finally arrived, Rich stood at the altar looking for Jerome out of the corner of his eye. He found him mingling with, of all people, Gene Haines. He was paranoid that Gene would share the bathroom story with his father; that was all he needed on his wedding day.

After the vows concluded and Peggy tossed her bouquet in the air, Rich felt a wave of guilt. He was about to have sex, and he hated that his father knew it. He spent a solid fifteen minutes wondering what Jerome was going to tell him on his way out the door, and his best guesses were, "Okay, where're you goin'?" or "What time are you gonna be back?" or "What hotel you stayin' at?" So Rich left without saying good-bye.

Their honeymoon was a weekend in Columbus, after which he was going to pack up and head to the Twins' minor league spring training site in Melbourne, Florida. The newlyweds got halfway to Columbus when their car's radiator blew, stranding them a couple of miles from the nearest gas station. Rich decided he had two options: call his father for help or walk two miles to the nearest mechanic. He walked the two miles.

They checked into their hotel that evening as Mr. and Mrs. Donnelly instead of Mr. and Mrs. Donaldson—at last. Once they were inside the room, Rich found himself peeking through the curtains, convinced Jerome would be sidling by in his Dodge DeSoto, much like he did at Marlene Swan's eighth-grade party. Once the coast was clear, they consummated their marriage.

The next day, they spent their first afternoon as a married couple at the bowling alley—Rich's idea. Peggy was expecting a candlelight dinner that evening, but Rich took her to the Scioto Downs racetrack to bet the horses. They ate hot dogs for supper.

Welcome to marriage with Rich—and Peggy was nonplussed. After the bowling and the racetrack, Rich was thinking, *Okay, I'm done. Let's go back to Cincinnati. I've got to get ready to go play baseball.* Peggy, on the other hand, wanted to shop, grab a pedicure, go out on the town, and have a white tablecloth dinner.

As married life unfolded, they agreed on only one thing: they wanted kids.

Letter from Amy

Dad,

I'm just double-checking.

Your biggest dream in life is to be in a World Series, right?

I'm just looking for things to pray for in church—and that seems like as good a thing to pray for as any.

So let me know when you get home. I'll file it away.

Love you!

Amy

Six

Minor Leagues, Major Issues

Minor league baseball in the 1960s was baseball on the cheap. The hotels were antiquated; the buses had rusty shock absorbers; and per diem got you a burger, some fries, and a Coke. After more than twenty years of being sequestered, manhandled, lectured, and objectified by Jerome, Rich Donnelly wondered, *It was all for this?*

The idea was to get to the big leagues, win a World Series, go down in history—and it had to begin somewhere. St. Cloud, Minnesota, was as good a place as any to start.

In some ways, ignorance was bliss. After spending ten days of spring training in Florida, Rich and Peggy enthusiastically relocated to the bedroom community of Sauk Rapids, Minnesota, not far from the minor league offices of the St. Cloud Rox.

This was rookie ball at its finest—an oxymoron if you've ever heard one. Rookie ball wasn't fine. Rather, it was seventy games in seventy days. And Rich somehow managed to be the Rox catcher for all seventy of them.

He learned fairly quickly that minor league baseball was a battle of attrition. The other catcher on the roster was a high draft pick named Mark Strader, who arrived in town with a sore throwing shoulder. That left Rich an opportunity he wasn't about to let go of.

The manager's name was Carroll Hardy, a former Red Sox reserve known as the only person in history to pinch-hit for Ted Williams (and later for Carl Yastrzemski as well). Hardy had also played pro football as a hobby for the 49ers and wanted players who would run through a brick wall for him. That was Rich to a T.

The one time Rich was supposed to take a day off that season, he still hustled to the bullpen to warm up the starting pitcher. Hardy had to order him back to the dugout. After Rich paced back and forth for two innings, Hardy finally reinserted him behind the plate.

This was the summer of 1968. Martin Luther King Jr. had been slain in April, and Bobby Kennedy had just been assassinated that June. Detroit was burning to a crisp. But news of the turbulence never quite made it up to Sauk Rapids. Rich and Peggy had a quaint apartment, a neighborhood church, and a nearby farmers market. They may as well have been living on another planet.

The baseball life was insulated. Rich had purchased a black Ford LTD with his bonus money, and their routine was simple. During homestands, he'd sleep in until eleven or twelve; she'd make him lunch at noon; and he'd drive the LTD to the ballpark at two. She'd feed him afterward at midnight—because, Lord knows, there was never a postgame spread in the clubhouse—and then he'd do it all over again the next day.

He was earning $500 a month before taxes, and the apartment ran $80 a month. They began to put together a nest egg. The hardest part was saying good-bye to each other for road trips, because these weren't exactly one-day or even three-day excursions. Traveling in the Northern League meant taking interminable bus rides to play the Duluth-Superior Dukes (a White Sox affiliate), the Sioux Falls Packers (a Reds affiliate), and the Aberdeen Pheasants (an Orioles affiliate). Compared to those places, Steubenville was a virtual metropolis.

Before their marriage, Rich had warned Peggy about the treacherous minor league travel. Romey's wife, Marlene, had been troubled and overwhelmed by it, so Rich wanted to make certain Peggy was on board. She assured him she was all-in.

So off Rich would go, in a rickety bus straight out of central casting. The team's driver was Norb Voigt, who picked the players up in an archaic cylinder tunnel bus that had a plastic interior and windows that took two hulking men to pry open. "It was like an old church bus," Rich says. "It looked like an oil tanker with seats."

Norb and Sadie Voigt had launched their bus company in 1947, transporting children to and from school, and they prided themselves on their personal touch. Norb did all the driving for the Rox himself, wearing a conductor's cap and suspenders for effect. He stocked the bus with hamburgers, while the team supplied the playing cards. From there, everyone just hoped Norb could stay awake.

Rich recalls one overnight trip, somewhere in the middle of nowhere South Dakota, where the players were awakened by the piercing sound of metal on metal.

"What happened, Norb?" somebody asked.

"I had to make a slight adjustment," he drawled.

"What?"

"A stop sign seemed to get in my way," Norb said. "No problem."

Norb had literally flattened the two-way stop sign in the middle of this country road, but he still ended up reaching Aberdeen on schedule. That was the minor leagues in a nutshell.

If Rich would return worn out, he'd never show it. Peggy would pick him up after road trips in the LTD, give him a lengthy hug, and chauffeur him back to the apartment. There they would resume trying to have a baby.

They may still have been newlyweds, but that's what young married couples did in the 1960s: produce children. Rich would check in with Peggy every so often, asking if she was pregnant yet. But she'd shake her head, and he'd move on with his day of baseball. By season's end, he was distracted by the playoff drive anyway. The team—with promising young players such as Rich, Jim Nettles, and Danny Thompson—took the Northern League championship. Norb and Sadie had front-row seats.

Rich decided the minor leagues weren't half bad—until he got word in 1969 he'd been assigned to the Class A Red Springs Twins. Red Springs was a miniature dot in southern North Carolina that considered its size (population 4,000) a compliment. It was more of a village than anything else, and when the Class A Wilson Tobs relocated there for the 1969 season, Red Springs became known as the tiniest minor league city in history. The chamber of commerce proudly dubbed itself "the world's smallest baseball town." But even though attendance was ten times Red Springs's population for the season—approximately 40,000 fans—Rich considered the place a pit.

Upon arrival, he and Peggy went searching for apartments and found that none existed. The team's owner, a construction entrepreneur named Matt Boykins, solved the issue by creating a makeshift trailer park on a remote plot of land. Rich and Peggy begrudgingly moved in. The climate was muggy, and the tin trailers weren't air-conditioned. Worse, Boykins dressed his players in heavy wool uniforms. Squatting behind home plate in this swamp, Rich lost virtually ten pounds a game.

Boykins, who reminded Rich of the portly Jackie Gleason, paid the players $600 a month in hard cash. He'd hand them their envelopes of money and slink away. Rich says the team flew a Confederate flag instead of an American flag outside the stadium, Robbins Park, which made him uncomfortable. His three African-American teammates weren't permitted to live in the trailer park and had to knock on doors, hunting for spare beds in the African-American neighborhood. They weren't allowed in restaurants either, and Rich would bring them food as best he could. This was the sort of minor league town that made Romey quit.

Rich's reprieve came on July 4, 1969—midway through that carnage of a season—when he was informed that the Twins were promoting him to advanced Class A Orlando of the Florida State League. "We packed in about ten minutes," Rich says.

He and Peggy sped the LTD straight down to Florida—back to civilization again. Compared to Red Springs, the Orlando Twins might as well have been the New York Yankees. The clubhouse was air-conditioned; the front office was competent; and the players' apartment complex had a modern swimming pool and barbecue pit. After games, the entire team would congregate at the pool, grill burgers, and attempt backflips off the diving board. Rich and Peggy never considered their trip to Columbus to be a true honeymoon, so this was their pleasant replacement. Orlando— and this was years before Disney World—felt like a resort.

Minor league life was tolerable again. Positioned so close to Cape Canaveral, Rich remembers he was able to witness the launch of Apollo 13 in person on July 16 and then, four days later, see Neil Armstrong walk on the moon on TV. The next red-letter date was August 1—when after just three weeks in town Rich was named starting catcher and captain of Orlando's eventual championship team.

The only downside was that his batting average was shrinking. Rich had never been taught correctly how to hit. Romey had always emphasized catching and throwing. Jerome had tried to provide some batting tips, but he was a relative amateur who would tell him to choke up on the bat and not much else.

The other issue was Rich's eyesight. He had needed glasses in high school and had transitioned to contact lenses after reaching the minor leagues. But the lenses on the market, circa 1969, were hard and caused his eyes to water. They would also cloud up on the humid, steamy days in Orlando. "I could hardly see," he says.

Eventually, his hitting became an impediment. In his high school years, he had gotten by on pure athleticism. But as he began to face more polished, flame-throwing pitchers, his confidence was shot. He remembers kneeling in the on-deck circle whenever there were two outs, praying to God that the batter in front of him would record the final out. "So I wouldn't have to hit that inning," he says.

His preference would've been to be a designated catcher. That's where he excelled the most—throwing runners out and crafting a game plan for the pitchers. But as the season in Orlando wound down, there was no fixing his offense. He says he must've "tried fifteen thousand different batting stances" and specifically emulated the swings of Roberto Clemente and Willie Stargell, his two favorite Pirates. He still aspired to be a Bucco someday, but with his batting average barely over .200, self-doubt had crept in.

He would wake up every morning at six to attend church, and his talks with God were 99.9 percent about hitting. He remembers whispering, "Look, God, I'm getting up at six to honor you. I'm making a sacrifice. Doesn't that count for something? The least you can do is help me out here with my baseball."

But it was of no use. The season may have concluded with a Florida State League championship, but Rich began to contemplate retirement. He felt exactly how Romey did way back when—mentally fatigued. Red Springs had turned Rich cynical, while Orlando had humbled him. He called his buddies back in Steubenville and lined up those same high school jobs again. He'd be a history teacher and defensive backs coach for the football team. Perhaps he'd enroll at nearby Franciscan University and get his master's degree in education. Peggy and he could make baby after baby.

His decision was made. But one day late in the fall, the Twins front office called to say they were inviting him to their winter instructional league in St. Petersburg, Florida—a stunner. Rich knew that only prospects were sent to the instructional league, so the Twins were apparently looking past his anemic batting average. He rushed to church to thank God for listening after all.

A bevy of catchers were ahead of him in the farm system, including future Baltimore Oriole stalwart Rick Dempsey. But by the time the instructional league was over, Rich was playing ahead of Dempsey and everyone else. The coaches adored all his intangibles—leadership, cheerleading, and the fact he found apartments for ten of his teammates. He gelled particularly with a young pitcher named Bert Blyleven, the future Hall of Famer, who had a curveball to die for.

He and Blyleven tag teamed fourteen times, and their record together as pitcher and catcher was 14–0. In the championship game, Blyleven hurled a 1–0 shutout to Rich. Dempsey sat and cheerleaded. Rich may not have been accumulating base hits, but he was orchestrating wins with his defense and baseball IQ. Somebody must've been watching, because in the winter draft, he was rapidly selected by the Washington Senators.

This beat instructional league by a landslide—because not only had the Senators drafted him, but they would be sending him to their 1970 major league camp. Just eight months prior, he'd been stuck in backwoods Red Springs, playing Class A ball and sleeping in an oven of a trailer. Now his manager was someone named Ted Williams.

Williams, the Splendid Splinter and arguably the purest hitter in baseball history, had become the Senators skipper the year before in 1969, a questionable choice, considering few felt he could tolerate mediocre batters. It was a valid concern, and Rich, of all people, was a most perfect test case.

Williams had read the scouting report on Rich—all field, no hit—and on the day Rich's taxicab pulled up to the Surf Rider Resort in Pompano Beach, Florida, he bumped straight into his manager by chance.

"Hey, who the heck are you?" asked Williams, who was standing curbside.

"I'm Rich Donnelly."

"Oh yeah, you're the catcher who can't hit worth a crap," hooted Williams, known to be one of the loudest, most sarcastic, most profane men in the game. In a shocker, the manager then offered to carry Rich's luggage.

"Okay, see you tomorrow!" Williams woofed.

Rich was eager to see where this relationship was headed, and it revealed itself during his initial session of batting practice. Every time Rich popped the ball up or rolled the ball over toward first base, Rich could sense Williams's glare.

Williams then ordered Rich over and deadpanned, "Who taught you how to hit?"

"My dad and my high school coach," Rich answered.

"Well, they were two horrible teachers," Williams said. "What did they tell you?"

"Take the first pitch; try to get a walk," Rich explained.

"Holy crap," Williams said. "How do you hold the bat?"

"I line my knuckles up," Rich said, having Jerome flashbacks.

"Screw that," Williams said. "Grab the (bleeping) bat and squeeze the (bleeping) pus out of it, and swing it. Swing your rear end off."

A strange thing happened the next time Rich swung the bat with all his might: the ball backspun to the warning track. Williams might have known what he was talking about.

The rest of that 1970 spring training was a revelation. With a little more pep in his bat, Rich began to resemble a major league player. The Senators were set at catcher with veterans Paul Casanova and Jim French, but Williams assured Rich he'd be starting the season with the Triple-A Denver Bears. Rich took Williams at his word. Now he'd be just one phone call away from his and Jerome's lifelong dream.

He spent the final weeks of spring training at the Senators minor league facility in Plant City. The outfield doubled as a soccer field, and the infield was uneven and choppy. There was no clubhouse. The players were forced to dress at the hotel and bus over. "It was like high school," Rich says.

It only magnified the difference between the majors and the minors: first class versus fifth. Rich was ravenous now for the big leagues, so imagine his dismay when the Senators told him he was beginning the 1970 season with Double-A Pittsfield in Massachusetts.

He decided Williams had flat-out lied to him about going to Triple-A, and a little bit of trust was lost. Because wives weren't permitted on team flights, Peggy had to attach a U-Haul to their LTD—which now had about 70,000 miles on it—and drive their belongings up to New England herself.

On the bright side, they were seeing another part of the world, and they again intended to treat it like an extended honeymoon. They found an apartment with a cobblestone driveway. Peggy decorated the place with a linen tablecloth and floral curtains. Perhaps she would become pregnant there.

On opening night, Rich was the starting catcher and went one for four, a promising debut. But the next morning, he received a call from the Pittsfield manager, Dick Gernert. There'd been a development. One of the catchers in Denver, Merritt Ranew, had loafed after a baseball and was being released outright. Rich, who had never loafed in his life, was the replacement.

So twenty-four hours into the Pittsfield season, Peggy packed up their belongings—linen tablecloth included—and drove the U-Haul from New England to the Mile High City. Rich had rightfully ended up in Triple-A after all. In his first at-bat, he held the bat with a death grip—channeling his inner Ted Williams—and hit a laser to left field. He was in Denver for the foreseeable future.

Peggy unpacked and redecorated. Their two-bedroom apartment—which they shared with Rich's teammate Tommy Ragland and Ragland's wife—had a view of the Rocky Mountains, with a babbling brook nearby. They also had a dog, a miniature beagle, that they bought at a pet store for $7.25. This dog was so petite Rich says she couldn't jump over a golf ball. So they named her Dinky. The only thing missing now was a baby.

But before long, Peggy had news: she was pregnant. They had tried for two years, and for that reason alone, a giddy Rich began handing out cigars while the baby was still a fetus. He was certain they would be having a boy because, in his worldly opinion, athletes always had boys. That was his scientific conclusion. He bought his would-be son a mini-baseball bat and mini-uniform. He would pat Peggy's bulging belly and whisper how he was going to teach this baby how to be a ballplayer, a gamer.

Every time he left on a road trip, he kissed her on the cheek and abdomen. But early one morning in Omaha, he received a phone call from Peggy that shook him to his core.

She told him the baby was gone. She had hemorrhaged in the middle of the night and suffered a miscarriage. She was in tears, but he was sobbing louder and harder than her. He hung up and literally walked five miles to the nearest Omaha Catholic church.

It was barely 6 a.m. when he arrived; he had the whole church to himself. He kneeled to say the Serenity Prayer. It felt like Romey all over again. He prayed for Peggy and asked God to heal her. She had wanted a child so badly that he ached for her, and he begged God to grant her peace.

But the more he prayed, the more indignant he felt. He thought, *How could God let this happen? How could God let me down?* He began to tremble, looked up toward the heavens, and whispered out loud, "God, this ain't fair. I lost my brother, and now my wife lost our baby. We waited so long. When we got married, we wanted a child, like, right now. I've been good, and Peggy's been good. We both waited until we were married to have sex. God, what did I do wrong?"

He left and walked the five miles back to the hotel. For some reason, he began to blame himself for the miscarriage. He decided he must have done something awful to turn God against him. He just didn't know what. He was so depressed that he skipped the game that night, sat demoralized in his room, and sobbed.

Once again, Rich didn't know what to make of what he thought was another cruel, confusing move by God. *What to do with death?*

Letter from Amy

Dad,

Did you think you were going to only have boys? Girls rock. You know that by now, right? Hahahaha.

Love,
Your daughter!!!!

Seven

Boys Will Generally
Be Boys

The church bells suddenly stopped ringing inside Rich's head. God took his baby, the same way he had taken Romey. So for the immediate and possibly long-term future, Rich was on leave from Sunday Mass.

He says he was "torn between putting my trust in God and giving up." He was leaning toward the "giving up," which, in the big picture, was monumental. Rich had prayed on his knees before bedtime every evening of his life—through college, through St. Cloud, through the trailers of Red Springs. He remembers his Xavier roommate, Ron Celnar, looking cockeyed at him that first night of their freshman year when he said the Serenity Prayer and then a whole decade of the rosary. But now that obsession was over.

He still considered himself a Catholic, but more of a "convenient" Catholic. He would go to church whenever it was *convenient*—meaning maybe in a year or two, if Peggy were ever able to get pregnant.

He was in a panic that her uterus was broken, that perhaps Peggy's diminutive size would keep her infertile. He had no facts to back this up, of course. It was just Triple-A clubhouse chatter, theories espoused by second basemen or outfielders who'd never been past high school.

Rich was so distraught that he confided in the Denver Bears general manager, Jim Burris, who assured him that women with a history of miscarriages can give birth to multiple healthy babies. Still, just in general, Rich's life had flipped sideways. His faith was waning, and his anger was at DEFCON 2. It's safe to say he was slowly morphing into Jerome.

His temper first revealed itself on a baseball field, although, in some ways, it wasn't a particularly horrible development. After being a sedate backup Triple-A catcher in 1970—sometimes even third string—he returned in 1971 with a scowl. "I became a mean player," he says.

And, curiously, a better player. The starting catcher, Bill Fahey, was injured four games into the year, and then around midseason, the other Denver catcher, Rick Stelmaszek, was promoted to the big league Senators. Rich felt Ted Williams had betrayed him again, that it should have been him instead of Stelmaszek headed for Washington. The starting job in Denver may now have belonged to Rich, but he was ticked off to be stranded in Triple-A—and about to take it out on anyone and everyone.

When his own pitchers would struggle with location—even thirty-six-year-old veterans like Garland Shifflett—twenty-four-year-old neophyte Rich would stomp out to the mound and berate them. "I'd chew their derrieres out," Rich says. "I never did that before. I mean, I'd go out and start screaming at 'em, 'Get the ball over the plate, let's go.' It wasn't very Christian of me. These guys would look at me like I was nuts."

He'd become the unofficial mouth of the clubhouse, to the point that one night his teammates were tempted to outfit him with a straitjacket. After a late extra-inning game, he tramped into the locker room still dressed in his catching gear, hollering expletives and generally acting possessed.

"I'll tell you one thing, you suckers," Rich scolded. "We don't have to lose if we don't want to. Every living one of you, we're winners. Let's go! I'm tired of this crap!"

The rest of the group was speechless . . . because they'd just won the game.

They walked up to him after his tantrum, single file, asking if he was okay. Rich told them, "Heck, yeah," and from then on, he was the unspoken captain of the team. His teammates admired his thirst for a W. The veterans adopted him as their own, and before long, they naturally insisted he come out on the town with them.

"Hey, Richie, come on, we'll buy you a beer," they'd beckon.

In a way, it was his initiation to the big time; they were breaking in the young kid. He had always aspired to be "one of the guys," but he was almost more than that now. The way he behaved on the field, he was *the man*. It was striking, for instance, how much the veterans kowtowed to him. These thirty- to thirty-five-year-old men—plus forty-nine-year-old pitching coach Art Fowler—would be all dressed up after the game, ready to hit the disco scene. But they'd patiently wait for their twenty-something catcher to shower and shave.

Once the group got to the bars, they became beer-guzzling machines. Rich had downed a few Iron Citys before in Steubenville, but he had been generally ambivalent about alcohol. He could take or leave it. But now, he was throwing them down to the point that he was going home drunk, home to a wife who was desperately trying to get pregnant.

Peggy rationalized that Rich's late-night soirees were simple cases of male bonding. She had no idea that the men—some of whom had been divorced twice or three times—were chasing "broads" too. She should have known better, but she was naive and single-mindedly focused on her fertility. Rich was just as focused on becoming a dad, which is why he never flirted or even looked at those women in the bar. Problem was, when he'd come home buzzed, he'd obsess on the baby issue.

"You pregnant yet," he'd ask over and over. "You pregnant yet . . . You pregnant yet . . . You pregnant yet?"

Peggy would have no clear answer for him, other than the obvious: "No, sorry." She was witnessing the same petulance and impatience his teammates were seeing on the field—and, as it turned out, his father and even Ted Williams were about to get a look at it too.

Once Jerome heard Rich was catching full-time and thriving, he scheduled a trip to Denver for a weekend. Rich was indifferent about his visit and just went about his business. During the first game, there was a collision at the plate, with the runner using a forearm shiver to try to jar the ball free from Rich. Rich was having none of it and tagged the guy high and hard with force, knocking the runner unconscious.

It was another notch in Rich's belt with his veteran teammates. Rich wasn't just giving 100 percent out there; he was giving 200 percent. The vets invited him to Eddie Bohn's Pig 'N Whistle that night so they could buy him a Coors or three. But Rich had to pass.

"Can't, guys," Rich said. "My dad's in town."

"Heck, bring your dad," a veteran player said.

Jerome didn't even know Rich drank, so this was going to be entertaining. As soon as they sat down in their booth, Bears pitcher Cisco Carlos bellowed to teammate Garland Shifflett, "Get Rich a beer, and get his dad one too."

Rich could feel Jerome's gaze on him, but it didn't feel at all contentious—it was more a look of, *Do I know you?*

"He looked at me like I wasn't even his son anymore," Rich says. "Like, 'What happened to this guy? He grew up overnight.'"

When Rich's teammates brought up the collision at the plate, Jerome finally broke his silence.

"Boy, that guy hit you, and you knocked the snot out of him."

"Yeah, I did, Dad."

That was about the extent of Jerome's comments. He bit his lip when the veterans pointed out a curvy blonde-haired girl to Rich, and he nodded when another vet profanely sang the praises of Rich.

"Your son, man, he's a baaaad dude on the field," they said to Jerome.

"Yeah, yeah, I know," Jerome answered.

But he didn't know, not in a trillion years. This was a new, sour, combustible, uncensored son of his he hadn't seen coming. Jerome had no idea about the miscarriage or about Rich's disagreements with God. But whatever had caused the transformation, Jerome was spellbound.

"All before, my dad was the authority figure, and I was under him," Rich says. "But after that beer and that game, I felt I was over him. He was looking up at me like, 'He's a grown man, and I'm just his dad.'

That's the first time I ever felt that way. My dad was under me for the first time. I wasn't scared of him anymore. And this sounds crazy, but if he had said something to me, I might have knocked the crud out of him."

It was Rich's brave new world—almost too brave. Late in the season, the big league Senators and their manager, Ted Williams, came through Denver for an exhibition. This was the game on the schedule Rich had circled. His payback game.

He had taken Ted's advice all season and squeezed the pus out of the bat. He was batting about .270, his career high by far. But the fact that Williams had chosen Stelmaszek over him—even though Stelmaszek was Rich's dear friend—still enraged him.

Rich told all the veterans in his clubhouse, "I'm not talking to that s.o.b." This was Rich's World Series. Just as the crowd at Mile High Stadium was settling into their seats, Rich threw out the speedy Dave Nelson trying to steal second. Next he threw out the speedy Lenny Randle. Next he gunned down the cat-quick Tim Cullen.

After the third caught-stealing, Rich wheeled toward Williams in the opposing dugout and howled, "Keep running. I'll throw every one of you out."

The words were barely out of his lips when Rich felt a sudden, *Oh no. What have I done? What is happening to me?* He left the field that night without shaking anyone's hand and drove home in the LTD to Peggy. They hugged, and he predicted out loud, "I think I'm done. I think I'm released. I just trashed Ted Williams."

It was no consolation that Rich helped lead the Bears to the 1971 Triple-A World Series later that season. In his mind, he had eviscerated his career. He spent the ensuing winter waiting to be axed.

He was also awaiting news from the fertility doctors. Peggy and Rich had both undergone tests to see if they could have a viable pregnancy, and the results finally came back favorable. Their doctor prescribed patience, which Rich had absolutely none of. For instance, if there were even two people ahead of him in line at the gas station or a fast-food joint, he would leave in a huff. Waiting for his son was maddening at best.

Eventually, just after New Year's Day 1972, there was good news and bad news. The good was that Peggy was pregnant. This time, Rich wouldn't buy baby gifts or talk to her belly or decide how many baseballs were going in the crib. He wasn't going to turn it over to God either. He'd tried that before with disastrous results. He just crossed his fingers that there wouldn't be another Omaha—a phone call to tell him about death.

The bad news was that the Rangers kicked him to the curb. It was his baseball death. The Senators, who had just moved to Texas to become the Rangers, called to say he was not welcome at their major league spring training camp in Pompano Beach. He would be going instead to the minor league facility in Plant City—as Denver's *backup* catcher.

From a pure baseball standpoint, it was a cruel demotion. In 85 games and 259 plate appearances in 1971, Rich's "squeeze the pus out of the bat" approach had produced a .267 batting average, some twenty points higher than Stalmaszek's. He had led the American Association in assists. Factor in his leadership, his advanced baseball IQ, and his age (twenty-four), and Rich should have had his own baseball card by then.

But there was that temper of his, plus those vulgarities he had hurled at Ted Williams. An organization considers the whole package, and Rich's package had stains and rips in it. He thought he was so close to a big league life, but now the Rangers wouldn't even let him come to camp and apologize to Williams face-to-face.

He arrived in Plant City with what he called "a bad attitude." And then some. If Rich was irascible before, multiply that by fifteen. Early in that spring training, on a Florida heat-stroke kind of day, he was catching one bullpen session after another. Tall pitchers, short pitchers, prospect pitchers, has-been pitchers—he caught them all. It was grunt work, and after two hours of it, Rich snapped.

He gathered his gear, and with a full head of steam, he walked three miles to the team hotel. Back in his room, he dialed the Rangers farm director, Hal Keller, and couldn't have been more direct.

"Hal, I've had enough. I quit."

"What do you mean, quit?"

"I played my butt off for two years, and I didn't get invited to spring training. You guys got me going back to Denver as a backup after I was the top catcher. I don't see any point."

"Hold on a minute," Keller said. "Don't leave. Just hold on. I'll call you back."

About an hour later, Keller telephoned him with a proposition straight out of left field, right field, and center field.

"Rich, would you like to be manager of the Greenville Rangers minor league team?"

(Silence.)

"Would you like to be manager of the Greenville Rangers? We talked to Ted Williams, and he recommended you. We think you'd be a great manager."

(Silence.)

"We'll basically double your salary. What are you making now—$900 a month for four months? That's $3,600. We'll pay you $7,500 to manage."

The offer had Rich in a cold sweat, stuttering again. He called Peggy back in Cincinnati, and together they went over the pros and cons. If he became a manager, he'd be free from the whimsical nature of the minor leagues. He couldn't be called up, sent down, released, or traded in the middle of the night. With the baby coming—sure to be a boy, of course—that sort of stability went a long way.

The downside—and this had him bawling in his hotel room—was that at age twenty-five his playing career would be over. He locked his door and wept for a full hour, reminiscing about all the sacrifices he'd made to reach the big leagues. All the Jell-O powder he slid into, all the rocks he hit with a broom handle, all the apples he threw in that cemetery, all the grief from Jerome, all the advice from Romey, all the praying to St. Jude—it was all for naught.

Still, managing was the prudent decision, and after conferring with Peggy and exhaling, he phoned Hal Keller to accept the team's offer.

Keller congratulated him and said there was one other thing he forgot to mention: the stadium in Greenville had just burned to a crisp.

So that's how hot-headed Rich Donnelly entered the coaching profession: with his home field on fire. The cause of the blaze on Valentine's Day 1972 was unclear, but talk about starting a career from scratch. Meadowbrook Park in Greenville, built in 1938 with a capacity of 8,000, was minus grandstands, minus concession stands, minus a ticket office, minus a clubhouse, and minus a backstop. All that remained was home plate, a charred field, and half of the brick outfield wall.

From the would-be infield, Rich says he could see a whorehouse to the left, a police station to the right, and a garbage dump in between. This was a rebuilding job if he ever saw one. The groundskeeper had to handcraft a backstop out of chicken wire—otherwise any ball that bounced past the catcher would've rolled all the way downtown. "And when I say downtown, I mean the balls skipped straight down Main Street," Rich says.

But the games must go on, and Rich's Greenville Rangers began the season with a standing-room-only crowd of fifteen—because, face it, there was no place to sit.

"This one woman came to every game," Rich says. "Her name was Ruby. She'd bring her lawn chair and plop it down in the middle of the ashes. If the umps were bad, she'd park her car in front of theirs so they couldn't get out. Then she'd walk to the nearest bar and be there for hours."

The ticket price was $0.00 because the owner, Vernor Ross (who ran a tire and battery shop), couldn't in good conscience charge people to stand and watch a ball game. So fans either walked in off the street to sit in folding chairs or entered by scaling what was left of the brick outfield wall. That's why Rich nicknamed the stadium "The Alamo."

One night in July, there was a torrential rainstorm, and the last remnants of the wall sunk straight into the mud. Once bulldozers cleared out the debris, Meadowbrook Park officially became an empty lot.

One of Rich's players, a catcher named Rich Revta, decided to build a makeshift clubhouse out of plywood so the players could have a shower and a toilet. But the drainage was faulty, leaving the shower knee-deep in water and the toilet perpetually clogged. Rich says the Rangers traveling instructor, Jimmy Piersall, took one look at the whole place and never came back.

Without an outfield fence, the stadium was also in dire need of ground rules. Rich told his two batboys to hold up a rope 325 feet from home plate. If a ball flew under the rope, it was a double. If it sailed over the rope, it was a home run. But that's where the home field advantage came in. The lighting was so poor there that Rich also told the batboys to drop the rope whenever the Rangers were batting—so the umpires would think a ground ball double was a home run.

With all this commotion going on, Rich thought it best that Peggy remain back in Cincinnati with her parents, Gene and Ruth. She was in the middle of her pregnancy, and Rich didn't want to risk her having another miscarriage sitting alone in a Greenville apartment.

Besides, he had his first-ever team to manage, and that was taking all of his energy. If Rich was irritable as a player, he was a regular George Patton as a manager. He didn't just do bed checks on the road; he'd do bed checks at *home*. He would literally drive to every player's apartment and knock on their door to see if they'd answer. It was unheard of and sounded a lot like the way Jerome used to spy on Rich.

Rich's pitching coach, Ed Nottle—a former White Sox farmhand— asked him to back off the players. "Didn't you go out in Denver?" Nottle asked. Rich thought back to those nights at Pig 'N Whistle and made a compromise: he'd only check curfew on the road.

It was a small gesture, but it went a long way with the team. The players were roughly the same age as Rich, and as soon as he showed flexibility as a manager, they played . . . just like Rich. They were a fearless, relentless group and took the second-half-of-the-season championship. Afterward, they bought Rich celebratory beers at a pub named the Keg House. He was one of the boys, and, not long after that, Rich was christened Western Carolinas League Class A Manager of the Year.

He returned to Cincinnati in October 1972, just as Peggy was going into labor. Her water broke on October 13, the day before Game 1 of the Reds-A's World Series. Rich took that to mean his firstborn (sure to be a boy, of course) didn't want to miss any of the Fall Classic.

And just as Rich predicted, Peggy gave birth to a male all right: Richard (Bubba) Donnelly Jr. It reaffirmed Rich's theory that athletic men have only sons—and Bubba was right away a boy's boy. He threw anything he could get his infant hands on: baseballs, tennis balls, rolled-up socks, or carrots.

For a minute there, Rich wanted to head to church and thank God for his good fortune. And when no one was looking, he did get down on his knees for a random Serenity Prayer. But other than that, Bubba's birth wasn't life-changing as much as it was a sigh of relief.

Of course, now that he'd had a sip of fatherhood, Rich wanted more sons. And now that he'd had a taste of a championship, he wanted more rings. Unable to salvage the stadium in Greenville, the Rangers moved their 1973 Class A team to Gastonia, North Carolina, where they provided Rich with a stud hitter named Mike Hargrove and a flame-throwing pitcher named Len Barker. Rich won another championship and another Manager of the Year award, and he was about to have another child.

Peggy had told him about her new pregnancy in that summer of 1973. Rich did the math and realized his second son—*of course* it'd be a son—would be born in April 1974, right around Opening Day. Peggy would have the baby in Cincinnati, and if the Gastonia Rangers happened to be playing when she went into labor, he'd have to miss the childbirth. He'd have to wait for another one of Peggy's phone calls.

Turns out, the baby cooperated and was delivered on a midweek off-day—enabling Rich to hustle up there. *What a sweet, considerate boy!* Rich thought to himself.

But then Rich looked down and couldn't believe his eyes.

This baby was a girl.

Letter from Amy

Dad,

    Will you teach me how to hit a home run?

    All the boys in school talk about home runs. They call them dingers, jacks, taters, round-trippers, bombs, grand salamis . . . Gosh, I'd love to hit one of those.

    Okay, whenever you get back home, let's talk about it.

Love,

Amy

SECOND BASE

SECOND BASE

Eight

Queen Elizabeth

The charm of having a baby daughter wasn't lost on Rich. Amy Elizabeth Donnelly had her father at hello, although it wasn't long before he was saying good-bye.

Rich was preoccupied with the 1974 baseball season in Gastonia, not to mention a potential climb up the Texas Rangers ladder. That spring training, just a couple of months before Amy was born, Rich was introduced to the Rangers newest big league manager, none other than Billy Martin. Just the name sent a shiver down Rich's spine.

Martin was a New York Yankees legend whose best friends were Mickey Mantle and Chivas Regal Whisky, not necessarily in that order. One of Martin's other sidekicks happened to be Art Fowler—Rich's old teammate and pitching coach in Denver—and one night during spring training 1974, Fowler started telling Billy about Rich.

When Billy heard that Rich once cussed out Ted Williams, he knew he had to meet this Donnelly guy. Billy despised Williams back from their Yankees-Red Sox battle royales in the 1950s, so any enemy of Williams' was a friend of his. Not that Rich was really an enemy of Williams' anymore—considering Ted landed him the job in Greenville—but if that scored points with Billy Martin, Rich was all-in.

Martin also heard from Fowler that Rich was a worker bee who threw a mean batting practice and wouldn't tolerate lazy players. All of this was right up Martin's alley, so he insisted that Rich work at the

95

Rangers major league camp all spring. Rich could simply join his Gastonia team come April.

Rich saw this as his path to a full-time major league job and enthusiastically came on board. His plan was to learn how to manage in the big leagues by shadowing Billy day and night. The night part was his mistake.

On the surface, Billy seemed to be a kindred spirit. Rich says Billy wore a metal crucifix on his ball cap and always tried to invite a priest or a band of nuns to the stadium. He says Billy would buy the nuns box seats and write out a check to the charity of their choice. At first, Rich sensed it was all genuine, until he found out that Billy "was the most unreligious of anybody I met in my life."

Once the spring training games ended, usually by 4 p.m., Billy and his crew began their evening procession. Together with his two bobos, Fowler and Jackie Moore, Billy had his happy hour(s) all planned out. They would have dinner and sake at Benihana until ten, followed by booze at the Tiki Hut until 2:30 a.m., followed by womanizing at Cheetah III—which happened to be a strip club—until dawn. Billy would pick up the tab and stagger back into the stadium by 6 a.m. He'd then shower, shave, and be ready for another day of baseball. And do it all over again.

Before long, they had lured Rich into their merry band of barhoppers. If Rich knew what was good for him—in other words, if he wanted a big league job someday—he'd have to go along with the program. He may have been only twenty-eight, but the all-nighters wore him out. "God, let's hide from him—Billy's relentless," Rich remembers Fowler saying. Rich's kryptonite was particularly the Chivas Regal, and his convenient excuse not to drink it was that he'd be Billy's designated driver.

"I had a room, but I never stayed in my bed," Rich says. "It was against what I believed in, but Billy Martin likes you? You don't want to piss him off. At the Cheetah, I sat there like, 'What am I doing here?' I'm embarrassed, and Billy's trying to hustle all the girls. I just wanted to go home."

But when it came to pure baseball wisdom, Rich realized Billy had it in spades. It wasn't just his instincts (such as when to pull pitchers) or his theories ("You gotta have balls to manage," he'd say) or his five Yankees World Series rings (thanks to Mantle and company); it was how Billy related to players. Billy would tear guys down and then build them back up, or vice versa. One day, he'd tell a player, "You're a five-tool player— and all your tools are horse manure." The next day, he'd give the same kid permission to skip curfew.

It was the education of Rich's life, and Rich took mental notes on how to be a leader of men. For instance, he never forgot the time a distraught Willie Davis came to Billy because the Surfrider Hotel wouldn't let him keep his pet Doberman named Dartanian in his room. Billy went to the hotel manager claiming that if Dartanian went, the whole Rangers organization went. An hour later, Davis and Dartanian had an adjoining suite.

Another time, during spring training 1974, Billy traded outfielder Elliot Maddox to the Yankees, only to learn the next morning that Maddox had called him "a liar" in the newspaper. Billy ordered coach Charlie Silvera to buy every paper in the general vicinity of Pompano Beach and Fort Lauderdale—and then hand them to any Rangers player who entered the hotel bar. That's where they would then find Billy, drunk off his rocker, wielding one of the newspapers himself. He told anyone who would listen that during a future Rangers-Yankees series, their hardest thrower, Jim Bibby, was going to drill Maddox with a pitch. Bibby eventually followed suit, pegging Maddox in the left shoulder to start a beanball war.

So Rich revered Billy and reviled Billy, all at once. On Sunday mornings, he didn't dare go to church—for fear that Billy would reprimand him. "I didn't want to make him mad," Rich says. This was Rich's initiation to the big leagues, and clearly it wasn't a place for choir boys ... or former altar boys.

At the end of the 1974 spring training, just as Rich was leaving to manage his Class A team in Gastonia, Billy patted him on the back and told him he reminded him of a young him. Rich took that as both a compliment and a detriment. Then Rich went out and won another championship and another Manager of the Year. Maybe he *was* another Billy.

Following the minor league playoffs that year, the Rangers offered Rich an $800-a-month off-season job in their ticket office back in Texas. He and Peggy decided that, with two toddlers, they could use the extra cash. They attached a U-Haul to the LTD and drove from Cincinnati to Arlington, Texas, with Bubba, Amy, and their dog, Dinky, in the backseat. They found a home on a cul-de-sac, complete with a two-car garage and a front and back yard to mow. Where were Jerome's steel-tipped shoes when he needed them?

To Rich, the value of suburbia was in the eye of the beholder. He felt it was the ideal place to raise his burgeoning family, and his off-season plan was to sell season tickets by day and be a loving, faithful dad by night. But that's when Billy Martin intervened.

Rich began working in the Rangers offices in September 1974, with a month to go in the big league regular season. When the team was playing at home, he'd sit with the sportswriters, and during one particular game, the phone rattled in the press box.

One of the Rangers beat writers, Randy Galloway, picked it up and said, "Rich, it's for you."

"For me?"

"Yeah, the dugout's calling; it's Art Fowler."

So Rich grabbed the phone to ask Fowler what he needed.

"Hey, Richie," Fowler said. "Billy wants to know if Hargrove can bunt. Can he run the suicide squeeze play with him?"

Billy's mind was always working like that. He knew Rich had managed Mike Hargrove at Gastonia the year before and wanted as much inside info as he could gather.

"He's a good athlete," Rich told him. "He's never squeezed for me, but I think he can handle the bat."

From Rich's mouth to Billy's ears. The suicide squeeze play went on for the next pitch, and Hargrove got the run in with a perfectly angled bunt.

Billy looked up at Rich from the dugout and gave him a thumbs-up. So much for a tranquil off-season.

From that day on, Rich was one of Billy's bobos—and Peggy, Bubba, and Amy were about to face the consequences. Over the winter months, Rich was essentially at the mercy of Billy. Art Fowler or Jackie Moore were the go-betweens, and at any hour of the day or night, they might invite Rich out to drink, play pool, and generally entertain Billy. They wouldn't take no for an answer, or at least that was Rich's perception.

Problem was, Peggy was working full-time as a nurse and would leave toddlers Bubba and Amy in Rich's care. He was selling tickets from home via the phone, so it was an ideal setup. But the minute Fowler, Moore, or Billy would reach out, Rich would call a neighbor to sub in as babysitter. It'd be 2 p.m., the shank of the afternoon, and Rich would be gone at the Red Apple Bar in Arlington until midnight.

"What I should've said was, 'I can't go, I've got my family here,'" Rich says. "But I went. I wasn't in the big leagues yet. I was still managing in the minor leagues. I said to myself, 'If I don't go, I'm going to ruin everything.' And that's why I went. I wasn't a drinker, but I was drinking beer, hanging out with them. I was afraid to tell them no. Because it might hurt my career as far as getting into the big leagues."

Peggy would arrive home to find the surprise babysitter and go bonkers. If there'd been cell phones in the 1970s, she'd have ordered him home. But she wasn't about to call the Red Apple Bar and deal with Billy. Upon his return, Rich would assure her he was doing it for the family, which was basically a crock.

"Family wasn't even close to coming first," he says. "Whatever I needed to do—regardless of my family—I would do. Like, I was supposed to take my family out to dinner with my wife. No. Billy called, I'm gone."

Rich was in too deep. The Rangers owner, Brad Corbett, wanted Billy spending much of his off-season in Texas, but Billy used to sneak away to New York City without anyone knowing it. How'd he get away with it? He'd have Rich pose as his body double. Billy would give Rich the keys to his Lincoln Continental—the one with the tinted windows and the Yankees license plates—and have Rich speed all over the Metroplex. People just assumed it was Billy.

For Rich, it was all in the name of reaching the majors. But what he ended up missing, to a large degree, was Bubba's and Amy's formative years. Before he knew it, the off-season would be over, and he'd be back in spring training again, back to barhopping in Florida with Billy, Art, and Jackie.

Peggy wouldn't let him escape the family completely. Rich began the 1975 season as manager of the Class A Anderson (South Carolina) Rangers—and Peggy brought the kids south to move in with him. It was an eye-opener for Rich. He had already bonded with Bubba, because they were both boys. Bubba would climb banisters, put his fingers in electrical sockets, and throw Nerf footballs, just how Rich liked it. Rich bought him a Pittsburgh Steelers outfit and had Bubba pretend to be Franco Harris. But early on, Rich still didn't know what to make of Amy.

One day, eleven-month-old Amy was standing happily in her portable walker, which had a food tray attached to it. Inside the tray was a sippy cup and cereal, which she was dipping in to. But before long, Bubba had dragged Amy into his room and began pretending to be Franco Harris. He decided Amy was the Miami Dolphins defense . . . and ran her over. First to go was the cup and then the cereal. Amy threw a conniption fit.

Rich, who was home from the ballpark, came fuming inside of Bubba's room to reprimand them. He warned Bubba to knock it off. But a minute later, Amy dropped the sippy cup herself and started wailing again—framing Bubba. Rather than deal with Rich again, Bubba began waiting on Amy hand and foot, scooping her cereal up off the rug and guarding her drink with his life. That's how Amy got her own Steubenville nickname: "Queen Elizabeth."

The question was, *Who is going to rule Rich?* Queen Elizabeth or Billy Martin? By July 1975, the decision was made for him: the Rangers fired Billy. Corbett accused Martin of being disloyal, and somewhere, Ted Williams had to be laughing. Billy immediately hightailed his Lincoln Continental back to New York, where George Steinbrenner hired him to be Yankees manager that August. Billy would eventually be fired, rehired, fired, rehired, fired and rehired by Steinbrenner, but that wasn't Rich's problem anymore. "I was kind of glad that Billy was gone," Rich says, "because that really wasn't me."

At least for the time being, that meant Rich wouldn't be spending his off-season nights at the Red Apple Bar. He could focus on baseball, family, and maybe even church—the latter being a whole other subject.

Regardless of where Rich's faith stood—and it was basically in limbo—he and Peggy had decided to raise the kids Catholic. Every Sunday morning during the winter, they would shine Bubba's shoes, iron Amy's pinafore, and sit together as one happy family in a pew. As far as Rich was concerned, there would be no misbehaving in church, period.

With Billy gone, he was free to walk into Mass without being judged. He found himself even praying occasionally. For that off-season at least, he was somewhat the old Rich. Then, around New Year's Day 1976, he found out about his promotion.

The Rangers front office, heading into that 1976 season, named Rich manager of the Triple-A Sacramento Solons—one breath below the major leagues. He could now see a clear path to a big league manager's job, and he didn't want to jeopardize that—so he stopped going to church.

"I thought the players would make fun of me if I went," he says. "I was convinced that church and baseball didn't mix."

God was on the outs again—just as one of Rich's prayers was being answered. As a high school kid, he had cradled a rosary and asked Jesus to make him a third base coach someday. And sure enough, at the Triple-A level in the 1970s, it was customary for the manager to coach third.

So in Sacramento in 1976—and then at Triple-A Tucson from 1977 to 1979—Rich got to stand in the third base coaching box and be the field general. He would flash signs to the hitters, runners, and would-be base stealers. It reminded him of his days at Forbes Field, watching the Pirates third base coach Frank Oceak wave in Bill Mazeroski.

One of his boyhood idols, in fact, had also been Frankie Crosetti, the old Yankees third base coach, whom Rich always considered to have the sweetest job in the world. The Yankees seemed to be in the Fall Classic virtually every year, and Crosetti was their third base coach from 1946 to 1968, winning nine world championships. Rich would've given his left arm to wave in one runner in a World Series, but lucky Crosetti got to send DiMaggio, Mantle, Berra, and even Billy Martin home. Rich used to pray at the foot of Crosetti instead of God.

So those four years managing at Triple-A Sacramento and Tucson were a fulfilling time in his life. He called all the shots and tried his best to bring Bubba and Amy to the stadium with him. Bubba was allowed in the clubhouse because he was older and the correct gender. He could hang out in the locker room around the half-naked men, firing dirty socks into the hampers like they were basketballs.

In fact, basketball—not baseball—was the sport Rich preferred for Bubba. Baseball was such a grind. Not only was hitting a ninety-miles-per-hour fastball probably the most difficult thing to do in sports, but Rich didn't want to expose his son to all-night bus rides, like the ones with Norb, and unkempt housing, like the dusty trailers in Red Springs.

Rich began to push Bubba into hoops the same way Jerome pushed Rich toward baseball. Rich may have been on the road half of the time, but he'd check in with six-year-old Bubba every night, asking him if he'd gotten his daily shooting in.

"Yeah, Dad," Bubba would say.

"What'd you do?"

"I shot Nerf hoops."

"That's not shooting! Drop down now and do twenty push-ups!"

Rich was looking like Jerome reincarnated, not that he realized it. Whenever he was around, he forced Bubba to run suicide wind sprints and shoot two hundred jump shots a day. Bubba was not likely to grow over five foot nine, not with diminutive Peggy for a mother, but whatever Rich was preaching seemed to be sinking in. By the time Bubba was seven, he was one of the premier shooters in Texas youth AAU basketball.

Amy was a whole different story. She wasn't allowed in the baseball clubhouse, as much as she'd beg to barge in. She was also still answering to the name Queen Elizabeth. One winter, when Jerome and Helen were visiting from Steubenville, they decided to go to a restaurant. Rich wanted the kids decked out in their Sunday best, except that Amy bolted out of her room wearing a sundress with cowboy boots.

Rich instructed her to march back into her room and change into more appropriate shoes.

"She's not wearing cowboy boots," Rich told Peggy.

"Well, okay," Peggy said, smirking. "I'll let you handle it, and I'll meet you in the car."

Ten minutes later, Amy climbed into the LTD still wearing the boots.

Amy was just a tough cookie. At her first dance recital at the age of three, Amy made it happily through the ballet portion of her evening. But just before the tap dancing segment, the instructor whispered some last-minute instructions—and Amy kicked her in the shin. Peggy never heard a clear explanation of what set Amy off, but her sense about her daughter was this: it was her way or the highway.

As Rich would witness more and more of Amy's petulance, he wasn't quite sure how to tame or discipline her. With Bubba, it was easy: he'd just take out his belt and whip him. Simple as that. With Amy, he had to behave himself. But then, on a day she talked back to him, he ordered her to pull her pants down. Off came his belt. He was about to semi-unload on her—not like Jerome had with him, yet enough to send a message—but could only bring himself to give her a light tap on her bare bottom. Either way, that set her off into wild tears. He was stumped. Another day, at the tender age of five, she uttered a profanity for the first time—maybe because she was mirroring him. Either way, the old altar was seething. But instead of wielding a belt this time, he borrowed his mom's old trick and wiped Amy's teeth with a bar of Fels-Naptha soap. That still didn't work.

Eventually, the all-time confrontation—the one Rich could never live down—happened at a church in Tucson. Amy was still about five and went to Mass one Sunday in a pristine yellow floral dress. "Cute as a button,"

Rich says. The problem was, she couldn't or wouldn't sit still. During the homily, she would jump over the pew or leap into some stranger's lap, all while making guttural noises. Rich airlifted her outside to the parking lot, stuck his finger toward her face, and gasped, "What are you doing?"

The next thing Rich knew, Amy's nose was bleeding "like a geyser." He had inadvertently jabbed her there with his finger, and blood had seeped all over her floral dress. Rich had no choice but to go fetch his wife. As soon as Peggy saw the gore, she went ballistic.

"What did you do? You hit her?"

"No, no, no. I was so mad at her that I just jabbed her with my finger," Rich said. "And I must've poked her in the nose."

"No, you had to have hit her."

"I *didn't* hit her."

The proof was Amy's face after Peggy had cleaned her up—it was pressed up sweetly on Rich's shoulder. There was never any question whether Amy adored her dad. She was so much like him at such a formative age that they appeared to be soul mates. As often as she could—whether it was summer, fall, spring, or December 24—Amy used to climb up on Rich's lap and beg him to recite her favorite poem, "'Twas the Night Before Christmas." And she was a champion beggar.

"Daddy, Daddy. Say it, say it," Amy would start.

He would rub her gently on her head and recite:

> 'Twas the night before Christmas, when all through the house
> Not a creature was stirring, not even a mouse;
> The stockings were hung by the chimney with care
> In hopes that St. Nicholas soon would be there;
> The children were nestled all snug in their beds,
> While VISIONS OF SUGAR-PLUMS DANCED IN
>   THEIR HEADS.

Not only would Rich shout the "visions of sugar-plums" line, but he would simultaneously muss up her hair and tickle her chin. It was a pure Rich-Amy moment that a jab to the nose could never erase. There was also nothing Jerome about it, and Rich took a level of pride in that.

Whenever he'd leave on road trips during the baseball season, the good-byes with Amy would last the longest. She'd want to sneak into his suitcase, and he'd have to tell her, "Sorry, but I'll call you tonight from the team hotel."

But one particular night, when Amy was still about five, Peggy ended up phoning *him* on the road. Something was wrong.

"Everything's okay," Peggy said, "but Amy got run over by a car today."

Rich assumed the worst, everything from a fractured skull to Amy at the brink of death. But Peggy informed him that she had only a broken arm. Amy had been riding her Big Wheel around the cul-de-sac when one of their neighbors backed out of a driveway and sideswiped her. At the hospital, a doctor told Peggy that if Amy had been an inch closer to the car's tire, she'd have been killed.

Rich heard this and had one prevailing thought: *he couldn't have lived without her.*

Letter from Amy

Dad,
    As far as I'm concerned, every day is Christmas.
    You agree?
    You can give me a noogie any time.

                                        Love,

                                        Amy

Nine

Family, God, and Baseball—Definitely Not in That Order

T he question was whether there was room for baseball, family, and God in Rich's life. The answer was, *Don't hold your breath.*

Baseball was his obvious No. 1. After capturing division titles as a manager in Greenville, in instructional league, and in Gastonia (twice), Rich was gaining a reputation as a winner. But when his teams in Triple-A had consistent second- and third-place finishes—all while his best players were being called up to the big league club—he gained a reputation as a wunderkind.

He was thirty-three years old by August 1979, and Peter Gammons of the *Boston Globe* had already pegged Rich as a major league manager-in-waiting, someone the Red Sox should consider hiring. The exact term Gammons used to describe Rich was "boy wonder."

Rich was a boy, all right, but that was half the problem. He still had the erratic temper he had inherited from Jerome and would sometimes scare the living daylights out of his young children. Bubba remembers driving to basketball practice with him one day and having his dad—not the car—blow a gasket.

Apparently, Rich had changed lanes without noticing a motorcycle in his path, barely avoiding a collision. The motorcyclist—fully bearded and dressed in black leather—responded by pointing a threatening finger toward Rich. The biker then pulled into an Elby's restaurant parking lot. Rich followed.

Immediately, Rich sprung out of his LTD, sprinted straight toward the man, and hissed, "Don't you ever stick your finger at me or I'll knock your a** out." Rich then returned to the car and went about his day. "That's him," Bubba says.

That said, the Rangers internal scouting report on Rich the manager read like this: *talented . . . intense . . . could use some maturity and seasoning.* So the Rangers manager Pat Corrales asked the boy wonder to join the major league club in September of the 1979 season—to get the education started.

It had been a dozen years since Rich was drafted by Pat Patterson and the Yankees and twenty-five years since he first kneeled by the side of the bed to ask St. Jude to take him to the big leagues. He'd finally arrived. This wasn't for Jerome; this was for him. Skyrockets went off in his head, and he called his first day in a major league uniform "a trip to heaven."

Because Rich was a former catcher, Corrales pointed him beyond the outfield wall, where he would serve as co-bullpen coach. One by one, the Rangers relievers introduced themselves, including the venerable former Cy Young Award winner Sparky Lyle.

"Congratulations, you'll be here for a long time," Lyle told Rich. "Anything I can do to help you, you let me know." Then Lyle turned around and mooned some fans in the stands.

Considering Lyle had played for Billy Martin in New York, Rich and Sparky each had war stories to tell about Mr. Chivas Regal. They bonded right away, just as Rich did with all the other pitchers. Billy Martin and Ted Williams stories tend to bring people together.

All in all, Rich's first thirty days with the Rangers were a rousing success. He had just the right velocity on his batting practice pitches and impressed Corrales with his energy and attention to detail. At the end of the season, Corrales offered him the job as lead bullpen coach for 1980.

It meant he'd be home in Arlington full-time, with a chance to engage his kids more. The question was whether he would. Just about a year prior, in 1978, Peggy had given birth to their third child—another boy, of course. The little guy's name was Mike, and all was right with the universe and athletic men again.

With more time to spend on his front porch, Rich became immersed in Bubba's basketball. Now eight years old, Bubba could already consistently beat his old man in driveway games of H-O-R-S-E, and they spent hour upon obsessive hour together working on three-point shooting. In fact, Bubba's range was so deep that one of Peggy's favorite trees was in the way of their makeshift three-point arc. So Rich, without alerting Peggy, cut the darn tree down.

Peggy barely spoke to him for two weeks, but Amy—peering out the window through the curtains—badly wanted into their games and workouts. Rich told her no, that these were serious male-only sessions. It was just how Jerome used to talk to Rich's sister, Patti, back in the 1950s. Sports were for boys; Barbies, kittens, and doggies were for girls.

Amy would curl up her nose at this ridiculous line of thinking. She also made it clear she was rough enough to handle anything Rich or Bubba might dish out. She had already more than held her own during their frequent games of "knee football" in the basement. She would horse-collar her dad and take a licking from Bubba—and keep on trucking. But nothing doing when it came to driveway games of basketball. She was reduced to the role of spectator.

Rich, although he wouldn't say it out loud, considered Amy the family "mascot." If she ventured outside while Bubba was shooting, hoping to finesse her way into the drills, Rich would tell her, "Hey, Amy, will you go shag the ball for us when it goes down the street?" She was subservient on the outside, but stewing on the inside.

What she really wanted to do was hit Whiffle balls with her dad in the backyard. Any time he was home, maybe watching a ball game in his Barcalounger, she would climb on his lap and ask him to pitch to her out back. He'd tell her, "I'll be out in a minute," but he'd never get off his duff.

The worst part was that whenever Bubba asked to hit in the back-yard, Rich would be out there in a flash—no questions asked. Amy eventually would amble outside to watch, hoping to get in a few swings of her own after Bubba wrapped up. As she'd patiently wait her turn, Rich would ask her to fetch any Whiffle ball Bubba hit over the hedges—grunt work. She was a glorified ball girl, except it was all worth it to her as long as she got her chance.

Eventually, Rich would wave her over, give her two swings, and call it a day. Still, you should have seen her face as Rich pitched her the ball; it was half smile, half concentration. She was swinging for the hedges herself.

"Yeah, but two swings and I'd hit the road," Rich says. "She always got the short end of the stick because the boys were the center of attention. I spent half my life with Bubba."

Amy was no dummy. Fairly soon, she stopped asking Rich out back. The sibling dynamic was clearly set, at least when it came to sports. Rich says it was almost as if "Amy was Peggy's baby and Bubba was my baby." But Amy wasn't giving up entirely. She devised a plan to penetrate Rich and Bubba's inner circle: she started a cheerleading squad.

At the time, Bubba was playing for a loaded AAU basketball team that was winning by an average of about fifty points a game. Its name: the "Green Machine." But the team was more mean than green. They pressed full-court, trash-talked, and generally ran circles around their opponents. And once Amy showed up with her cheerleading crew, they felt like they were on par with, say, UCLA.

"Amy organized the whole thing," Bubba says. "She'd get these girls who were sisters of the guys on the team—girls older than her. But she took charge and ran the show. They had uniforms and pom-poms. Once we had cheerleaders, people thought we were the Lakers and Harlem Globetrotters all in one."

She may have made Bubba's day, but it also solidified Amy's place as family mascot. Unfortunately, Rich couldn't see it for what it was: sexism, gender profiling. He was too busy with his impending big league life to address it. Besides, six-year-old Amy was having a blast at Bubba's games, content to just be a part of the mean Green Machine.

Once spring training 1980 came around, Rich was gone again anyway. It was his first full season as a big league coach; he was finally going to get to see how the other half lived. He found out that big league per diem ($45 a day) was enormous, that hotels were plush (real feather pillows!), and that no one went to church.

One Sunday in Pompano Beach, he thought he should go to Mass, thought his soul needed some cleansing. But he was so paranoid that someone would see him there—and potentially ostracize him—that he literally crawled on his hands and knees through the church parking lot. Just in case someone like Sparky Lyle might be driving by.

Rich was falling into a trap, a hole, or a bottomless pit, at least in the spiritual sense. Certainly the major leagues wasn't the place to snap him out of it either. Not with Sparky and company in the bullpen.

Lyle was one of the most affable, genuine guys he'd come across, an immediate friend. But Sparky also exposed Rich, just as Billy Martin had, to everything that was sophomoric and irregular about the big leagues.

One night in Detroit, Sparky was being nagged by an obnoxious fan in the bullpen. It's part of the game. But when that same fan leaned over the railing and asked Sparky for an autograph, Rich says Sparky peed in a foam cup, hid it behind his back, and said, "Sure, buddy, be glad to"—and then doused the fan's face.

Another day, a kid leaned over to beg Sparky for a souvenir—asking for his hat, his glove, or his shirt. Sparky said, "Here, take my shirt, my glove—take everything." Rich says Sparky then proceeded to strip down to his jockstrap and throw all his gear into the stands. The fans gave Sparky a standing ovation.

Another time, he invited Rich, Peggy, and the kids out on his boat. Rich drove over to Sparky's house, where he saw the boat attached to Sparky's car in the driveway.

"Hop in the boat," Sparky said.

So Peggy, Amy, Bubba, Rich, and Mike all climbed in—carrying sodas and sandwiches. Sparky and his wife stepped in soon after, with their own snacks. After about fifteen minutes, Rich asked, "Are we going to go to the lake?"

"I didn't say nothing about going to the lake," Sparky said. "I asked if you'd like to sit in my boat."

The kids enjoyed the concrete boat ride nonetheless, and so did Rich. But the major league lifestyle—every day and every night spent with the mischievous men—just made Rich more detached from his kids, especially Amy.

She may have given up on backyard baseball with her father, but on the plus side, she'd adopted her two-year-old brother Mike. She'd carry him on her hip, feed him, burp him, pick out his clothes. "She was a mother hen," Peggy says. She was just a natural caretaker, a born leader, Queen Elizabeth. When she was babysitting Mike, *she* was calling the shots—not her dad. She was in her element.

But Rich, as the 1980 season wore on, was not. It was odd, because from Opening Day through about June, he had been awestruck by his surroundings. One day during batting practice, the Yankees megastar Reggie Jackson had come over to him, shaken his hand, and said, "Nice to meet you—Jackson." Rich's stammering comeback was, "Uh . . . Donnelly."

"I don't think I washed my hand for about a month," Rich says.

But by July, the pregame grind of warming up the starting pitchers, coupled with the mid-and late-game grind of warming up relievers, took its toll on Rich's knees. He still had aspirations of managing in the big leagues or at least coaching third base. To him, the only fun part of being boss of the bullpen was the "*bull*" going on in the bullpen.

He and four of the pitchers—Lyle, Ferguson Jenkins, Gaylord Perry, and Charlie Hough—were all about the same age and would often have a beer after the game at a seafood place called Mr. Catfish. One night, they convinced the restaurant's owner—whom they nicknamed 'The Codfather"—to bring some fried fish to the bullpen. So that next evening, Lyle, Jenkins, Perry, Hough, and Rich put a piece of plywood over some concrete blocks in the bullpen, placed a towel on top, and, voilà, they had a dinner table. The Codfather then showed up with catfish, cole slaw, hush puppies, and French fries—and they had a feast during a live game.

"I have a bib on, and we're having dinner in the third inning," Rich recalls. "Fergie, Gaylord, and Charlie—they could give a crap about the game. I said, 'What's the score?' They said, 'Who cares, pass the tartar sauce.' Then I'd go out to warm up a pitcher—with mayonnaise stains on my uniform."

It was entertaining and unfulfilling at the same time. By the end of the season, an exhausted Rich informed the Rangers front office that he preferred to return to Triple-A as a manager. The team agreed to make it happen, but that didn't mean Rich was any less stressed.

Peggy had just given birth that September to their fourth child (of course, another son), this one named Tim. Rich's rule—jocks have only boys—was holding up . . . unless you counted the anomaly, Amy.

It was a chaotic time. Rich had given up his big league dream for Triple-A, all while Peggy had to care for two boys under the age of two. Rich was taking his frustrations out on Bubba, it seemed. If Bubba didn't work hard enough developing his three-point shot or didn't buckle down in school, Rich would make him run around the block or, worse, get up in his face. He wanted Bubba to be perfect.

"I remember when a situation would arise, he would ball up his fists," Bubba says. "He was a mixture of Billy Martin and Bobby Knight right in their prime."

Peggy noticed "marks" on Bubba one day and reminded Rich of how the whippings used to sting with Jerome. Rich would be contrite, but this behavior had been steamrolling—since the miscarriage, since Ted Williams, since Billy Martin, etc.

The saving grace in their household had been seven-year-old Amy. What was it with this girl? She began to write letters or notes to Bubba, to her mom, and to her hero Rich—just chatty reminders that she was thinking of them. Better yet, she took the load off Peggy by taking care of little Tim. He was her personal project.

Wherever she went, Tim went, and vice versa. Amy carried the baby around for hours on end, to the point where one of their family friends thought Amy might injure her hip. "We used to tell her, 'Amy, put him down before you drop him,'" Rich says. "But no. They were as close as a brother and sister could be. She raised him. She fed him, changed his diapers. She did everything."

One day, little Tim waddled and jumped into a puddle at a mall, drenching himself. Rich yelled at him, scooped him up, and tossed him in the backseat. Amy spent the next half hour telling Rich off and hugging Tim.

She was basically Tim's second mom, the person he most often crawled on top of.

She'd recite, "'Twas the night before Christmas"—and rub his little head.

Amy told everyone she had one prevailing thought: *she couldn't have lived without Tim.*

Letter from Amy

Dad,
    When you come home after the season, I want you to come straight to the garage.
    You won't believe your eyes.

Love,

Amy

Ten

Convenient Catholic

A lot went on in the Donnelly household while Rich was away coaching baseball—none of it dull.

What their father didn't realize was that Amy ruled the roost in his absence. She wasn't known only as Queen Elizabeth anymore; she now answered to the name Mrs. Guthrie.

The real Mrs. Guthrie was one of Amy's favorite elementary school teachers in Arlington, Texas. So Amy—starting at the ages of seven and eight—decided to replicate her classroom at home.

She first borrowed one of her grandmother Ruth's dresses and gussied up her hair. After that, all she needed was some students.

She took a quick look around the house and saw four-year-old Mike and two-year-old Tim throwing Cheerios at each other. The lightbulb went off in her head. She would teach the boys their ABCs, their arithmetic, or at least how to write their names. She announced out loud, "I'm Mrs. Guthrie," and that her little brothers needed to report to school immediately. Tim did anything Amy asked, so he was all-in. Mike said, "Forget it."

As was her way, Amy wouldn't take no for an answer. So she paid Mike forty cents to show up.

Now that that was settled, Amy began to teach. She adored the authority that went with the job and decided teaching would be her occupation someday—and that someday might as well begin right now.

After ruling her two-boy classroom with an iron fist, she set her sights much higher as the months and years went on: on the entire neighborhood. By the time Amy was in the fourth grade, she was recruiting every elementary school kid on her block—and the next block—to her garage. This would be after school or in the summertime, and the kids on her cul-de-sac would have no idea what hit them. They would come outside to simply play basketball, kickball, Whiffle ball, jump rope, or hide-and-seek. But Queen Elizabeth—uh, Mrs. Guthrie—would wave them over and say they'd have to get their spelling and math done first. "Then she would give them written permission to go play," Peggy says.

Not only did the kids acquiesce, but they also gave her at least a solid half hour of their undivided attention, sometimes more. Amy would teach using a whiteboard—until Peggy surprised her one Christmas with her own blackboard—and she was always on the lookout for any other school supplies she could get her hands on.

Before long, Amy was using her own money to rent overhead projectors. She'd also purchase worksheets, a receipt book, Post-it notes, and, God forbid, a red marker.

"Once she got the red marker, it was trouble," Mike would often say.

The kids may have thought it was make-believe, but Amy was dead serious and a taskmaster to boot. On their way out of the garage—and if they were misbehaving, they weren't allowed out—the kids would be given mandatory homework that had to be signed by their parents. And if the work was filled with mistakes, that's when she'd freely express herself with the red marker.

Her main feedback to the kids would usually be on Post-it notes she'd slip them in the garage—comments like "stop goofing off" or "you're failing this class." She would make some of them stay afterward and write sentences over and over on the chalkboard. The kids would be mortified and would diligently do their work at home. By this point, she didn't answer to Mrs. Guthrie anymore; she was Miss Donnelly, with the emphasis on Miss.

This soon became a topic of conversation at the annual neighborhood

Christmas party. Peggy was approached by a concerned parent who told her, "I'm having to sign more papers for Amy than I am for the real teachers at school. Could you talk to her?"

Peggy, knowing her daughter, said, "Sorry, it won't do any good." If anything, Amy was going to start assigning *more* homework. The only solution, Peggy suggested, was to steer clear of the cul-de-sac. Because once a kid was out in the open, they were Amy's.

Eventually, some kids were bound to start skipping class, and the first one to try it was her mercurial brother Mike. But Amy was prepared for that as well. One night over dinner, she proposed making Mike her principal, Mr. West. He would be in charge of detention and rounding up any kids who were playing hooky from the garage. The receipts from the receipt book she bought would serve as the detention slips.

Mike jumped at the chance, if only because it gave him free rein to smack a couple of kids on the rump with a ruler. Either way, her classroom was full again for the foreseeable future. The only conceivable way a kid could get excused from classwork was if he smelled or had bad breath. That was Amy's nonnegotiable pet peeve, and she wasn't afraid to say out loud that a kid stunk or had yellow teeth and needed to go home.

When Rich came back from managing the Triple-A Wichita Aeros in 1981 and the Triple-A Denver Bears in 1982, he finally saw for himself that Amy was a lot like . . . him. He saw what she'd done with the garage—creating her own universe where there used to be balls and bats lying around—and realized she was looking for her own identity away from baseball and her brothers. "It was the one place where she was the center of attention," Rich says. "Because she didn't get—well, she *got* attention from me, but she didn't get *proper* attention from me. Only if it was really convenient for me."

He could tell she craved being a star, craved being called "Boss Woman" by Rich and the boys. Teaching was the perfect outlet.

Rich praised her for her efforts and soon learned she had found another outlet: soccer. Rich knew little about the sport and had never played it. But that only meant it was her game, and hers alone. That was a crucial benefit—because basketball and baseball already were a Bubba-Rich team effort. Maybe soccer could become an Amy-Rich effort. She joined an elite team called the Twisters that played up to thirty-five games all over the Metroplex, and Rich went to one of her early matches out of curiosity to see what a girl's sport looked like.

Right away, he was stunned at how feistily Amy played, the way she slid in dastardly and low to steal the ball from other girls. She reminded him again of himself because he'd always played a million miles an hour too. But the clincher that day at the soccer field was when someone accidentally kicked a ball into her face.

It was a shot on goal, one of those line-drive, at-close-range kicks that can break a nose. She collapsed in a heap, and Rich winced as she writhed on the turf, expecting her to be sobbing uncontrollably. "I mean, it was a rocket kick that hit her flush in the face," Rich says. "The referee came, and out came the coaches. It looked like her face had gotten hit by a Mack truck."

But Amy—after about ninety seconds—rose up, dusted herself off, straightened her ponytail, and offered a thumbs-up. Back into the scrum she went. "She didn't even blink," Rich says. "She didn't cry. I said, 'That's one tough girl right there.' If you talk to any of my boys and ask about Amy, the first thing they'll say is she didn't take crap from anybody. I think it's because she was raised with boys and took the brunt of everything."

He could see she was one of the swiftest and most athletic girls on the squad, but pound for pound—and there wasn't a lot of weight on her—she was assuredly the fiercest. She also had the mouth of a truck driver to accent her whole package. Rich and Peggy's quaint little blonde Amy was known to drop an F-bomb or two.

"People would ask me how many boys I had," Peggy says. "I'd say, 'I kind of have four.'"

Rich tried not to miss a game, but it was more for his amusement than anything else. He was a product of his era and also the way he was raised by Jerome—women's sports didn't matter. Remember, this was circa 1981, 1982, and 1983; the infrastructure of Title IX was still being waged in the courts. Rich enjoyed Amy's foray into soccer, but he didn't exactly think it would get her a scholarship to Texas Tech either.

"That's the part that's so terrible," Rich says. "Because what happened, to my surprise, is that Amy became one of the best soccer players in Arlington. She would've been a really good soccer player had I encouraged it and worked with her—but I didn't."

Still, Amy beamed every time she saw Rich on the sidelines for one of her games; for the next hour or so, she felt she had her hero/dad all to herself. "She so badly wanted his approval," Peggy says. But deep down, he was the same old Rich—obsessed with winning and getting back to the big leagues on his own terms. He was self-absorbed, and everything other than baseball was a distant second to him: the kids, church, his marriage, and so on. Bubba's basketball career was about the only other activity he was tuned in for. Otherwise, he was in full baseball mode, unable to focus for long on anything else.

It was as if he walked around in a baseball trance. Bubba, as a ten-year-old, remembers visiting Rich in Denver in 1982 and going to a Bears-Iowa Cubs contest. There was going to be a postgame fireworks show at Mile High Stadium, and Bubba asked, "Dad, can we stay for the fireworks?"

Rich, whose Bears had lost the game, ignored him and tramped straight to the car. They drove fifteen miles to a house they were renting, still without a word being spoken. Rich then parked the car in the driveway, turned to Bubba, and finally answered, "No, we're not staying for the fireworks"—twenty-five minutes after the question.

Following the 1982 minor league season, Rich remained in a foul mood, certain he was stuck in the minor leagues for eternity. At the time, the major league Rangers had just hired the eccentric Doug Rader as their manager, and Rich badly wanted to be part of his staff. Rader was a six-foot-two version of Jerry Lewis, with bright red curly hair and a firm belief in slapstick. Turn your back on Rader—nicknamed

"The Red Rooster"—and he might pull down your pants or take a match to your cleats. Rader was occasionally serious, the kind of man who would regularly hand $100 bills to the homeless. But when it came to baseball, Rader was convinced that he who laughs . . . hits the ball farther and harder. From what Rich heard, he was the ultimate manager to work for. So imagine Rich's disappointment when he picked up the *Dallas Morning News* and read Radar's list of potential coaching candidates. Rich's name was nowhere to be found. Snubbed again.

Rich turned to an old reliable: religion. He was still a "convenient Catholic"; he still went to church when it was convenient or if he had a favor to ask. This time, he asked God to have Rader call him.

Voilà, several days later, the phone rang at Rich's home.

It was the middle of the day, midweek. Peggy was at her nursing job, while Bubba, Amy, and Mike were at school. So Rich was alone with two-year-old Tim when he picked up the phone. He whispered hello because Tim was napping and heard an urgent voice on the other end of the line.

"What are you doing?" asked the caller.

"Who's this?" asked Rich.

"Doug Rader."

"Hi, Doug."

"Can you get a yard pass?" Rader asked.

"A what?"

"A yard pass—can you get the heck out of the house?"

"Yeah."

"Well," Rader said, "if you want to be the first base coach of the Texas Rangers, you get to the downtown Holiday Inn in the next ten minutes."

Either the phone went dead or Rader hung up—because there was a sudden silence. Rich grabbed his car keys. He wasn't getting to coach third base, but first base coach was better than crouching in the bullpen all season. He backed his car out of Amy's school—the garage—and hightailed it to the Holiday Inn. He pulled up to the front circle and suddenly saw a man with flaming red hair, sprinting full speed for Rich's car—as if he was running from a gun. Then this Ronald McDonald look-alike did a hook slide into Rich's front tire.

"Safe! I'm safe!" howled Doug Rader.

Rich did a triple-take, while Rader kept yapping.

"Listen, I gotta go. I've got a flight," Rader said. "But you're going to be the first base coach; you're going to be on pension; you'll get licensing money. I'll call you tonight with more."

And just like that, Rader was hoofing it back into the hotel. Rich thought, *This guy's nuts*—until Rich realized *he* was the one who was nuts. He'd left Tim alone at home.

He imagined Tim opening the front door and parading through the neighborhood half-naked. In a mad panic, Rich called his neighbor Gary Reston from a phone booth.

"Gary, oh my gosh, I left Tim in the house. There's no one home, and I left the door unlocked. Can you go over to make sure he hasn't run out in the street?"

"I'm on it," Reston said.

Reston found Tim still fast asleep. Rich knew Amy was going to ream him out for leaving her baby unsupervised, but all of that would be overshadowed by his news: he was back in the bigs.

Of course, there were two ways this could go. Either Rich would avoid the debauchery of the major league life and stay devoted to his family and church. Or . . . he wouldn't. Rader would provide the comic relief, for sure, but it was up to Rich to figure out his path, one way or another.

Certainly, coaching first base kept him focused during games. Three years before as the Rangers bullpen coach, he was eating midgame meals courtesy of the Codfather. But the only thing he was eating in the first base coaching box was dirt.

His main objective there was to get the runner from first base to second base, and a lot of the time, the runner would kick up a cloud of dust en route. It was a far cry from his dream job of getting runners from third base to home, but this was a start—and a little bit of mud on his lips was worth it.

He learned fairly quickly that he had four priorities: (1) pick up the elaborate sign sequence from the third base coach, (2) make sure the runner wasn't dozing off and picked it up as well, (3) let the runner know how many outs there were, and (4) let the runner know about any tricky pickoff moves. Everything else was basically runner instinct—such as whether to take off for second on a ball in the dirt—which is why first base coaching was a relatively low-stress job. Rich had coached third base in Triple-A; compared to that, coaching first for the Rangers was a picnic.

It *was* a picnic in the most literal sense. Before the last spring training game of 1983 against the Yankees, Rader sent his clubhouse manager, Joe Macko, to a store to buy thirty-five beach blankets. When Macko returned, Rader asked Rich and all of the coaches to lay the blankets down in right field. Rader then huddled the team together in the clubhouse and walked them single file out to right field, where the blankets awaited.

"Hey, guys, take your shoes off, relax, and go get a blanket," Rader instructed. "The coaches are going to serve you hot dogs and Cokes instead of batting practice. We're gonna have a good time, fellas."

Problem was, no one informed Billy Martin's Yankees players, who strolled out an hour later, only to be told that batting practice was canceled because of blankets in the outfield. Rich says Billy probably just went back to his office for a snooze.

But that was just another day in the life with Rader. Another time, the team was about to play the Red Sox on Patriots' Day, the same day as the Boston Marathon. As Rader and Rich loped toward the team bus, they saw runners in the lobby stretching and jogging in place. So Rader—in a classy suit—lit up a cigarette, inhaled, started doing jumping jacks, and then blew smoke everywhere. "What, are you crazy?" said some runner, who started coughing.

Another day, back in Arlington, Rader and Rich participated in a charity golf tournament together. But Rader grew annoyed when the group behind them kept driving their ball into Radar and Rich's space.

Finally, Rader said, "Hi, fellas, you havin' fun?" He then reached into his golf bag, pulled out a shotgun, and blew one of their golf balls to smithereens. He put the shotgun into his bag and drawled, "Enjoy your day, boys."

Still another time, Rader drove his Cadillac—which he'd nicknamed, "The Love Boat"—to Rich's cul-de-sac and parked it in Rich's driveway. Bubba had been outside shooting hoops, so Rader asked him whether he had a hose.

"Yes, Mr. Rader," Bubba said.

"Well, hook up the hose—I gotta wash my car."

Once the hose was set, Rader opened all four doors of his "Love Boat" and doused the interior with water, full blast. When it was good and soaking wet, he tossed the hose back to Bubba and thanked him.

"Come on, Rico, let's go," Rader said. "Car's all clean."

Rich says every day with Rader was like going to the circus. Rader swung by the house another time, on a Monday off day, saying, "Rico, come here. Do you want to go to Wet 'n Wild, the water park?"

"Yeah, I'll get the kids," Rich said.

"No, the kids ain't goin'," blurted Rader. "Me and you are goin'!"

"Me and you are goin' to Wet 'n Wild?" Rich queried. "We start a big series with the Angels tomorrow, and I thought we were havin' batting practice today."

"Nope," said Rader. "We're goin' to Wet 'n Wild. We're gonna relax. Bring your bathing suit."

Little did Rich know that the water park wasn't open to the public on Mondays, and the general manager of the park had given Rader the keys. The two grown men had the entire place to themselves.

"We went on the waterfall three thousand times," Rich says.

As they were leaving dripping wet, Rader brought up the big Angels series and how he needed to figure out a way to get the players pumped up.

"Listen, when I was managing," Rich advised, "I did a victory cheer once—I spelled out V-I-C-T-O-R-Y—and the players loved it."

"Could you do that tomorrow?" Rader asked.

"In the clubhouse? With all the players?" Rich responded.

"Yes," Rader said. "And when you do the 'Y' of your Victory Cheer, do you fall down and put your legs up in the air like a Y?"

"Yeah, that's what I do."

"Well, it'd be neat if you had Peggy tattoo your butt cheeks with a 'TR' for Texas Rangers," Rader said. "You could drop down, do your 'Y,' and really get the players going."

When Rader and Rich arrived back at the house, Rader asked Peggy if she was willing to draw a "TR" on Rich's rear end. She laughed and then meticulously painted it on with blue and red markers the next day—purposely while Amy was away teaching in the garage. The only concern was whether it would smear off on Rich's commute to the stadium. So Rich crouched—never sat—while he drove.

That afternoon, he did his V-I-C-T-O-R-Y cheer for the whole team in his jockstrap, dropping down on the clubhouse floor to show off the blue and red "TR." He received a standing ovation from the fellas. Anything for the fellas. Anything for Rader. The Rangers took two out of three from the Angels, and Rich solidified his place as one of the most revered, likeable coaches in the organization.

But that was the issue: anything for the fellas, but not anything for Amy. At first, Bubba, Mike, Tim, and especially Amy were enjoying Rich's tenure as Rangers first base coach. Every summer, the team would have "Family Day" at Arlington Stadium, where the players' and coaches' children would wear a Rangers uniform with their names on the back and play a game against their dads. The Donnellys lived for that Family Day.

Amy was on cloud nine; she had a uniform of her own and was finally on equal footing with her brothers. "Now she was queen of Arlington Stadium," Rich says. Three-year-old Tim stole the show by hitting a ground ball and then running past first base all the way to the right field fence. The thirty thousand fans roared as Amy chased Tim down the line to fetch him back. For weeks, not one of the kids wanted to take their jerseys off.

"Amy and the boys wore them to school every day," Rich says. "They slept in them. They did everything in them. Peggy somehow got them to take 'em off once a week so she could wash them. I had spent thirteen years getting to the big leagues, and they felt like they were in the big leagues with me. They were so proud to be like a Rangers player. They thought they were on the Rangers team."

But the equal footing didn't last for Amy; it rarely did. Mike and Tim were growing older and more athletic—so Rich had two more guinea pigs to train. Bubba had already chosen basketball, but now Mike was toying with the idea of being a football kicker, and little Tim a baseball player. Rich intended to mold them.

Amy, meanwhile, was left in the garage, rounding up her students from the cul-de-sac. Either that or she was hanging out with her best friend and confidante, Cindy Gambrell.

She had met Cindy in kindergarten, back when Amy wore barrettes in her hair and barely made a peep at school. Year by year, they had grown closer, and by 1984, Cindy says they were like Frick and Frack. "Amy tricked people into thinking she was shy," Cindy says. "She just was quiet until she knew you—then she was a crazy person."

Since Peggy was working full-time, she had a rule that no friends could come into the house until she got home. But Amy would usher Cindy in anyway. When Peggy arrived, Amy would hide Cindy behind a nook in her room. Then the minute Peggy was inside, Cindy would sneak out through a side door and ring the doorbell.

"Oh, Mrs. Donnelly, can I play with Amy?" she'd ask.

Peggy was on to them but ultimately let it slide. Amy needed Cindy, and Cindy—whose father wasn't heavily involved in her life—needed Amy. They would attend Rangers games together, ogling the cutest players, and would head home afterward with the boys and Rich. In fact, Cindy thought they were a model family. One day, Cindy watched Rich tell Amy to take a whiff of a sweet-smelling banana cream pie. Amy leaned down to do so—until Rich shoved Amy's face down in the middle of the cream.

Everyone was cracking up except Amy, who punched Rich sternly in the arm. Cindy, though, was jealous of the jocularity. She told Amy she wished she had a dad like that, and she meant it. "The part I saw—I always thought how lucky she was, what a great family, what a great dad," Cindy says.

But none of them—not even Peggy—realized how conflicted Rich really was. It had been fourteen years since Rich truly trusted God, fourteen years since he'd been down on his knees saying a decade of the rosary.

He was afraid if Rader saw him praying from his knees, he'd light Rich's hair on fire. Rader was a Catholic too—but not a "convenient" Catholic as much as a "comedy" Catholic. He'd go to church or pre-game chapel for the laughs, and he'd bring Rich along for the ride in his Love Boat.

During spring training 1984, Rader decided they should go to Sunday Mass for old times' sake. Rich says he reminded him that they had a Sunday game at 1 p.m., which meant they had to be at the stadium by nine.

"It won't work, Doug," Rich said.

"Okay, then we'll go to 4 p.m. Mass on Saturday on our way to the game," Rader said.

"In our uniforms?" Rich asked.

"Yep—in our uniforms, Rico."

So into the church walked Rader and Rich, in full Texas Rangers regalia. Rader, in fact, ambled in wearing spikes.

As he entered, the clicking sound of his cleats turned the heads of the entire congregation. Rader's face was red with sunburn, while Rich's face was red with embarrassment. Eventually, the priest delivered the homily and then said, "The first collection today is going to be for the general fund. The second collection will be for the church renovation."

Rader, on cue, opened up his wallet, started ripping out five-dollar bills, and fluttered them toward the middle aisle. People chuckled.

The priest then said, "The third collection will be for the missionaries in Guam." Rader flicked some more money from his wallet.

The priest said the final collection would be for upcoming Easter festivities, at which point Rader tossed his credit cards and about $800 in meal money into the center aisle.

"Ah, take it all," Rader said out loud.

And off he and Rich went to the game.

After that, Rader agreed it was more practical to attend Mass during the season when the team would host Sunday chapels at the stadium. One Sunday, Rader showered after BP, blow-dried his red hair straight up so he resembled Bozo the Clown, and walked naked into the service. The speaker was the esteemed Dallas Cowboys coach Tom Landry.

"Hi, coach! Whatcha been up to?" Rader bellowed.

Landry's response: "Guess we'll start today with a prayer."

Rich would leave the stadium on days like that torn and confused. He didn't know whether to be Billy Martin and Doug Rader . . . or to be young Rich from Steubenville.

He didn't have the answer, and soon he wouldn't have a family.

Letter from Amy

Bubba,

Let me know if Dad comes over today. 'Cause if he does, I'm leaving.

Love,

Amy

Eleven

Infidelity

The best and worst part of spring training was the night life. The bars stayed open late; the exhibition games started early; and only the serious—or the ones with a conscience—survived.

In spring training 1984, Rich was primed to be one of the casualties. He was coaching first base by day and was uncoachable by night. In baseball terms, he compares his behavior that spring to rounding first, heading for second, and wandering outside of the baseline. Rich was about to be called out.

It started on a night he'd been stuck on the phone with Peggy and couldn't go partying with the boys. The boys, by the way, happened to be his roommates: the Rangers trainer Bill Zeigler and the country music singer Charlie Pride. Pride was the wildcard, in more ways than one. He was a friend of Zeigler's who came to spring training to hide from the music industry and his agent. He also loved baseball—being a former pitcher in the Negro Leagues—and slept on a cot in Rich and Zeigler's room. But above all, Charlie Pride was a celebrity who knew all the decadent country bars in town.

On the night Rich couldn't go out, Zeigler and Pride came home raving about a waitress who had served them at one of Charlie's rowdy country joints. There had been about fifteen Rangers players there, plus Charlie and Zeigler, and they'd run up a humongous tab. This girl had waited on them hand and foot—with the cheeriest of attitudes—and Zeigler, the next day, realized they'd forgotten to tip her.

That evening, Zeigler told Rich and Charlie they should go back and slip her some cash. So the trio returned to the bar, and for Rich, it was lust at first sight.

All those nights at Cheetah III with Billy Martin, he hadn't talked up a stripper or requested a lap dance. All those nights out as a Denver Bears player, he'd resisted the groupies. But his faith was wavering now, his morals eroded. Either baseball had brought this on or the death of Romey or the miscarriage or the emotional scars from Jerome. Or all of the above. But Rich was about to choose the life of Mr. Chivas Regal—and nothing good was likely to come of it.

The waitress—let's call her Lucy—was a brown-haired, brown-eyed bombshell who was all of twenty-one years old. Rich was thirty-seven and no slouch himself. When he was first a Rangers coach in 1980, he'd had his own fan club of about twenty women who would sit down the right field line adjacent to the bullpen. They'd eyeball him all game long and eventually wore T-shirts with Rich's picture on them. The caption: "Is this Robert Redford or Rich Donnelly?"

Lucy must have noticed the resemblance too, because after Zeigler tipped her, she stared at Rich almost as much as he stared at her. "You weren't here last night, were you?" she asked him. By midnight, their small talk turned into large talk. Zeigler eventually told her that they had to get going, and her response was, "Why do you have to go? Why don't you stay for a while?"

Rich mentioned he had a game in the morning, and Zeigler said, "Yeah, seriously, I gotta take him home."

"I'll take him home," Lucy said—stopping the conversation dead in its tracks.

This was the same Rich who wasn't allowed to date girls, eyeball girls, ogle girls, talk to girls, or breathe on girls in high school. The same Rich who was stalked by Jerome at Marlene Swan's house party. He'd had one real girlfriend in his life—his wife—so, in the simplest terms, he had never truly sowed his oats. It was Jerome's fault perhaps. But Rich didn't use all of that as his excuse, because Rich wasn't capable of that kind of self-analysis. The fact was, he was not going to pass up Lucy's pretty face. Not as tortured as he was as a man.

"Baseball—yeah, you're supposed to be a tough guy," Rich says. "You can't go to church. You gotta drink and smoke, gotta chew tobacco, have girlfriends, and act like a big leaguer. That's what I thought.

"I should've been happy, but I was at my most miserable. You think you have everything you ever wanted: you have a good job; you have kids. But you get into baseball, and you see these guys with beautiful models, and you think, *Who in the world would want me?* And here she is. She was the one everybody looked at, everybody wanted—and she liked *me*."

He went home with Lucy that night, and it wasn't terribly long before they were living together in Pompano Beach. She was a dental assistant by trade, and for the final thirty to thirty-five days of spring training, they fell into the rhythm of being a couple. When it was time to start the season, he figured he would leave, and that would be that. She was so drop-dead gorgeous that he assumed she'd have another boyfriend in a matter of hours, maybe ten boyfriends. He was based in Arlington; she seemed ensconced in Florida. He saw it as just a fling.

Back home in Texas, Amy greeted him with a hug, while he greeted her with a "'Twas the Night Before Christmas." She was ten now and had basically outgrown the poem, but she grinned her way through it nonetheless. She was still teaching in the garage, still playing soccer for the Twisters, still mentoring Tim, and still consorting with Cindy. Last but not least, Rich was still her hero.

One day early in the season, the whole lot of them—Bubba, Amy, Mike, and Tim—had a dentist appointment down the street from their house. Upon returning, they raved about the new dental assistant who had given them Scooby-Doo stickers.

"That's nice," Rich said.

"Her name is Lucy, and she's really pretty, Dad."

"What?"

Rich told everyone he had to go to the grocery store, but instead rushed over to the dentist's office. Sure enough, he saw Lucy's car—with the Florida license plate—in the parking lot. He was beside himself. He walked in, asked the receptionist if he could see Lucy, and then pulled her to a private spot behind the desk.

"What the heck are you doing here?" he asked.

"I want to be close to you."

"So you got a job a mile from my house?"

"And an apartment," she said.

She had brought everything she owned in a U-Haul—her clothes, her furniture, and her man crush. She hadn't asked him for permission ahead of time; she had just decided to invade his space and put his marriage in immediate jeopardy. A stronger, more honorable man would have ended it right then and there. Rich did the opposite.

"It was awful," he says, "but I'd found a girl who paid attention to me—and was beautiful."

Using every excuse in the book—"Rader wants me to come over and talk about the lineup . . . One of the players needs a lift home from the bar"—he would escape to Lucy's apartment to continue their affair. It was easier when Peggy had to work a late nursing shift. After the kids went to bed, he'd simply hustle over to Lucy's, knowing he had to be back by midnight.

Occasionally, Peggy would beat him home, and he'd have to think up another whopper—such as he'd been out getting gas for the car. He realized he had to get creative. After road trips, he'd tell Peggy his charter flight was landing at 3 a.m. when it was really arriving at 11 p.m. That gave him and Lucy five hours alone at her place—before he'd head home at 4 a.m. All this from the former altar boy.

For a long while, he made his dual life work. He'd take Lucy on an occasional Rangers road trip, and in New York, he treated her to the Broadway show *Cats*. He bought the cast recording while leaving the theatre and played it day and night in his car. Whenever Amy rode with him, she'd hear the *Cats* show tunes and became enthralled with the music too. She asked Rich if she could see the show with him, and he couldn't dare tell her he'd seen it with Lucy. That would've been parent suicide. He just told Amy that someday they could maybe go—but for now to enjoy the show tunes.

His little game started to unravel as soon as Lucy began to cross boundaries. One night from the road during the 1984 season, he called Peggy to see how Bubba's Little League game had gone. "Oh, I don't know," Peggy said. "The kids did well, I guess." He was desperate for more detail, wanted the complete play-by-play. But Peggy must've been disengaged or talking to a friend during Bubba's at-bats. He hung up frustrated and decided to phone Lucy.

He asked her how her day went and she mentioned she'd been to a baseball game—specifically a Little League game.

"What?"

"I went to watch Bubba," Lucy said. "He went two for three and made a good play at short."

It turned out Lucy had been sitting right next to Peggy the whole night. Peggy hadn't recognized her from the dentist's office, but that was beside the point. Rich knew his secret wasn't safe.

It went on like this for months, this little game of cat and mouse. Rich would bring Lucy on the road—which should have been less stressful, except that Lucy would hop on the team bus on the way to the ballpark wearing short shorts.

"Holy crap, who is that?" Rich remembers third baseman Buddy Bell asking.

"That's my girlfriend," Rich answered.

Before long, Lucy was acquainted with Rader and all the players. One night, she danced on top of a hotel bar, and another player started hitting on her. Part of Rich wanted to tell him, "Go ahead, take her. Get her away from me."

Rich was in over his head. The unspoken rule among ballplayers was, "What happens on the road stays on the road"—so nobody spilled the news to Peggy. But Rich's wife was no dummy; there were too many alleged trips to the gas station, too many alleged trips to see Rader. One night, he returned home from Lucy's apartment just minutes before Peggy arrived at the house from work. Rich hustled into bed. But when Peggy entered the bedroom, she asked him what he'd done that night.

"Oh, I stayed at home and watched TV," he said.

"Is that right? Then how come the hood of your car is hot?" she said.

Now it was a full-fledged game of hide-and-seek—because Peggy began to spy on him. On a night after a road trip—when he'd told Peggy his flight would be landing at 3 a.m.—Rich looked out of Lucy's apartment window and noticed Peggy parked outside in her car. It was officially panic time; she had found them.

Peggy said absolutely nothing the next morning, biding her time. Rich went to the ballpark that day ashen-faced and confided in his friend Dave Stewart, one of the Rangers pitchers. He says he told Stewart that Peggy was following him, so Stewart—trying to be helpful—offered to swap cars with Rich.

"Here are the keys to my Lexus," Stewart said, according to Rich. "You take my car, and I'll take your car. She'll *never* find me."

So Stewart would speed off in Rich's station wagon, while Rich would speed over to Lucy's place in Dave Stewart's Lexus—all with the intention of throwing Peggy way off course. He says Peggy would park outside of Lucy's, see the unfamiliar Lexus, and bail. Rich and Stewart would then swap the cars back at 12:30 a.m. It kept Peggy at bay.

But Lucy just didn't know when to let up. One game day in 1985 at Arlington Stadium, Rich jogged out to his first base coaching box in the first inning and trained his eyes on the leadoff hitter, Wayne Tolleson— and then he spied Lucy sitting in the front row. She had somehow finagled a season ticket on the third base side, directly in Rich's sight line to the batter's box. She was *stalking* him. Every time he looked at a batter, he would see Lucy's face. She would wave or blow kisses; it was borderline fatal attraction.

He asked her afterward, "What the heck are you doing?"

"I bought a season ticket so I can see you every night," she answered.

He was rattled, but if he dumped her, he was certain she'd go to Peggy and backstab him. How could he have gotten himself into this deviant mess? He was on a road trip to Kansas City, pondering what to do, when the phone rang in his hotel room.

It was Peggy, and her opening line was, "Hi, I'm out having lunch."

"Who are you having lunch with?" Rich asked.

"A friend of yours—Lucy."

The marriage was as good as over at that very second. Rich says Lucy had outed him to Peggy, for whatever reason, and Peggy countered by telling Lucy every sordid detail about Rich. It was the obvious low point, and Peggy decided she was through. When Rich returned from the road trip, he found all of his belongings stuffed inside bags and suitcases on the front porch. She had booted him out.

"Hey, if you want to be with her, go ahead," Peggy scolded him. "Go ahead. I can't stop you. Come back in a year, and maybe we'll talk."

It sounded a lot like good-bye. Two decades earlier, he and Peggy had checked into a hotel as boyfriend and girlfriend, as the Donaldsons. They had ended up abstaining from sex that night, and Rich had raced to confession simply for lusting after her. Now was the time he *really* needed confession. But he didn't race to see a priest at all; instead, he floored the station wagon and headed to Lucy's apartment, permanently.

A few nights later, Rich says Lucy pulled out a shoebox from her closet. "I want to show you something," she said. She then opened the lid and pulled out two handfuls of assorted credit card bills and utility bills.

"Can you pay these off for me?" she asked.

He was fuming, embarrassed. He'd been had. The kid from Steubenville had been stung. He thought to himself, *So this is what this was all about; it was about money.* He made a beeline for the door.

He kept his distance from her after that and heard later she was dating a Rangers player. But all he could think about was his family. It was bad enough that his marriage was history, but what about Bubba, Mike, and Tim? What about Amy?

All they knew was that Dad wasn't living in the house on the cul-de-sac anymore. Bubba was too wrapped up in his basketball to dwell on it, and Mike and Tim were seven and five years old, respectively. But Amy was old enough and astute enough to realize that her father had been a heel. She had witnessed her mother's tears. She may have been only all of eleven, but Amy was in touch with her emotions—and the one that wasn't exiting any time soon was her anger.

In Amy's mind, her father had replaced her and her mom with some floozy. She'd spent her whole life aching for his attention, and he'd chosen someone else. Amy didn't want to write Rich letters or notes anymore; she wanted to write him out of her life, at least for the time being. She had inherited Rich's temper, and he was about to get a load of her wrath.

He remembers driving down a street near the cul-de-sac one day and seeing Amy and Cindy walking together. He rolled down his window to say hello. Amy gave him her dirtiest look, gave him a scrunched-up face, gave him a death stare.

"She doesn't want to talk to you, Mr. Donnelly," Cindy said.

Amy just kept on walking.

Letter from Amy

Bubba,
   I would rather let my teeth rot than go back to that dental chick.

                                        Love,

                                        Amy

Twelve

A Daughter Scorned

Time was going to have to heal the wounds, because sorry wasn't working.

Rich had only one family left—his baseball one. Each family was equally dysfunctional, although his baseball brothers seemed to prefer it that way.

When Doug Rader heard what happened, he assured Rich he had his back. It's the way of the locker room, which is why a clubhouse is such a sacred place to the teams. During spring training, for instance, child welfare officers had barged into Rader's manager's office looking for a certain John Milton Rivers, who was lagging behind on child support payments.

"John Milton Rivers? Nope, we don't have no John Milton Rivers here," Rader said.

"We were told he was here, sir," the officer said.

"Listen," Rader said, "if I find John Milton Rivers, I'll call you."

The agents left, at which point Rader went and found Rangers outfielder John Milton (Mickey) Rivers in the clubhouse laundry room playing a game of Spades.

"Well," Rader told Rich, "if the officers had asked for *Mickey* Rivers, I'd have helped 'em."

In other words, baseball coaches and players could be the most determined enablers out there, which offered Rich a degree of comfort.

No one scolded him for cheating on Peggy; they praised him for dating a woman sixteen years his junior. If Rich was going to learn his lesson, it wasn't going to happen in the depths of Arlington Stadium. He was on his own with this one.

Unfortunately for Rich, the 1985 baseball season just piled on to his misery. Exactly thirty-two games into the year, with a record of 9–23, the Rangers fired his sidekick Doug Rader. The team was in Chicago when the news broke, and Rader called his coaches into the manager's office. He sat them down at a table and began to read his baseball will and testament:

"To Merv Rettenmund, I leave my old glove . . . To Twig [Wayne Terwilliger], I leave my old awful fungo bat . . . And to you, Rico, I leave my steel cup 'cause you got balls and you're from Steel City Steubenville."

Rich remembers the scene being "hilarious and sad at the same time." Then, before another word was spoken, Rader got up—without a hug, without a tear, without a handshake—and walked out. His replacement, Bobby Valentine, happened to be walking in at that exact moment. Valentine tried to shake Rader's hand, but Rader pulled back and said, "Anybody but you."

Considering his ties to Rader, Rich thought Valentine might fire him at season's end—and he wore the stress on his sleeve. Rich was ejected from his first-ever major league game after telling umpire Tim McClelland, "You couldn't make a good call with a fistful of dimes in a phone booth!" It was a nice zinger, all right, but it was Rich whose fuse had been shorter than McClelland's.

At the end of September, Valentine assured Rich he had nothing to worry about, that his job was safe. But on the night of a 1985 World Series game—Cardinals versus Royals—Valentine phoned Rich to tell him he'd changed his mind and was dumping him. After sixteen seasons with the Senators/Rangers, it was a sobering development. Rich was officially on the outs with his wife, his three sons, and his only daughter—and now with baseball. He needed the healing and reconciliation to begin as soon as possible, but Amy was certainly not going to be the one to initiate it.

Her stress level was through the roof too, because she'd found there was nothing more inhumane than a single-parent household. Amy craved being in charge, of course, but with Peggy working full-time, she was losing a chunk of her childhood. While her older brother, Bubba, was in the gym every day after school, she'd be the one taking care of Mike and Tim—fixing them snacks, making sure they washed behind their ears.

She was only eleven going on twelve, but she might as well have been twenty. Peggy would buy adorable clothing for Tim at The Gap, but it was Amy who had to dress him up in it. Tim still insisted on wearing his Rangers jersey to first grade every day, so Amy conned him into his Gap clothes the Steubenville way—with cold, hard cash.

"I'll pay you a dollar to wear them," she said.

"Deal," Tim blurted.

The only way she could get things done around the house was with these bribes. And it was mostly her brothers' poor hygiene that had her going broke. Amy still refused to tolerate bad breath, brown teeth, or odorous feet, and—just as with her students in the garage—she would offer cold, hard cash to get Mike and Tim to take a bath.

Mike wouldn't listen much to her, and she used to wag her finger at him because of it. She'd then tease Mike because of his unusually large head and make up nicknames for him like "Bucket Head" or "Melon Head"—or "Mel" for short. That was Amy's M.O for Mike, though it wouldn't work much. But considering that Amy was Tim's surrogate mom, Tim would acquiesce—most of the time. The one thing Tim fought her on was digging the dirt out of his fingernails. He said the nail file hurt, and he was so dead set against it that he wouldn't even take a dollar to let her do it.

"Okay, I'll clean your room if I can clean your fingernails," she offered.

"Amy, why do you care so much?" Mike interjected.

"Because those nails are disgusting."

Tim hardly minded—because the one thing he hated more than cleaning fingernails was tidying up his room. So he took the offer. "Tim was like her little pet," Mike would say.

Amy's only real source of sanity came from her friend Cindy, who had issues with her own father. They would commiserate with each other on their way to and from school, which gave Amy someone to bash Lucy to. "Amy had names for her, that's all I'll say," Cindy says. But day by day, week by week, month by month, Amy's temper wasn't defusing.

She hadn't forgiven Rich, but she was becoming Rich. At least a part of her. She was still the sweet Amy deep down who would volunteer to do the dishes and rub Peggy's sore feet after work. She was still a giver. But her parents' breakup had unleashed something inexplicable inside of her.

One day, she and Cindy were walking home from school as usual when some boorish girl began to follow them and bully them. Having been taught to turn the other cheek, Amy ignored it—until it happened the next day and the next. She then alerted Peggy to it, at which time Peggy gave Amy the green light to be Rich Donnelly.

"If she touches you, knock her you know what out," Peggy said.

Sure enough, the bully showed up again the next afternoon and made a wisecrack. Amy promptly turned around and smashed the girl's nose with her books, a knockout if you ever saw one. The girl ended up flat on the sidewalk, her nostrils bleeding. While Cindy screamed, Amy simply said, "That oughta do it."

The boys at home were proud of her—"We're not a family of derelicts, so it was amazing she stood up for herself," Bubba says—but it illustrated the scope of her anger. As much as her father was still her idol, his absence meant she might be out of chances to win him over, to be on equal ground with her brothers. And that perturbed her to no end. Rich would call the house to speak to Bubba about his basketball or to Mike about his kicking or to Tim about his baseball swing. He'd ask to talk to Amy as well, but she'd make herself incommunicado.

"Oh, she stopped all communication," Peggy says. "Cold turkey. She wouldn't talk to him on the phone; she wouldn't have anything to do with him."

If the silent treatment hurt Rich—and it did—then mission accomplished. How long her grudge would last, nobody knew. Especially Rich.

"It was awful," he says. "Her silence was deadly. Not once did she say, 'What are you doing, Dad?' Never. Just dirty looks. Oh, she had a temper. Don't get her riled up. I mean, she'd fight with those brothers of hers all the time. She'd fight with them about whatever. When she got going, phew, she was the roughest one in the family. Like Bubba always said, 'Dad, she won't take mess from anybody.' And I believe it."

All of this turned Rich into even more of a lost soul. All he knew was that he needed a job, because without family and baseball he was a nothing, a zero, a waste. His best friend in Arlington—a Rangers fan and self-made millionaire named Vince Genovese—couldn't bear to see Rich so depressed. So he flew Rich in his private jet to the 1985 winter meetings in San Diego with some instructions.

"Rico," Vince said, "you're going to sit in that hotel lobby. And every farm director and general manager who walks by, you're going to stand up and tell 'em you're looking for a job and you're the guy they should hire."

Rich agreed to give it a try. As he sat in the lobby that first day, he read in the newspaper that his hometown Pittsburgh Pirates had just hired an old acquaintance of his, Jim Leyland. It took Rich way back. He had first heard of Leyland in 1968 after he'd signed with the Twins. As he was about to join the team, a buddy from Xavier named Smokey Knorek—who was in a popular campus rock and roll band—said, "If you ever run into a guy in pro ball named Jim Leyland, tell him I said hello. He's from Perrysburg, Ohio, and I'm from Rossford, right next door. I know the man."

Sure enough, a year later when Rich's A-ball team in Orlando took on the Lakeland Tigers, Jim Leyland was the opposing catcher. When it was his turn to hit, Rich stepped into the batter's box, looked down at Leyland, and said, "Hey, Smokey Knorek says to say hello."

"Okay, that's nice—now get in the (bleeping) box," Leyland responded.

This was Rich's kind of guy. They eventually managed against each other at both A-ball and spring training and bonded over their Ohio roots and their love for the University of Notre Dame. Later on, Leyland had ascended to third base coach for the White Sox at the same time Rich was first base coach for the Rangers. Not only were they pals by this point, but they also both coached baseball with their teeth clenched. Leyland smoked two packs of cigarettes a game, while Rich chewed four packs of bubble gum a game. They were kindred spirits, and when Rich saw that Leyland had landed the Pirates job in 1985, he called his hotel room.

Leyland was glad to hear from him, but could promise nothing. He had an opening for a bullpen coach, but the Pirates general manager, a behemoth former scout named Syd Thrift, was permitting Leyland to hire only one member of his staff sight unseen—third base coach Gene Lamont. So all Leyland could do was mention Rich's name to Thrift and hope that Thrift would grant him an interview.

Three days passed in San Diego with not a call from Thrift or even a sniff of a job offer elsewhere. Rich and Genovese were about to fly back to Arlington that afternoon empty-handed when the phone rang in Rich's room. It was Leyland.

"Can you be up in Syd Thrift's room in an hour?" Leyland asked.

"Sure, yeah," Rich said. "I'm on it." A few minutes later, Thrift called Rich himself. He had a thick drawl to go with his booming voice, and their conversation began like this.

THRIFT: "What do you say there, boy? How you doin' there,
        boy? Why don't you come up here, boy? I'm up in Suite
        2206, boy. Boy, you wanna talk about a job, don't you, boy?'
RICH: "Yes, sir."

THRIFT: "Well, I tell you what you do, boy. You come up to
Room 2206. And you want to do me a favor, boy? Why don't
you stop at that bakery down there in the lobby, boy, and get
me twelve blueberry muffins when you come up here."

RICH: "Yes, sir. I'll be right up."

Rich rushed to the bakery, bought a baker's dozen worth of blueberry
muffins, and had them boxed. When he knocked on the door of Suite
2206, Thrift opened up and ripped the box right out of Rich's hand.

THRIFT: "Hey, boy! Come on in, boy!"

RICH: "Mr. Thrift, here are your blueberry muffins. I got you a
baker's dozen."

THRIFT: "Boy, that's great, boy. Why don't you sit down here,
boy?"

The general manager proceeded to ask Rich thirteen questions and,
according to Rich, stuffed one full muffin in his mouth after every one
of them.

THRIFT: "Boy, when you're in that bullpen, boy, what will
you do?"

RICH: "Well, sir, you can't just let them warm up. You've got to
chart 'em and let 'em know who they're gonna face."

THRIFT: "Boy, that's great, boy. Where did you come from, boy?"

RICH: "Well, sir, I managed in the Rangers organization, and
I was a coach for the big league club the last three seasons.
I managed against Jim Leyland."

After both the thirteenth question and thirteenth muffin were history, Thrift said, "That's great, boy. Well, boy, if we're interested, we'll
be calling you."

With that, Rich exited Suite 2206 wishing he'd bought two baker's dozens. "Then I would've gotten twenty-six questions," he says. He hopped on his flight home with Genovese, convinced he'd never again hear from Thrift in his life.

Later that night, back in Texas, Rich's phone rang. It was Leyland, who asked him how the interview played out.

> RICH: "Well, Jim, I'm not sure. I couldn't understand him much—he asked all the questions with his mouth full of blueberry muffins."
>
> LEYLAND: "Well, are your parents going to come to Opening Day?"
>
> RICH: "Opening Day where?"
>
> LEYLAND: "Don't your parents live near Pittsburgh?"
>
> RICH: "Yes, Steubenville."
>
> LEYLAND: "Well aren't they going to come to the Pirates opener and watch their son coach in the bullpen?"

The pause lasted about five seconds, whereupon Rich let out a "holy moly." After a childhood of listening to KDKA, of living and dying with Bob Prince, of storing tattered Pirates box scores in his dresser drawer, of idolizing Bill Mazeroski, Roberto Clemente, and Bill Virdon ... Rich was a Bucco. His dream of winning a World Series in black and gold was suddenly feasible. He wasn't a third base coach, but he was in the building and on the payroll.

He dialed the phone number at his old house on the cul-de-sac to give them the low-down. After a year-plus of the Lucy affair and silent treatments and evil glares, he considered any sort of good news a blessing. He spoke to Bubba, who could sense the exhilaration in his dad's voice. He spoke to Mike and Tim. The Donnellys were back in the bigs. Amy still wouldn't come near the phone, but she couldn't help but overhear Rich's good fortune.

She then walked alone to her room ... smiling.

Letter from Amy

Hey, Bubba,

Who'd you say your favorite Pirate was? Sid Bream? I hear he's nice. I wish I could go in the clubhouse with you all sometimes so I could get to know these guys.

Love,

Amy

Thirteen

"Amy, What Do You Want to Do?"

Peggy asked for a show of hands on whether the kids wanted a summer vacation in Pittsburgh/Steubenville. There were three yeses and one maybe.

The one on the fence, of course, was Amy. Not that there was any doubt which way she was leaning. The prospect of her letting Tim go anywhere without her was slim to none. But first she needed to find the inner peace to forgive her father.

Peggy stressed to Amy that the breakup had nothing to do with her, which was much of what Amy needed to hear. Amy was already insecure about her place in her father's heart, and she unnecessarily blamed herself for being born a girl, for being a burden on Rich, for making him want to abandon the family. Every bit of it was a fabrication, an untruth. But if Amy was truly sold on any of this, Peggy had to step in right away. She—and even Cindy—tried all they could to sway her thinking.

Peggy ended up telling Amy ten times a day that she loved her, that her father loved her—that the day she was born was one of the most glorious days of their lives. Amy being Amy, she was cynical. She asked her mom how she even knew how her father felt. So Peggy broke the news to Amy with a firm whisper: Peggy and Rich had been talking . . . Peggy and Rich might be getting back together.

The plan was for Peggy and the kids to join him in the Steubenville area come June or July, once Rich had settled comfortably into his baseball season and his new job as the Pirates bullpen coach. Amy heard all of this and began her thaw. She voted yes on the summer vacation in Steubenville, voted yes to laying eyes on her father again.

Peggy, deep down, knew this was a risky move. She could only cross her fingers, hoping Rich would somehow return to being a devoted family man. She was willing to take him back for the kids, for Amy. But she had no illusions it would go smoothly or that they'd all be one happy family again, guaranteed.

She couldn't get inside Rich's head, which was probably fortuitous. One day, Rich would be pining for Peggy and the kids; the next, he'd be feeling "depressed" and "miserable." Lucy was still calling him from time to time, which flustered him. With the Pirates season fast approaching, he needed to hit the reset button, needed to rediscover who he used to be. So he did the unthinkable: he moved back in with Jerome and Helen.

Why he would subject himself to his father again after two-plus decades of emotional abuse had everything to do with Steubenville. Not only was it just a short drive from Pittsburgh, but all of his old buddies— all of his goodfellas—were still living there. Donnie Teramana and Dewey Guida were on their way to becoming self-made millionaires, either through construction or the restaurant business. They'd all go to the high school football games together for old times' sake. He would wake up every morning and head to the Spot—a breakfast joint where you could place a bet, have a shot of bourbon, or hang out with Tennis Shoe Ernie, all before 9 a.m.

Not to mention the fact that Rich was returning as sort of a conquering hero. He was about to be a Pirate, a Bucco, a source of free tickets for everyone in town—and everyone in Steubenville was backslapping him, including Brucie Boggs and Mousy and Ratsy Gaylord. Dean Martin and Jimmy the Greek suddenly had company on the celebrity totem pole there. The chatter around town became, "Duke Donnelly is in the big leagues. Pass it on."

For all those reasons, living under his father's roof again was tolerable. For one thing, Jerome had mellowed a bit in his advanced age, didn't nag his son as often anymore, and was eager to see his grandkids come visit. Rich had stopped being afraid of Jerome eons before in Denver anyway. The other upside—besides not having to pay rent—was that Rich got to sleep in his boyhood room again, the same room that had been his safe haven after Romey's death, the same room where he used to build a May altar. Maybe all of this would restore his faith, or at least a miniscule bit of it.

Of course, once the 1986 baseball season started, Rich wasn't going to be home full-time anyway. He was about to belong to Jim Leyland—and get the education of a lifetime.

Leyland was a humble, chain-smoking baseball savant who simultaneously struck fear and good tidings into every ballplayer he ever met. He could be abrasive and a forgiving confidant in the same breath. He was *everyman*. His brother was a priest, yet he adored racetracks and casinos. His father was blue-collar, yet he could charm the front office suits. Leyland had the good qualities of Billy Martin and Doug Rader in him, not the loose cannon qualities. He would never embarrass a franchise; he'd never dive into a Chivas Regal at eight in the morning or take a shotgun to a golf ball.

Not that Leyland was a finished product. This was his first big league managing job, which meant he needed to lean on lieutenants such as Rich, Gene Lamont, Milt May, Ray Miller, and Chuck Tanner. They were all cut from the same cloth—baseball men who could communicate with their players as well as each other. That came in handy, considering how godawful a team they inherited.

The year before, under Tanner, the Pirates had lost 104 games. They were the worst possible combination—old, slow, and apathetic. Right fielder George Hendrick was thirty-five; third baseman Bill Madlock was thirty-four; first baseman Jason Thompson was thirty; left fielder Steve Kemp was thirty—and all four needed to be replaced pronto. Leyland knew the rebuild could be painstakingly slow and hoped Thrift and company would be willing to gut it out. He figured the team could be respectable in about three years, depending on how swiftly he could change the lousy culture.

Opening Day showed Leyland how horrific a challenge it would be. On April 8, 1986, as the Pirates were about to take on the eventual World Series Champion New York Mets, Leyland stood with his team awaiting the national anthem. Just as the singer was about to bellow out, "O say can you see?" right fielder Mike Brown turned to Leyland and said, "Hey, Jim, every time I hear this song, I have a bad game."

"What?" Leyland chirped.

If that didn't set the tone for an exasperating season, nothing else would. The way Rich describes it, the 1986 Pirates were so pitiable that a fan had the following mid-year conversation with a ticket office employee:

FAN: "Hey, I need four tickets for the June 28 Expos game."
EMPLOYEE: "Okay, I'll get 'em for you."
FAN: "What time is the game?"
EMPLOYEE: "What time can you be here?"

Rich heard that story secondhand, but he's convinced it happened more than once. "How bad were we? Guys would run out a ground ball to first base and get a standing ovation," Rich says. "That was the big thrill of the night."

By the first of July, the Buccos were well on their way to a ninety-eight-loss season and no longer in playoff contention. But on the plus-side, a youth movement was underway. The new first baseman replacing Jason Thompson was a twenty-five-year-old power hitter named Sid Bream. The new corner outfielder replacing Mr. National Anthem Mike Brown was a twenty-three-year-old stud named Bobby Bonilla. And the new rookie centerfielder was a grumpy, mercurial, skinny, prolific twenty-one-year-old dynamo named Barry Bonds.

Around that same point in July, another set of youngsters came rolling into town as well: fourteen-year-old Bubba Donnelly, eight-year-old Mike Donnelly, and six-year-old Tim Donnelly. And along for the ride, effervescent and upbeat, was twelve-year-old Amy Donnelly.

Peggy, after arriving with the four kids in tow, was curious how the reception would go between Amy and Rich. Quite naturally, Rich himself was expecting the arrival of a winter storm, unsure whether Amy would give him the icy stare and the scrunched-up nose she had given him through his car window the year before.

But their greeting proved to be the antithesis of that—evidence that underneath that caustic exterior, Amy was the same angel she'd always been. They had hugged the minute their eyes met, and Rich's first words—which he would repeat a hundred times all summer—were, *I love you, Amy.*

"Amy's wrath was like no other, and I was waiting for her to unload on me," Rich says. "But she was like normal, fun-loving Amy, snuggling up to me all the time. A true miracle."

The embrace between Rich and Peggy was a little more measured, which, in reality, was equally as pivotal. After the Lucy affair, Peggy needed Rich to be devoted to the marriage times twelve, and on the surface, he was willing to give it his best shot. For the month of July, he rented an apartment in Weirton, West Virginia, just outside Steubenville and conveniently on the road to Pittsburgh. The six of them had designs on being a harmonious family unit—naive as it may have been—but Rich remembers the dynamic between him and Peggy as being "tense."

The kids, bless their hearts, couldn't sense their parents' ambivalence. They were having too much fun at Three Rivers Stadium. They rode with their dad to many of the home night games, arriving at about 12:30 p.m. to a relatively deserted ballpark. The boys couldn't wait to charge into the clubhouse, where there was all the bubble gum they could chew and all the sunflower seeds they could spit. That was the good news; the bad news was they weren't allowed to touch it.

Rich wasn't going to put up with any monkey business in there.

On the day of their first clubhouse visit, Rich explained the house rules to his boys—the same way Jerome used to issue edicts to him.

- Number 1: They couldn't embarrass him; if they did, they would be whipped.
- Number 2: They'd better not break anything; if they did, they would be whipped.
- Number 3: Whatever foul language they heard in the clubhouse had to stay in the clubhouse; if they spoke profanely anywhere else, they would be whipped.
- Number 4: Once the players arrived in the locker room at about 2 p.m., they had to get the heck out; either they sat calmly on a couch next to the indoor batting cage or they would be whipped.

It could've been worse—the boys could've been Amy. Because she was female, it was sacrilege to let her in the clubhouse or even near the batting cage. At least the boys could inhabit the field, sit in the dugout, play catch with their dad, and mingle with the players. Amy had to stay put in the Green Room, or Wives Room.

It may sound restrictive, but compared to every other kid they knew back home, it was a dream scenario. Their playground was a big league stadium, and they'd have been nuts to complain. A few weeks into the visit, the boys became virtually part of the locker room furniture. From a distance, they had watched a rotund clubhouse attendant nicknamed "Chuck E. Cheese" pick up stray jockstraps with a clothes hanger and toss them into a hamper. So the boys began to pick up towels and soiled socks—ingratiating themselves to everyone.

Before long, the players knew the kids by name and would send them on errands. The boys would fetch the players coffee or, in rare cases, dart out of the stadium to buy them a hamburger and fries from a nearby McDonald's. One time, Bubba brought Bonds back a burger that had pickles on it. "Don't you know I hate pickles?" Bonds scolded him. So Bubba flicked the pickles off of it.

The upside was that Bonds had given him twenty bucks to buy the burger—and let Bubba keep the $15 change as a tip. Bonds wasn't such a sourpuss, after all. But the most gracious player of all was Bream, the religious first baseman who hailed from faith-based Liberty University. Bream struck the boys as the kind of the guy who would fit in on their cul-de-sac. When they shined the cleats of other players, they'd be critiqued for smearing the black polish. But Bream couldn't have cared less how bright his cleats looked. He was never negative; he'd always say hello, good-bye, please, and thank you. They gravitated to Bream for just that reason.

By and large, the players couldn't have been kinder. On travel days, when the team would be leaving on a road trip immediately following a home game, the boys would volunteer to carry players' luggage to the bus—receiving handsome tips. Bobby Bonilla was another of their favorites because of his toothy grin and propensity to shell out $20 bills for suitcase services rendered. The three boys would often leave the stadium with up to $50 each.

Amy was somewhat jealous about being left out, although the summer was more about repairing her relationship with her father than anything else. If ever the Pirates lost a home game in 1986—and they lost a lot—a word would never be spoken on the Donnelly car ride back to Weirton. No one was a lousier loser than Rich. But if ever the Pirates won, these rides back were full of Amy's wondrous, unfiltered, uncensored banter. Rich might spend much of the car ride demanding that Bubba get in a basketball workout the next day or telling Mike to stop talking back all the time. But if he ordered Amy around in the slightest, she would tell him, "Nope, I'm not doing that" or "Oh, hush it, Dad"—and wait to see how he'd respond.

The boys would cringe at how she talked back to their father, knowing if it had been them, their dad would have pulled over to the side of the road and brandished his belt. But with Amy, Rich would just give her his patented glare—the same sort of glare she'd given *him* that one day—and leave it at that. "She wasn't scared," Tim says. "Wasn't scared of anything. She could just get away with some things we boys had no shot of getting away with."

She likely was testing limits, and Rich—knowing the two of them were in healing mode—let her slide. The truth was, Amy enjoyed being suddenly part of her father's inner sanctum and on somewhat of an equal ground with her brothers. She was finally one of them. As unsettled as Rich was in his marriage, he had decided this was the summer of Amy, bar none.

In mid-August, he made certain to include her on a Pirates road trip to Philadelphia—where she'd get to barge her way inside his world even more. The road was where the team truly bonded, and even though Amy was ineligible to enter the clubhouse, sleeping at the team hotel was the next best thing. The players would all stay on the same hotel floor, and Leyland would often have pizza parties up in his suite. And on this particular trip to Philadelphia, Leyland had the presidential suite.

The suite was a doozy—two adjoining rooms, a living room, a dining room table, and a state-of-the-art television. To show you what kind of person Leyland was, he just flat-out handed the room over to Rich, the boys, and Amy. "We'll just swap, and I'll take your room," Leyland said.

The kids were over-the-top thrilled, and Amy—Queen Elizabeth—announced she would be sleeping in Leyland's king-sized bed. The boys argued with her over that one. But Rich had the final say on the sleeping arrangements and agreed that Amy had called the bed first. She and the boys would hop up and down on the enormous mattress and then call all their friends back in Texas, saying, "We're Ronald Reagan; we're in the presidential suite." If that didn't have Amy in love with baseball and Uncle Jim Leyland, nothing would.

By the end of August, it was time for the kids to go back to Texas for a new school year. Amy winked good-bye to Rich, and little Tim cried his eyeballs out all the way to the airport. What they didn't realize was that Rich was ready for them to go.

He and Peggy hadn't reconciled, not in the least. In fact, she had returned home to Texas earlier that August—leaving the children alone with Rich—after she'd witnessed still more of Rich's indiscretions. On nights the kids hadn't gone to the game or were staying overnight with Jerome and Helen, Rich would go out looking for girls at an all-night bar/restaurant in Steubenville called Angelo's. He had hardly learned his lesson, and Peggy knew it. So she made up a white lie and told the kids she had to return to Arlington ahead of schedule for work.

Once the kids joined Peggy in Texas, Rich went somewhat into Billy Martin mode. The other Pirates coaches nicknamed Rich "The Man Who Feared Sleep" because for a while he never even considered shut-eye. He would leave Three Rivers Stadium after weeknight home games at around 11:30 p.m. and be in Angelo's until dawn. "The cops would come in for coffee at like four in the morning," Rich says, "and I'd still be chasing girls. Because of the way I was raised and having gotten married so young, it was all new to me."

Weekends were different. After Saturday night home games, when the Pirates would be playing an afternoon game in mere hours the next day, Rich would stay at Leyland's place in the Mount Washington area to avoid the thirty-mile trip to and from Steubenville. Late one Saturday night after the kids and Peggy had left for Texas, the two of them were in Leyland's apartment, bored off their rockers.

"Hey, Rich," said Leyland, who was single at the time, "can you get any of them girls from Angelo's to come up our way tonight?"

Rich then called Angelo at the bar: "Hey, Ang, any girls down there tonight?"

"Everybody sort of left," Angelo said, "but there's two girls over in the corner having dinner. And if you met the one girl, you'd marry her—she's gorgeous. I'll talk to 'em."

"Okay, call me back," Rich said.

Ten minutes later, Angelo phoned back to put the pretty girl on the line. She had seen Rich's picture over the bar, resplendent in his Pirates uniform.

"I see your picture," the girl said. "You're a coach for the Pirates?"

"Yeah."

"And you're with Jim Leyland right now?"

"Yeah, he's right here. I'll put him on the phone."

Leyland spoke to the woman briefly before handing the phone back to Rich with instructions: "Tell her and her friend to get some bologna, salami, and some bread and bring it up to Mount Washington," Leyland whispered. "We'll have a picnic."

Rich passed along the request, to which the girl exclaimed, "You mean right now?"

"Yeah, come on up. We're starving, and we don't want to go out."

For the next twenty seconds, Rich and Leyland heard some giggling on the other end of the line . . . and then finally a voice.

"We're not normally these kinds of girls," she said. "This is totally out of character for us. But we'll go to the store and see you in a bit."

An hour later, at about midnight, Roberta Guydosh entered Rich's life. He was never the same. She was brunette, quiet, genuine, and unpretentious, a divorced mother of four who liked to hang out at one of his favorite bars in Carnegie, Pennsylvania, called Oldie's.

They said their good-byes that night, but a few days later, he specifically went to Oldie's to hunt her down—and found her on the dance floor jitterbugging. They slow danced three songs and ended up at her home later that night in Toronto, Ohio. They just kissed—nothing more. He told her he was going to marry her someday.

"She had these big, beautiful eyes," Rich says. "But the thing that made me want to marry her was she was wearing blue jeans with white socks. White socks! I said, 'Oh my gosh, that's what I want.' She wasn't all dressed up, and that's what got me."

She rolled her eyes at his marriage proclamation, thinking it was just a phony pick-up line. Rich told her he was leaving on a nine-day road trip to Houston, Cincinnati, and Atlanta, and to prove he was serious, he would call her once a day. She said if he did, she'd be willing to date him when he got back. So he called her *twice* a day.

He was so smitten with Roberta that when he moved back into his parents' house that fall, he raced to tell Jerome and Helen all about her.

He flew to Texas to finalize his divorce with Peggy, who he thought was better off without him anyway. Rich and Roberta then moved in together. That was his good news; the bad news was that he had to tell Amy.

By that point, the summer of Amy had long since passed. The news of the divorce hadn't exactly crushed her; she had long been aware of the dysfunction. Still, Peggy took her to a seminar on how to cope with a broken home—in case her daughter had residual anger. Amy fidgeted, tugged on Peggy's sleeve, and asked to leave. "I get it, Mom," she said.

But no one was expecting Rich to have another girl already lined up, another Lucy. That was the real blow to the stomach. Rich called Texas and first got on the phone with Bubba. He told his son he was living with another woman, who happened to be raising four kids of her own. Bubba remembers that it broke his heart.

"Dad, I don't understand," Bubba told him. "I mean, I understand, but I don't get it."

Amy heard the commotion and grabbed the line. *Here we go*, Rich thought. He told Amy about Roberta and her four children—and Amy combusted. She was the female Rich; he was convinced of that now. She held nothing back at first—and then she held everything back.

"She was yelling at him, telling him, 'What is wrong with you?'" Bubba says. "I mean, she was yelling, which is something I didn't even think about doing because I'd get my tail kicked in. She probably felt, *I'm a good girl, but you screwed us over, and I'm going to tell you what I think*."

But her closing line is what stuck with Bubba, Rich, and anyone within a mile of the cul-de-sac who probably heard it.

"I'm not going to talk to you for the rest of your life," Amy said.

She then slammed down the phone, slammed her bedroom door, and slammed the book shut on Rich.

Letter from Amy

Bubba,
    Why would you move up to Steubenville to live with those nuts?

Love,

Amy

Fourteen

Amy Wants to Rage

So father and daughter went their separate ways. How long it would last, nobody knew. But if there'd been an over-under at the Spot up in Steubenville, the over might've been 1995. And this was 1987.

With Peggy working double shifts and Bubba immersed in high school basketball, the center of Amy's universe was Tim and Cindy. One of them was her quasi-son; the other was her soul mate. She couldn't live without either one of them—and she didn't have to.

If Amy and Tim were close before, the divorce made them a brother and sister in arms. Amy took responsibility for his entire well-being, whether it was folding his laundry, bribing him to take a shower, sticking up for him during his fights with Mike, or helping him ace his homework. The schoolwork was obviously right up her alley. Although she was now a seventh grader, she was more than ever luring stray neighborhood kids to her garage classroom. She had to be home anyway to babysit Tim, and Tim's friends—unlike Mike's older buddies—were still naive enough to do all the spelling and arithmetic she assigned.

"She was teaching me multiplication when my real class at school was only doing addition and subtraction," Tim says. "She got us way ahead."

By this point, Amy was giving the neighborhood kids report cards and term papers, and she bragged that her cul-de-sac probably had the highest collective grade point average in their Arlington zip code.

She would spend all her spare cash on whiteboards and would stay up at night drawing up a curriculum. This wasn't a fad anymore. Amy was going to go to college to be a teacher; her mind was made up.

Of course, when Peggy was home on weekends, Amy could be an ordinary teenager again and hang with Cindy. Cindy's mom, Brenda, would carpool them to movies or to the mall or to cheerleading. In public and at school, thirteen-year-old Amy was cute and spunky, the stereotypical sweet bubbly blonde. Boys were starting to show an interest in her, which was an intriguing development. She ended up with a boyfriend for a bit and told only three people about it—Cindy, Tim, and Peggy. But eventually, Bubba got wind of what happened: The boy ticked Amy off one day, and she dumped him, with zero regret.

"Usually that can be traumatic for girls, but not Amy—she moved on like it was nothin'," Bubba says.

The more difficult breakup was the day fifteen-year-old Bubba moved to Steubenville permanently to live with Rich and Roberta. It only made Amy more furious at her dad—for reopening her feelings of abandonment. But the truth was, it was all Bubba's idea. In junior high school, Bubba had been the most prolific three-point shooter in Texas basketball history, draining seven threes in a game multiple times. But his dream was to be a Division I college basketball player, and in football-crazy Texas, playing hoops was too far down the totem pole for his taste. Bubba thought he would receive better exposure and coaching at Steubenville High—not to mention the Rich factor.

Rich, like his father Jerome before him, wasn't going to rest until Bubba perfected his craft. He'd have Bubba shooting three-pointers at all hours of the night or running laps in the snow and sleet of Ohio. He created "Left-Handed Tuesdays," meaning the right-handed Bubba could only shoot or dribble with his left hand every Tuesday, all Tuesday long. If Bubba used his right hand, he was in trouble and would have to do 250 pushups. Bubba thought he knew what he was getting into, but he didn't know the half of it. Rich would pore through every piece of homework Bubba did as well. One night, Bubba showed Rich a term paper he'd written—and Rich tore it up because Bubba had forgotten to sign his name on top. Rich forced him to rewrite it from scratch.

Amy wrote letters to Bubba, asking how it was going, and Bubba would never admit to her how cruel and demanding their father was. He would only tell Amy that his overall basketball skills were blossoming and that he was already being recruited to play in college. That got Amy thinking: maybe she should try basketball too.

She was doing all she could to gain her father's approval; that was a never-ending obsession of hers—whether she'd admit it even to herself or not. But she did notice how much Rich fawned over Bubba, and deep down—even though she wasn't ready to call her dad—she wanted Rich to call and fawn over her.

Her only prior experience with basketball was taking random shots in the driveway when she was little or occasional two-on-one games with Bubba and her dad. In fact, those two-on-one games were some of the most glorious times of Amy's young life. It would be Rich and Amy versus Bubba—and her dad would refuse to let her lose. Rich would set screens on Bubba, leaving Amy with open shots. Or Rich would call fouls on Bubba all game long and never let Bubba call fouls on him and Amy. Bubba would complain to no avail, and Amy would just laugh in response. Her dad was on *her* side for once.

So junior high basketball seemed like a smart idea, and the shocking development was that she dominated. "She had her father's intensity when she played," Peggy says. "She put her game face on." Not only did Amy play the sport like she played soccer—a trillion miles an hour—but she wasn't afraid to shoot any time and from any place. One afternoon, she sank nine three-pointers, shattering Bubba's family record. She called her brother in Steubenville that day to brag, and her father overheard their conversation. He was floored—"It just didn't ever cross my mind that she'd be an athlete—never," Rich says . . . but it's not like he grabbed the phone to congratulate her either.

Amy never came out and said the rift between her and her father still enraged her. But her actions seemed to tell a whole other story.

After Amy broke Bubba's record, Peggy made it a point to get out of work early and attend one of Amy's games. But what Peggy saw that day stunned her. A girl on the opposing team was streaking for a layup, and Amy intentionally shoved her with two hands into a padded brick wall under the basket. "Amy had five fouls to use, and she was going to use them," Cindy says. "She was a spitfire. I'm not saying she was mean— well, maybe she *was* mean at basketball."

It was a scary moment, although everyone assumed it was just Amy being Amy. But Peggy wanted her reprimanded. "I went down to talk to her coach," Peggy says. "And I said, 'You've got to say something to her. You've *got* to.'"

It was the Rich in her, boiling over. Bubba was easygoing like Peggy; Mike was a troubled loner; and Tim was happy-go-lucky. But Amy was practically Rich reincarnated—which is maybe why they clashed. It was almost as if the two of them had an extrasensory connection. In fact, not long after Amy's basketball incident, Rich was in a melee of his own.

He'd been minding his business during a game in late April 1987 when two drunken fans invaded his bullpen. "You guys can't come in here," Rich shouted, at which point one of the men blurted a profanity toward him.

That set Rich off. He put the intruder in a chokehold and slammed him to the turf, breaking the guy's collarbone. He then punched him in the face maybe twenty times for good measure. It was obsessive and gory, and as it was going down, pitcher Bob Walk told Rich, "Stop, you're going to kill him!"

Eventually, the police arrested the men for trespassing. But while Rich tried dusting himself off, he realized he couldn't move his thumb. He had torn ligaments in there during the body slam and needed surgery the next morning. He was afraid the man might press charges for assault, and, sure enough, a police officer entered the clubhouse a week later, looking for Rich.

"You the guy who beat up my son?" the cop asked.

"Yes," admitted Rich, his head down and his hand in a cast.

"Thank you," the cop said. "He needed his butt kicked."

So Amy and Rich were definitely a pair of live wires, and it was only a matter of time before they reunited. And it ended up happening all because of baseball.

As the summer of 1987 approached, Tim and Mike began counting down the days until the trip to Steubenville and Three Rivers Stadium. All year, they couldn't stop talking about Sid Bream, Barry Bonds, Bobby Bo, $50 tips, Leyland's pizza parties, and the road trip to the presidential suite. Amy heard them, and at some point, she needed to clear the air with Rich or simply stay behind in Texas.

The year before, she had come to her senses easily—because she was never going to let Tim out of her clutches and because Peggy was traveling with them. But this time, Peggy wasn't going anywhere. They'd be staying with Rich, Roberta, and Roberta's kids—an entirely new and awkward dynamic. Amy couldn't bear the thought of that at first, but the more she mulled it over, she also couldn't imagine a summer without the Pirates.

On a night Rich called Texas to speak with the boys, Amy grabbed the phone and broke the ice. She said she'd like to spend the summer with him, but only on one condition.

"I'm not coming if Cindy can't come with me," she told him.

Her brothers had never been allowed to bring a buddy, but Rich knew *yes* was his only option. The boys were allowed in the clubhouse, and Amy wasn't. So it seemed fair to all involved. She needed a partner in crime at the stadium, and Cindy—Amy's shadow all school-year long—was the perfect sidekick. It was settled then.

They arrived the first of June and dove right back into their routine. Mike and Tim would scoop up dirty towels, fetch pickleless hamburgers for Bonds, and shag fly balls in the outfield. Amy and Cindy, meantime, had to get creative.

On a typical day, Rich would arrive at Three Rivers Stadium around 12:30 p.m., and turn the girls loose downtown. Amy and Cindy would find places to shop and have lunch—and then mosey on back to the stadium by mid-to-late afternoon. For the rest of the night, they'd rule the Green Room.

The Green Room was a family room where the players' wives could spread out among themselves on couches. It was also a place where the wives could drop off their young children—so the moms could watch the games unburdened in the stands. That's where Amy came in.

According to Rich, Amy became the "den mother" of the Green Room. If she could tame Tim's hyperactive friends in her garage, she could certainly handle the Pirates toddlers. Early that June, she was already playing with Tonka toys in the family room with Scott Van Slyke, the one-year-old son of newly acquired Andy Van Slyke, while telling the pregnant Katie Drabek—wife of pitcher Doug Drabek—that she would gladly babysit after their baby was born.

When the games were over, both married and single players would sidle into the Green Room to mingle, which is how Amy and Cindy got to meet a dreamy new Pirates reserve named John Cangelosi. Cangie, as he was known, was a 5-foot-8, 145-pound twenty-four-year-old who could have almost passed for a high school junior. Amy's and Cindy's eyes met the minute he loped into the room—they each had an instant crush.

One by one, more players would file in—including the man-child Bream, who would always ask Amy if there was anything he could do for her. Just the fact that he remembered her first name was enough. "We were friends with all of them," Cindy says. "Well, we weren't really, but we thought we were. We talked to them all. Amy just loved that part of being around her dad, which is basically what it came down to."

At the end of the evening, Amy and Cindy patiently waited outside the clubhouse door for Rich, who was usually one of the last to leave. On their way out of the stadium, kids would be camped out for autographs, and Amy intently watched them plead to her dad, "Will you sign for me? Will you sign?" That warmed her heart. As soon as Rich stopped, she would go into teacher mode, telling the kids, "Don't push; wait your turn . . . He'll sign for all of you."

The challenge was getting Amy to loosen up at home around Roberta. From the minute Amy heard Rich had a new live-in girlfriend—with her own kids to boot—she lumped Roberta in with Lucy. To Amy, the women were one and the same—both trying to hijack her father away from her, both trying to sabotage her family. Before Amy had come up for the summer, she had discovered a Donnelly family photo album titled "Our Happy Family." She laughed a sarcastic laugh and wrote a big "NOT" across it.

"*Betrayal* might be a good word for how she felt," Cindy says. "Amy wasn't one to be sad and mopey about it. She was more like, 'I hate these women, and I'm never going to talk to them.'"

Amy was defiant and distant from the moment she got under Roberta's roof. Eye contact was at a minimum; yes and no answers were the norm. Prior to the trip, Rich kept assuring Amy that Roberta was no floozy, telling her, "I think this is the girl I want to marry." That had only Amy more conflicted—until the day she and Cindy uncovered Rich and Roberta's wedding album. "That's how we found out they were married," Cindy says.

At first, Amy was furious about being kept in the dark. Bubba was the only one who'd known about the matrimony—because he lived there full-time—and Amy had just about had it with the secrets and the sneaking around. But every day she was around Roberta, Amy would thaw just a little. She could see how contented her father seemed and how Roberta was slaving to work three different jobs.

Roberta had literally been on welfare after her own contentious divorce, and there was a work ethic and a humility about her that connected with Amy. Rich may have been a big league coach, but there were eight kids' mouths to feed between the two families, and Roberta was chipping in as best she could. She had also taken in Rich's four kids, no questions asked, a fact not lost on Amy. As a ninth grader-to-be, Amy was mature enough now to let bygones be bygones.

She began to help around the house and became more of her smiling, verbose self. Then in mid-June—when Rich, she, Cindy, and the boys were driving home from Three Rivers Stadium after a day game—Amy told her father to slam on the brakes.

"Dad, we need to stop at the mall over there to buy Roberta a present," she told him. "It's her birthday tomorrow."

At that very moment, any remaining tension between Rich and Amy ceased to exist. It was as if she was on his lap again, listening to "'Twas the Night Before Christmas." The minute Amy had decided to accept Roberta, to go out of her way to acknowledge her birthday, she was essentially accepting her father's imperfections, once and for all. "It blew me away," Rich says, "because I'd been walking on eggshells with Amy for a long time."

With her own money that day, Amy purchased Roberta a clock radio—to help her rise and shine for her trio of jobs—and Roberta cherished it as much as Rich did. They weren't the perfect family by any means, but there was peace under their roof for the rest of the summer.

Letter from Amy

Dad,
    Is it okay if I watch some of these games in the stands instead of in the Green Room?
    I adore this team!

Love,

Amy

Fifteen

Amy Wants to Win

With the acrimony gone, Amy's baseball team took center stage. Leyland was doing everything he could to build a juggernaut, albeit incrementally, and the first indisputable gains took place in 1987.

On April Fool's Day, just as the season was beginning, Leyland convinced the general manager Syd Thrift to swing the trade that would seal the Pirates infrastructure. The deal involved one of the Buccos' most popular players, four-time all-star catcher Tony Pena, and it was a move Thrift and the front office had been patently against from the start. But on a car ride back with Thrift from a spring training game, with Leyland smoking the whole way like a chimney, Rich says the two came to an understanding.

Leyland proposed sending the thirty-year-old Pena—a player he'd long admired—to St. Louis for center fielder Andy Van Slyke, catcher Mike LaValliere, and pitcher Mike Dunne. All three of them were under twenty-six, and the two position players in particular—Van Slyke and LaValliere—were pure hitters and born leaders.

"But Tony's our captain and on the cover of all of our publications," Thrift said.

"Well, you finished twenty-five games out with your captain," Leyland said. "Plus, there's only one captain in here, and that's me."

Both Leyland and Thrift hated to see Pena go, and Leyland publicly gave Thrift all the credit for having the guts to pull the trigger. But the trade not only made the Pirates younger and deeper; it woke up their budding superstar Barry Bonds. Van Slyke became his nemesis, in a productive, unspoken way. Before Van Slyke arrived, Bonds was a sometimes-lackadaisical center fielder who got by on his uncanny raw talent. But the smooth Van Slyke—nicknamed "Slick"—superseded him in center, forcing Bonds to shift to left field, and it seemed to stick in Bonds's craw.

As far as Leyland was concerned, that was for the better. Most players wouldn't stand up to the moody, condescending Bonds, and Leyland loved how Van Slyke and even Cangie took Barry to task. Van Slyke, in fact, was behind one of the more cunning clubhouse pranks Bonds ever endured.

The backstory was that Bonds hated pregame workouts and almost never took extra batting practice. He barely even participated in regular BP before the games; he'd just take a few hacks, chill in the dugout, and then take a pregame nap on the clubhouse couch. What bothered the other players—while they played cards or ate a pregame meal—was Bonds's snoring. It was considerably loud.

So Van Slyke had an idea. While Bonds was sleeping/snoring at about 5:45 p.m. one day, Slick told a locker room attendant nicknamed "Red" to move the three clubhouse clocks forward to 7:05 p.m. Then Van Slyke instructed everyone to clear the room. Once they had all exited, Red shook Bonds awake to tell him he had missed the game's first pitch at seven o'clock.

"Hey, Barry; hey, Barry," Red said.

"What . . . what . . . what do you want, Red?"

"I think you better get up. It's 7:05."

Bonds took one look at the clock and shouted, "Holy crap!" He then inadvertently pulled his jersey on backward, hopped out into the hallway with one cleat on, one cleat off . . . and bumped into the entire Pirates team, laughing their heinies off.

"You suck," Bonds hollered.

After he'd processed it all, Bonds flip-flopped and decided he enjoyed the prank—"because now he was part of the team; he was one of the guys," Rich says. "That's all he ever wanted."

That was the Pirates team that turned the corner in 1987. The clubhouse was a relative zoo—right down to their weekly kangaroo court sessions. Rich, of all people, was the judge, in charge of fining players and coaches for even the slightest, most petty indiscretions. He would wear a judge's robe, to go with his custom gavel, and, one night, he went after Bonds—who used to practice taking pitches in the cages to help himself see the ball better.

"It's been brought to my attention," Rich crooned, "that our left fielder was in the batting cage but wasn't hitting. He was practicing taking a third strike. That'll be five dollars!"

"That's bull," shouted Bonds, who ended up handing over the five-spot.

It was all for a good cause. Midway through the 1987 season, the team had accumulated $900 cash in kangaroo court fines. And considering Leyland was about to marry his girlfriend, Katie, that year, they called him into court.

"It's been brought to my attention," Rich said, "that a complaint has been filed against our manager for only smoking two packs of cigarettes during yesterday's tight game when he should've been smoking three or maybe four."

"That's bull!" shouted Leyland.

"Well," continued Rich, "your fine is in that box behind you."

Leyland twirled around to find a hefty box in the corner of the clubhouse. He ripped it open to find a big-screen TV, paid for by the kangaroo court. It was his wedding gift from Bonds, Van Slyke, Bream, and company. Leyland was so touched that he wept.

It was simply a team with love-hate relationships. For instance, the only times Bonds and Van Slyke ever basically spoke was when Van Slyke said, "I got it!" on a fly ball to left-center. But it gave them a constructive edge that showed up in the win-loss column. After finishing 64–98 in 1986, they improved to 80–82 in 1987, with LaValliere batting .300, Van Slyke hitting .293, Bonilla hitting .300, and Bonds crushing twenty-five home runs.

Amy bore witness to it, and of all the aforementioned players, Bonds was her favorite. "Barry just connected with her—Barry loved Amy," Rich says. From the outside looking in, it was a peculiar choice. But there were multiple factors at play. One, Bonds was charming away from the clubhouse and particularly in the Green Room. He would fraternize with the wives and tickle the little kids. He was a kid in a man's body himself, so it made sense. And anyone who was a friend to a little child was a friend to Amy. "They just connected," Rich says.

The second reason was obvious only to Rich. "Amy was a punk, just like him," he says. It was by and large the truth—neither Amy nor Bonds liked to be disrespected, and neither hesitated to bare their teeth. They would tell you to your face you needed deodorant or you were too much up in their business. They could stir it up in one breath and make you melt in the next. Amy was more popular with the players, of course—in fact, the whole Pirates team was smitten with Amy—but it was clear to Rich why the two gravitated toward each other.

One night after a game, Rich finished dressing and walked out of the clubhouse expecting to find Amy and Cindy waiting in the stadium tunnel. But they were nowhere to be found. He searched for them in the indoor batting cage and in the Green Room—nothing. Finally, around a corridor, there they were with Bonds. He was doing all the talking, and they were doing all the nodding.

On the drive home, Rich asked what that was all about.

"He was giving us advice," Amy said.

"On what?"

"On ballplayers—that we shouldn't date 'em and shouldn't trust 'em," she said.

That was Bonds and Amy to a T—no-holds-barred, opinionated, nothing off-limits. Rich could only exhale and roll his eyes.

Either way, it hadn't just been the summer of Amy this time around; it had been the summer of Leyland, Thrift, Van Slyke, LaValliere, Bonds, Bonilla, Rich, et al. The groundwork had been laid not only for a future playoff run, but also for Amy's fanaticism toward the team.

When she left for Texas that August, she left immersed in the roster, in the personalities, in the box scores, and in the major league standings. She considered herself the No. 1 Buccos fan.

The clubhouse must have rubbed off on her because, in the ensuing couple of school years back home, she was acting like Barry Bonds herself. To pick up extra spending money, she took a job at the popular children's pizzeria and arcade, Chuck E. Cheese's—a job she apparently quit twice. According to Bubba, Amy was responsible for standing by the front door to make sure the little kids left for home with their correct parents or guardians. That suited Amy perfectly because no one cared more for the safety of a child than she did. It was the Sid Bream in her. But one day, her manager told her to leave her post to fill the salt and pepper shakers. Aghast, she quit.

"Well," she apparently told the manager on the way out, "salt and pepper is not what you hired me to do."

Eventually, the good people of Chuck E. Cheese's took her back. But, according to Peggy, the manager ordered Amy to "close" the restaurant one night—clean the tables, clear the salt and pepper shakers—and Amy said, "I'm not closing. I closed last night." The manager tersely repeated, "No, I said you're closing tonight." To which Amy responded, "I quit," and threw her apron at him. That was the end of that.

Next, according to Bubba, Amy took a job at an insurance office, taking phone calls and leaving messages. It was a heady job for a high school student, and she took pride in her meticulous note writing. But one day, Bubba says her manager asked her to print out copies at the Xerox machine. Aghast, she quit.

"Wait a minute," she apparently told the manager on her way out, "copying is not what you hired me to do."

Bubba and everyone else agreed it was Amy being Amy—"She wasn't afraid of anything," Bubba says. It reminded Peggy of the time Amy kicked her ballet teacher in the shin. Amy was sweet until you crossed her. Then she became Barry Bonds.

She wasn't oblivious to this either. Amy was well aware of how she could come across—tough, caustic, unforgiving, her way or the highway. She even hung a poster in her room that read, "Heaven doesn't want me, and hell's afraid I'll take over." She found it to be apropos, and everyone else in the Donnelly family—except maybe Tim, who thought his sis was perfect—nodded and chuckled.

She just couldn't wait for her summers in Steubenville and Pittsburgh, when she'd be reunited with Rich, Roberta, Bubba, Leyland, Cangie, Bonds, Bream, Bonilla, and the Green Room. In that stadium, with that team, she was in her element—babysitting the players' kids, cheering on the wives' husbands . . . and hoping somehow, some way, her father's dream of a World Series would come true.

In fact, she was so certain that 1990 was going to be *the* year that she asked her dad whether she and Cindy could fly down to Bradenton, Florida, for spring training. This way, Amy wouldn't have to wait until summer. "She just ached to see her dad," Peggy says. The plan—which Rich approved—was for Amy to finish her tenth-grade basketball season and, along with Cindy, head to Florida over spring break. But just about a month before the trip, she had a scare.

Amy was running sprints during basketball practice when, out of nowhere, she fainted. The high school coaches contacted Peggy, and the assumption was that she was dehydrated or hadn't eaten enough before the workout. Since Peggy was a nurse, she was able to swiftly arrange a doctor appointment. One of the possibilities that came up from a urine test was peculiar: diabetes insipidus.

According to the Mayo Clinic, diabetes insipidus is a disorder related to a person's water imbalance. The symptoms are excessive thirst and the frequent need to urinate—all of which Amy was experiencing but wasn't telling Peggy. The tests had been inconclusive, and neither Peggy nor the doctors saw any reason to pursue that diagnosis further. "I said, that's ridiculous; it can't be that," Peggy says. The doctors urged Amy to drink Gatorade; no one seemed too alarmed. She returned to the basketball court, and, more importantly, got her wish to attend spring training.

The Pirates team she encountered in Bradenton was confident, lively, and obnoxious, even more so than usual. From a pure baseball standpoint, Bream and "Spanky" LaValliere were healthy after being injured in 1989, and the team finally seemed to buy into what Leyland was selling. In spring training, Leyland told the group "No alley ball"— meaning, don't take careless, needless chances with the baseball. "He was saying, 'Don't throw the ball all over the place,'" Rich says. "Forget the pickoffs and the thirty-two bunt plays. Just throw strikes, catch the ball, throw in some hits."

Rich booked a hotel room for Amy and Cindy to stay in on their own, and Amy babysat all of her usual suspects at the field: little Scott Van Slyke, little Kyle Drabek, and the LaValliere kids. She always had coloring books ready for them, and they wept whenever "Aunt Amy" had to leave.

Before she flew from Bradenton back to Texas, she told her dad she'd continue to write him during the season and that he'd better write back. He said he'd try, but he and the team had the New York Mets to deal with.

No question, the Pirates were obsessed with the team from the Big Apple. These were the Mets of Dwight Gooden and Darryl Strawberry, and Leyland would never forget how in his rookie season of 1986, the Mets coldly took seventeen of eighteen games from his club, scoring ninety-nine runs. This was going to be payback, or so he and his players hoped.

They had a few things on their side—arguably the best pitcher in baseball (Drabek), arguably the best switch-hitter in baseball (Bonilla), arguably the best double-play combination (shortstop Jay Bell and second baseman José "Chico" Lind), arguably the best young manager (Leyland), and arguably the best overall ballplayer in the stratosphere (Bonds).

That year, 1990, was Bonds's breakout year, and Amy had foretold it. She had pointed out to her dad that Barry seemed more focused and arrogant than ever, and from one "punk" to another, she knew that was a good thing.

Amy went back to finish up tenth grade, scouring every Pirates box score and counting down to yet another summer in Steubenville and Pittsburgh. She seemed more serene than ever, partly because her grievances with Rich were history and partly because she had turned sweet sixteen that April. She was maturing. Rich and Peggy presented her with a used Mitsubishi Mirage to drive, and it meant she could drop Tim off at his Little League games or chauffer him home from school. She could run errands for Peggy. Better yet, she and Cindy could motor anywhere their hearts desired.

The graveyard was one of the places Amy would drive to. One of Cindy's and Amy's longtime friends had lost their mom, and Amy, who remained fascinated with cemeteries, would regularly stop there to clean the mother's headstone with Clorox. She told Cindy a soiled tombstone showed a lack of respect. She would dig up weeds or add trinkets to the vase of flowers nearby, unbeknownst to their friend. For whatever reason, the tombstones brought out a certain tranquility in Amy. They never frightened her.

Obviously, Amy felt even more at peace around the Pirates, and the summer of 1990 was when she witnessed them become relevant. It wasn't just that Drabek won the Cy Young Award or that Bonds became the first major leaguer in history to bat over .300, drive in a hundred runs, score a hundred runs, and steal fifty bases in the same season—to go with thirty-three homers and a Gold Glove. It's that they were never uptight.

Other than the tension between Bonds and Van Slyke—which the team had accepted by now—the Pirates clubhouse generally needed a laugh track. For instance, second baseman Chico Lind, their mouth that roared, kept three machetes above his locker and wasn't afraid to wield them.

One afternoon, Sid Bream was blaring country music on his brand-spanking-new $800 stereo, at which point Lind shouted, "Turn that crap off." Lind then whipped out a machete and sliced the stereo to shreds—wires sprouting every which way. Bream, a man of faith and composure, simply laid the machine to rest in the trash can. The next day, Lind handed Bream nearly twice as much money, $1,500, to buy a new and better one.

Between Lind and newly acquired Wally Backman, there was never a dull moment. One weekend, broadcaster Tony Kubek was interviewing Drabek when Lind snuck up behind Kubek, took three giant steps, and leapfrogged Kubek's head. "Chico had some serious hops," Rich says. As for Backman—a former member of the dreaded Mets—he instantly became bosom buddies with Bream, which made no sense at all.

Bream and Backman were polar opposites. Backman was the most profane player on the roster, and Bream would ask him repeatedly to stop the cussing. "Okay," Backman would say. "Now pass the (bleeping) mustard."

Backman eventually told Bream, "I'll stop cussing if you go and drink with me at night." Bream never went out with him, and Backman never stopped cursing. "They were beautiful together," Rich says. "Nobody could figure it out."

Leyland had his eccentric moments as well. Every trip into Houston, he'd request a high floor at the Westin Galleria so he could drive golf balls out of his balcony window into a deserted parking lot. Van Slyke would be panting down below trying to catch them.

All of this put together—talent plus machismo—led to an irrepressible season. The team was in first place for all but twenty-two days during the season, and Amy and Cindy were incessantly waving black and gold pom-poms from the stands. They each wore a T-shirt that depicted the city of Pittsburgh peeing on the Mets home field, Shea Stadium. Amy didn't design them, but she seconded the notion and wore hers to bed sometimes.

She was also once again the queen of the Green Room. She'd politely tell the three Van Slyke boys—Scott, Jared, and A. J.—to put their crayons away before leaving, and they naturally obeyed her. Since she now had her driver's license, she could drive to babysit the LaValliere kids at their Pittsburgh home—for five dollars an hour. The Drabeks heard that and requested her services as well. Amy would throw in free math lessons.

She had also fallen in love with her father's coarse hometown of Steubenville. She knew all the characters—Bible Bill, Barking Barry, Tennis Shoe Ernie, et al.—and loved when Rich would wax poetic on the mob, Dean Martin, and Romey. Amy's favorite Steubenville restaurant was the Federal Terrace Bar and Restaurant, where the owner, Robert "Pango" Panganelli, would walk around wearing an apron stained with meat sauce. She would order Pango's grilled cheese and laugh at the salty language emanating from their lone waitress, eighty-year-old Minnie.

In fact, Amy might've been tempted to relocate to Steubenville herself, but she never could've left Peggy, Cindy, or Tim. Her brother Mike, however, was about to move up to Ohio to join Bubba, who had just received a basketball scholarship to Robert Morris University in Pittsburgh. So the summer of 1990 was the last time all four kids were together before Bubba left for campus. And to be able to witness a Pirates pennant race was the cherry on top.

The team eliminated the Mets on September 30 in St. Louis, after Drabek pitched a complete game three-hitter for his twenty-second victory. Rich raced in from the bullpen to tackle the first player he could find—out of utter disbelief and joy. He had once jumped up and down on his childhood bed after Bill Mazeroski's seventh game World Series walk-off home run in 1960. He wanted his own Mazeroski moment, and this was his chance.

He says he didn't own a cell phone back in 1990—"only the rich players did." So he borrowed outfielder R. J. Reynolds's mobile and called Roberta directly from the Busch Stadium infield. He told her they could finally buy the house they were renting. Playoff money was on its way—and job security presumably with it.

Rich's next call was to Texas, where Amy and Tim both hollered superlatives into the phone. They begged to come to the National League Championship Series against the Reds, or at least the home games. Rich said he wished they could, but he didn't want them missing school. But he made the following concession: if the Pirates reached the World Series, then they could *absolutely* go—school or no school.

When the Pirates landed in Pittsburgh, twenty thousand fans were waiting to pay homage at the airport, with thousands more flooding the streets to greet the team bus. With all that hullabaloo just for a division title, Rich imagined a World Series parade would be over the moon. He reiterated to Amy and Tim how much a Fall Classic would mean to him, and Amy—before bed every night—prayed on her knees for that to happen. That was fortunate because Rich himself still didn't pray at all.

The series started with a dreamy Game 1 in Cincinnati. Sid Bream hit a clutch two-run homer in the fourth inning to tie the game at three—which had his buddy Wally Backman dancing a jig—and the Pirates scored the eventual winning run in the seventh when Reds outfielder Eric Davis misplayed a simple fly ball. The Bucs now had their ace, Doug Drabek, lined up to pitch Game 2. While he was shaving after the game, Pirates third base coach Gene Lamont slyly told Rich, "We are going to sweep these guys."

Amy badly wanted to see it all in person, but Rich called her to say Reds owner Marge Schott had made the Pirates families sit in uncomfortable wooden folding chairs on the second deck—just so she could sell more seats. "Roberta felt like the chairs were from a card party," Rich says. "We were furious." Given all that, Rich told Amy she was better off watching on TV. Amy said she'd have sat on thumbtacks to be there.

The next day, Amy raced home from school to watch Game 2, an afternoon affair. But the Pirates lost, 2–1, when her buddy Bonds lost a fly ball in the sun off the bat of Paul O'Neill. She was sick about it, and for the rest of the series, the Reds kept getting timely hits and played flawless defense.

Nothing went the Pirates way again. In the ninth inning of Game 6, trailing the series three games to two, Pittsburgh's Carmelo Martínez appeared to have tied the game with a two-run homer. But Reds right fielder Glenn Braggs deftly reached over the wall to rob him.

There were no words to soothe Amy, who slumped in her chair back in Texas. Once again, an empty October. Once again, a despondent father. Once again, no World Series.

Letter from Amy

Dear Dad,

   Why would Sid Bream do that?

                           Love,

                           Amy

THIRD BASE

Sixteen

"Dad, I'm Sorry"

T he news blared on December 5, 1990—Sid Bream had signed with the Atlanta Braves. In Pittsburgh, there wasn't outrage as much as there was a knowing nod, a degree of resignation.

The Pirates front office wasn't big on doling out the cash. Leyland and Rich felt they had the best young roster in baseball, but also knew they were on borrowed time. Bonilla would be a free agent after the 1991 season, and Bonds after 1992. It was now or . . . well, never say never.

Amy and Cindy made their regular pilgrimage to spring training, and it was business as usual—until Bonds and Leyland had one of the more public spats in memory. Bonds, the reigning MVP, was pouting over his contract impasse and loafed one day during outfield drills. The Pirates legend Bill Virdon, who served as outfield coach, chastised him, and Bonds barked back. Leyland overheard the fracas and lit into Bonds profanely—all of it caught on film. He told Amy's buddy, "If you don't want to be here, get your (stuff) and quit." Leyland added, "I don't want to see it no more."

It may have appeared the team was unraveling, but it only reinforced Leyland's standing among the players. Bonds was an asset on the field and divisive off it. But when Leyland stood up to him—which Van Slyke had already been doing for years—there was finally a sense that no one was bigger than the team. Except the manager, maybe.

Bonds later agreed that Leyland was right to tee off on him. Amy

179

admired Barry's honesty on that. She wasn't giving up on her fellow "punk" at all.

Either way, 1991 was another sustainable season for the juggernaut Pirates. With Bream and Backman both gone (Backman bolting for the Phillies), the sideshows were Lind's machetes, Lloyd McClendon weight lifting in the buff, and, of course, Bonds versus Van Slyke.

There was little doubt that the latter two respected each other as players. It was just Bonds's moodiness that grated on Van Slyke. Rich says it finally came to a head after a game that season when, just like Bill Virdon, Van Slyke accused Bonds of loafing. Rich says Barry threw the first punch at Slick, while the rest of the team rubbernecked. According to Rich, Bonds and Van Slyke landed about ten punches each. Bonilla broke it up, grabbing each by the shirt and saying, "Guys, guys, that's enough." No one from the media had seen it or filmed it, so it was kept in-house. The team just went out and won again the next day.

"After the brawl, everybody had a meatball sandwich and went home," Rich says of the tiff. "Not really a big deal. No matter what happened in that clubhouse, when we hit the field, all was forgotten for two and a half hours."

Meanwhile, Rich and Leyland were tighter than ever, to the point they became roommates every road trip. That season, someone had broken into Leyland's hotel room in Chicago and lifted $4,000 out of his pants pocket. The robbery unnerved Leyland, who told the team's traveling secretary, Greg Johnson, "From now on, here's what I want—I want Rich with an adjoining room to my suite. I want somebody with me."

So the two old Ohio catchers were as close as Amy was to Cindy. "It got to be kind of a joke," Rich says. Rich would wake up and order the two of them breakfast every morning while Leyland filled out the lineup card for that day's game. After games, their rooms became a quasi-hospitality suite. The coaches Bill Virdon, Ray Miller, Milt May, and Gene Lamont would convene there, sometimes followed by Pirates beat writers—such as Bob Hertzel and Paul Meyer—who'd been invited in by Leyland. There'd be soda, whiskey, beer, peanuts, and pizza at everyone's disposal. If Amy, Tim, Bubba, or Mike were on the trip, they'd swagger in as well.

Leyland would usually get up out of his chair at 1 a.m. and go to bed first, without saying good night. But on his way out, he'd always cock his head toward Rich and say, "Lock that door. Lock that door before you go to bed."

Before long, a playoff berth was locked up, as well. Starting on April 16, 1991—Amy's seventeenth birthday—the Pirates won eight out of their next nine games and eventually twenty-eight out of thirty-nine to take control of the National League East. Their outfield of Bonds, Bonilla, and Van Slyke drove in a combined 299 runs, and the team carved out a league-best 98 wins. Only one pitching staff had silenced them all year—the Atlanta Braves trio of John Smoltz, Tom Glavine, and Steve Avery. And that's who they had to face in the NLCS.

Rich made the same deal with Amy he did the year before: if they reached the World Series, everyone was definitely going. She, Tim, and Cindy rooted vociferously from Texas. Amy gave them assigned seats in the living room, and in the pivotal Game 5, she jitterbugged after Chico Lind's RBI single gave the Pirates a 1–0 win and a three-games-to-two series lead.

Games 6 and 7 were at Three Rivers Stadium—they *had* to take at least one. Tim and Amy were tempted to start packing for the World Series, but there were two issues: her buddy Barry Bonds wasn't hitting, and her buddy Sid Bream was good karma for the Braves. The Bucs were shut out 1–0 and 4–0 in Games 6 and 7 by Avery and Smoltz. It was maddening, and it was over. Bonds finished a pitiful 4 for 27 (.148) for the series with no home runs, and although Bream had a bum knee much of the season, he did have three hits in ten NLCS at-bats, almost as many as Bonds. Amy and Tim were inconsolable; at this point, a World Series seemed unfathomable.

Rich was still moping around at Thanksgiving when Leyland called with numbing news: Pirates third base coach Gene Lamont was leaving to become the White Sox manager.

"And I want you to replace him," Leyland said.

It was as if an orchestra had erupted inside of Rich's head—cymbals exploding. One of his most sacred major league dreams was coaching third base for a World Series-caliber team, and here was his opportunity at the age of forty-six. Not only that, it was the Pirates … the Buccos … KDKA … Bob Prince … the team of Clemente, Stargell, Mazeroski, and Groat … the team of his Steubenville youth. Better yet, he'd be coaching for his best, most trusted friend in baseball: his suitemate Leyland.

Once Lamont resigned, it took all of a nanosecond for Leyland to promote Rich. Leyland knew Rich had spent eons coaching third base as a manager in the minors. They had coached third against each other during the 1970s—each trying to steal the other's signs—so Leyland understood exactly what he'd be inheriting in Rich: a devoted, feisty, smart, athletic, hyper partner in crime.

Leyland assured Rich that other than the manager, the third base coach is the most important, revered figure in the ballpark. But more pertinent than that, once a ball game begins, the third base coach is *on the field*—and the manager isn't. The two may communicate via a coded sign language, but it is up to the third base coach to coordinate the game plan, to make certain the players navigate the bases properly. "A third base coach doesn't necessarily win games for you, but he definitely can lose 'em," Rich says.

The manager had Rich meet him for breakfast that winter to discuss his two-word third base coaching philosophy: *send 'em*. Leyland wanted Rich to be uber-aggressive. He told him, "Stopping a runner at third has nothing to do with the score." In other words, if it was 11–0 or 0–0, Leyland wanted Rich to err on the other side of caution. He wanted Rich to rev up his arm, to get ready to wave those suckers around third. "Sneak some runs in for me," Leyland said.

Leyland also assured Rich he would never ever stomp his feet in anger if Rich got a runner thrown out at home plate. He wanted him relaxed, egotistical, indestructible, and free. "If you have to get on your third base coach a lot about making bad decisions, then you should get a new third base coach." Leyland says. "Because what happens is you get 'em paranoid when you're on 'em all the time."

Leyland closed by telling Rich a story from the winter meetings. He had sat with all the managers, some of whom were eventual Hall of Famers like Joe Torre, and asked, "Who's the best third base coach you ever saw?"

Somebody mentioned an old-timer, perhaps the Yankees Frankie Crosetti—Rich's idol.

"Why him?" Leyland countered.

"Because he never got anybody thrown out," somebody said.

"Then he was the worst third base coach in the history of the game," Leyland deadpanned. "Good third base coaches get guys thrown out."

With that, Rich returned to Steubenville feeling liberated. He would have the job of a lifetime, working for the manager of a lifetime. He called Amy and his boys to tell them his grand news, and Amy's response was rousing applause. She was heartily in favor of wishes coming true, and Rich had often talked about aspiring to one job and one job only: third base coach. He wasn't bucking any longer for a major league managerial position; being first lieutenant to Leyland was gratifying enough.

As spring training approached, the anxiety naturally crept in, and as type A as Rich already was, everyone around him was walking on eggshells. In December, he drove to watch Bubba's Robert Morris team play a Saturday afternoon game at the University of West Virginia, and Bubba—normally a 42 percent three-point shooter—missed too many shots for Rich's taste. So Rich wouldn't talk to him. Their plan was to drive together afterward from West Virginia to Canton, Ohio, for a Steubenville High School playoff football game and then back to Steubenville. It was just the two of them in the car for virtually eight hours, and still not a word was spoken. "Literally, nothing," Bubba says. "He wouldn't even put the radio on. That's the way he was."

Rich had third base coaching on the brain, 24/7. He did the math and found there were "seventeen places I could touch on my body without going to jail." So he memorized those seventeen places and decided those were the spots he would graze when giving signs to the players—elbow, forearm, ear, forehead, nostril, etc. By the time he arrived for spring training in February, he felt he was prepared for anything. Except he was wrong.

Back in Texas, Amy had begun training exuberantly for her senior season of high school basketball, with so much to look forward to. She and Cindy would often talk about their upcoming graduation and about finding an apartment together down the line. They had already purchased quaint dinner plates and place mats. Potpourri was bound to be next. In the short term, Cindy was thinking about attending Texas Tech, and Amy the University of Texas-Arlington, majoring in education. Before long, she'd officially be a teacher.

But as basketball season commenced, Amy's dehydration was flaring up. Even though she'd plow through a jug of Gatorade a day, she was still ravenous for fluids, dry in the mouth. She wasn't regular with her period and would have to urinate at all hours of the day and night. Problem was, she'd almost accepted it as routine and wasn't telling anyone. She was Rich's daughter; she had taught herself to be Teflon Amy. She didn't want to burden anyone, didn't want to alarm Peggy, much less her father.

Later, that February 1992, Peggy took her in for a routine, random optical checkup to see if her eyeglasses prescription needed updating. The ophthalmologist performed a peripheral vision screening and found that the reactions from her right eye were negligible. It was a red flag. The doctor told Peggy that to be safe, Amy should undergo more tests.

Peggy assumed it was nothing and was somewhat annoyed to be driving all over the Metroplex. But this time, Amy flunked a more advanced peripheral screening that had sensors and flashes. The next step was an MRI, and the general practitioner Peggy worked for—Dr. Donna Baker—recommended a neurosurgeon in Arlington, Dr. Jeffrey Heitkamp, who purportedly had a kind bedside manner with teens. That was a plus—because Amy kept missing basketball practice and wasn't in a fine mood.

The MRI was conducted with everyone's fingers crossed, and when the results returned, Dr. Heitkamp pulled both Amy and Peggy into a side room. There was no delicate or tactful way to say it: she had a brain tumor.

Before either of them could burst into tears, the doctor tried to change the narrative. He thought if he entered through her nose, he could surgically and unobtrusively remove the tumor. Whatever he couldn't get, he believed could be shrunk with medication. Either way, no one knew if the tumor was malignant yet, and the doctor refused to give them a prognosis until he referred Amy to one of the more reputable neurosurgeons in the state, down the road in Dallas. "This guy he sent us to supposedly walked on water," Peggy says.

At that moment, Amy had a request: she wanted to call her father at spring training. Rich had just come off the field from an intrasquad game and was lying on the floor of his Bradenton apartment. He preferred the rug to the couch; it was cooler down there after a humid Florida workout. When the phone rang and he recognized Amy's voice, he perked up.

"Hey, how ya doin'?" Amy said.

"Good, Am," answered Rich.

"Dad, there's something I gotta tell ya," she said.

He remembers thinking, *Oh boy, this ain't going to be good,* that maybe she broke her arm in practice or had an issue with her grades in high school. But what he heard next floored him, even though he was already on the floor.

"I have a brain tumor—and I'm sorry," Amy said.

Why she apologized only she knew. According to Peggy, it was probably from years of trying to be the perfect daughter to an imperfect man, years of thinking she was a burden, years of thinking her dad wanted her to be a boy. Amy even asked Peggy before the phone call if she thought her dad would be angry that she'd have to miss the basketball season. Peggy answered, "No, Amy, no."

Rich was in such a fog that he barely heard what Amy said next. He was still stuck on her "I'm sorry" line, consumed by it, overwhelmed by it, enthralled by it. "If that had been me and I was seventeen years old in the prime of my life and you tell me I have a brain tumor, I'd have been bitter," Rich says. "I would've been, 'Why me? How come me?' And that's why when she said, 'Dad, I'm sorry,' that resonated with me.

"Why would you say that to your dad? Why wouldn't you say, 'Dad, I got a brain tumor and I might die.' But, no, she goes, 'Dad, I'm sorry.' She's apologizing to me. It's not her fault. But she felt like it. She's sorry she's gonna put me through this, and here she is, going through it. It should've been about her; somehow she made it about me."

In the midst of this harrowing conversation, Rich flashed back to the Big Wheels mishap, how he couldn't have lived without Amy then and couldn't live without her now. He then subconsciously flipped into denial mode, telling himself the brain tumor would be all better in the morning, that it was like nothing more than a case of the sniffles. He wasn't being rational.

He asked to speak to Peggy, who told him, "They want to operate." That snapped him out of his stupor. She told him the tumor was behind Amy's right eye and that there was one more specialist to see—the big whopper in Dallas. She suspected the surgery would happen within a week, and Rich promised he would be there to hold Amy's hand before and after. Then he hung up sobbing.

Amy seemed to be holding up. Later in the afternoon, she heard from Cindy, who was calling from the pay phone at their high school gym. Amy had left campus that morning for the MRI, and Cindy had expected her back in class that day.

"Where you at? What's going on?" Cindy asked.

"I have a brain tumor," said Amy, no-holds-barred as usual.

"*What?*"

"Don't be upset," Amy said. "It's going to be fine. It's no big deal. I'm going to have to have surgery. Don't be freaked out. It's okay."

"What? What are you talking about?" Cindy said.

"No, really, it's okay; it's okay," Amy continued. "They're going to take it out, and it'll be fine."

Cindy was in tears throughout and was still in tears when her mother, Brenda, picked her up from school. She told her mom the situation, and when Brenda asked how Amy was coping with it all, Cindy remembers thinking, *Amy was the one consoling* me.

It was uncanny how calm Amy was, how undeterred she was by the diagnosis. When she arrived back at the cul-de-sac, she said, "What's going on?" to Tim, as if nothing monumental had occurred. Tim was a twelve-year-old sixth grader by then, and when Peggy sat him down and tried to explain what a tumor was, it didn't truly register. He nodded and went outside to play kickball.

Up at Robert Morris University, where the basketball team was chasing an NCAA tournament bid, Bubba knew all too well what brain cancer was. Peggy called that same night to tell him the bitter news, and he found it striking that, just months before, Amy had begun writing him weekly letters. "She must've known something was wrong," Bubba says. "She must've felt it."

Fairly soon, Amy had her appointment with the highly respected neurosurgeon in Dallas, Dr. Bruce Mickey, who was not as upbeat as his peer in Arlington. There was no clean way to remove the tumor, no entering through her nasal cavity. Dr. Mickey told them he would need to open up her cranium, that it was the most efficient way to carve out the cancer.

Peggy told Rich to fly in, ASAP, and Jim Leyland couldn't have been more supportive. He told Rich to take as much time as required in Texas, that the third base coaching box would be waiting for him when he returned. One by one, the coaches and players slapped Rich on the back— Bonds, Van Slyke, Drabek, LaValliere, and so on. Amy had been the team babysitter, the den mother of the Green Room, the crooked smile always waiting outside the clubhouse door. They were hurting over this too.

Rich arrived the day before the operation and walked into the hospital expecting a melancholy, frightened Amy. She was having brain surgery in a matter of hours. But when he entered her room, he sensed a strange, remarkable vibe. "She was the same Amy," he says. "She was cheerful. She had her hair, her beautiful hair. She was laughin', like, 'Dad, everything's gonna be fine. Everything's gonna be good. Don't worry about nothin'."

It was nonsensical. But he had plenty of time to psychoanalyze it during the operation the next morning. That surgery dragged on for two hours, four hours, six hours. During that interminable wait, he decided that perhaps Amy—in a backward kind of way—enjoyed being the center of attention for once. Not only were her mom and dad reunited, working in unison on her behalf, but she had them all to herself. That was Rich's amateur analysis as he sat practically paralyzed, wondering if his daughter would emerge from surgery with all of her faculties.

While Rich waited and waited, his only respite was the NCAA college basketball tournament game on TV. In fact, it was Bubba's game. Robert Morris was taking on heavily favored UCLA in the first round at Tucson, and Rich hated that the biggest day of his son's athletic life was arguably the worst day of his. Robert Morris ended up losing by twenty points, but Bubba, all of five foot ten, knocked down two three-pointers that day and thought of Amy after each one. It was bittersweet.

When the brain operation finally ended, seven hours after it began, Dr. Mickey entered the family waiting room with a blank expression on his face. "His look was just awful," Rich says. He sat down next to Rich and Peggy, who were accompanied by Dr. Baker, the general practitioner Peggy worked for. Then he launched in.

Dr. Mickey explained it was a rare mixed tumor—part germinoma, part teratoma—and that he and the assisting surgeon were unable to extract it completely. As soon as Peggy heard *germinoma*, she teared up. Being a nurse, she knew too much; she knew it was malignant and dangerous. She remembers Dr. Mickey comparing the tumor to the inner core of a baseball, that the mass was essentially "rubber bands stuck together with heat." Worse yet, the tumor had attached to nerves inside her brain, and if they had dug it out too aggressively, she could've been paralyzed or worse. The mass was just located in an unlucky spot.

He went on to say that it was the tumor that had triggered Amy's fainting spell, her obsessive thirst, her dehydration, and her frequent need to urinate. In other words, Amy did have diabetes insipidus, which had been spurred on by her cancer. She would need to be treated for that as well.

Rich asked what Amy's prognosis was, and the doctor said there were no guarantees and no fail-safe treatment plan. Whether Rich heard any of this is up for debate, because he simply rose and headed for the elevator.

Dr. Baker chased after him, almost enraged. "Where are you going?" she asked Rich. He turned and gave her the answer Peggy was expecting.

"I've got to get back to work," he said.

"You're not leaving here now," Dr. Baker stated emphatically. "We're in trouble, and you're going to be here for this part of it."

Rich hadn't slept the previous night, and it took him a minute to regain his bearings. He then pulled Dr. Mickey to the side because he wanted no ambiguity at all, no mixed messages. He wanted to know, in no uncertain terms, what was going on. So he asked the doctor his most honest question: "Tell me straight. Tell me straight up; don't sugarcoat nothin'. Tell me straight up."

"Rich," the doctor said, "she has nine months to live."

If Rich needed a slap in the face to wake him up, here it was. "Are you sure you can't get all of the tumor?" he asked. "Can you try again? Please try again."

"Rich," the doctor said, "you know how players chew tobacco and then wrap it around bubble gum?"

"Yeah."

"Well, picture that," Dr. Mickey said. "But we've got to get rid of all the bubble gum without breaking the tobacco. There are nerves around there we just can't touch."

"What's the best-case scenario?" Rich asked.

"I don't know if there is one," the doctor answered. "But we'll do everything possible. It's not something I can tell you today. In two months, I can tell you. Chances are 90 percent it's a nine-month deal. We're going to try radiation; we'll try chemotherapy. I'm sorry."

The finality of it all reminded Rich of Romey, some thirty-odd years before. It reminded him of their deathbed chat when Romey urged him to work his tail off in baseball, to not get an F in Religion. It reminded him of Peggy's cruel miscarriage. It reminded him of cemeteries. If ever Rich needed a priest or a church, it was right then. But he wasn't near to being in the right frame of mind. He was a lost soul. He was miffed that God chose the wrong person to take. *He* was the one who cheated on his wife, who ignored his daughter, who latched on to Billy Martin, who trash-talked Ted Williams. *It should be* me *suffering. Amy did nothing to deserve this*, he thought, seething. So Rich's one question to God was this: *Why her, and not me?*

The next morning, when he walked in on Amy, it was arguably the cruelest moment of his life up to that point. Her head was shaved, her face unrecognizable. The scar across her forehead looked like the laces of a football—all seams and stitches . . . an elongated zipper. An iron crown was attached to her head as well. Her body was crisscrossed with wires and tubes, and she had no ability to speak.

He could barely stomach it, and after a few minutes, he barreled out of the room to get some air. He asked someone where the hospital chapel was—he was going to give God a try again. There he got down on one knee, and instead of praying for Amy's brain, he just bawled his eyes out.

"I felt guilty," Rich says. "I felt about *this* big. All that stuff about me and my career meant nothing to me. I felt like nothing. She's going through that, and you're worried about a baseball game? You're worried about your job? Really?"

He had waited his whole life to coach third base in the big leagues—he could wait a little longer. He hunkered down at the hospital, hoping for a squeeze from Amy's weakened hand or a wink from Amy's swollen face. He was there for the long haul, and any gradual improvement, any morsel of normalcy, was worth a celebration.

Before long, Amy could speak, albeit hoarsely. For close to a week, she had watched her dad fidget and pace in the room—his mind clearly someplace else. Rich had always been impatient, but Amy could sense he was feeling both trapped and distracted inside Children's Hospital. She knew this because she told Peggy that she'd heard him speaking to Jim Leyland.

It's not as if this was pleasant for her either. She had been catheterized, which was embarrassing enough. She wanted to escape from the hospital just as much as Rich did. But more than anything, she couldn't bear to keep her father from the third base coaching box, from the Pirates' inevitable World Series push. "Yeah, she knew it was my dream to get to a World Series, to win a World Series," Rich says. "She knew everything about her dad and what he wanted. We'd talk about it; we'd talk about it all the time. She had an inherent knowledge of what it was like to be a big league coach. She knew. She knew."

Amy did the noble thing: she pointed her dad in the direction of the airport. She was still Queen Elizabeth, still unable to censor herself. She flat-out told him, "Go back to work. Go back to coaching third. You'll be a mess. You can't do anything for me here. I love you, and I know you love me. So go back and do what you've gotta do. And when you guys come to play in Houston in May, I'll see you there."

Rich followed her instructions, but he left with his head down. "I just felt so useless as a human being," he says. His guilt engulfed him the entire flight to Florida, but he reminded himself that she was the one who told him to go—no, *ordered* him to go. "That's why I felt okay about doing it," he says. He and Amy also made a deal to write each other four or five times a week and to chat on the phone as well. She told him she would be scouring the Pirates box scores, that she would be there in spirit. "You're not getting rid of me," Amy told him.

By the time the 1992 baseball season began on April 6, Amy was back sleeping in her own bed. The poster on her wall—the one that read, "Heaven doesn't want me, and hell's afraid I'll take over"—was cringeworthy. But life had to go on, and that meant chemotherapy.

The first round of chemo was scheduled for April 16—Amy's eighteenth birthday. Peggy could've requested an alternative date, but time wasn't on their side. Peggy wanted to attack that tumor sooner than later. It meant Amy had to spend her first few hours as a legal adult with poison in her veins. She had been so positive for the first two months after her diagnosis, but this was the one day Peggy felt her wrath. Amy, the spitfire, told her mother off. "It was a sucky birthday," Peggy says.

Still, Peggy tried her best to salvage it. She invited Cindy, Tim, and her own mother, Ruth, to join them for a makeshift birthday party at Children's Hospital. As soon as the chemo was over, Peggy served pizza and a ginormous birthday cake with nineteen candles—the extra one for good luck. At that point, Amy just rolled with it.

"She feels horrible, and she's just letting us have this party," Cindy remembers. "We're like, 'Here, have cake.' She's like, 'I don't want any cake.' But she wanted us to be able to celebrate, even if she didn't feel like it."

After the pizza and cake, it was time to open presents. One was a package that came via the US Postal Service. The person who sent it: Sid Bream.

Bream was an Atlanta Brave now, but that was irrelevant as far as Amy was concerned. The sight of his handwritten note reenergized her a slight bit and put a wan smile on her face. She unwrapped the box to find a red and black T-shirt bearing the slogan "No Fear."

It couldn't have been more fitting. Because the one thing Amy Donnelly refused to exhibit as she began this battle was fear.

Letter from Amy

Dear Dad,
    Tell Barry I said hello.

                                    Love,

                                    Amy

Seventeen

"What Is He Cupping His Hands and Telling Them?"

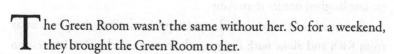

The Green Room wasn't the same without her. So for a weekend, they brought the Green Room to her.

It was on the last day of April 1992, two weeks after Amy's eighteenth birthday. The Pirates had flown to Houston to play the Astros, and Amy, Cindy, Peggy, and Tim had driven the 255 miles from Arlington to see them play. But the Buccos were just as interested to see *her*.

None of them knew how she was going to look, especially Rich. It had been almost two months since she had shooed him back to the Pirates, and although they had written their brief letters and spoken almost daily, he was secretly hoping the cancer hadn't overtaken her.

But the minute she walked into the team hotel, Rich says, he almost cried. Her medication had bloated her; he immediately surmised she had put on thirty pounds. She looked ashen, and there was something odd going on with her hair. "It just wasn't my Amy," he says. "It was hard. Last time I'd seen her, even though she had just gotten out of surgery, she was still my little Amy. But now she looked like somebody who was having chemo."

But once she opened her mouth, not a sour word was spoken. She

193

squealed out, "Dad, I missed you," and kissed him on the cheek. She then pulled back and gave him a toothy, glowing smile. It wasn't a forced, phony, or crooked grin either. She was as upbeat as Rich had seen her in God knows how long, and it downright confused him. "I'm saying to myself, *Geez, how are you so happy going through this? You look beat up,*" Rich remembers. "But she loved me. She grabbed me. She said, 'Dad, good to see you. Can we get a pizza after the game?' 'Yeah, we can get a pizza.' It was like she had a head cold instead of a tumor."

He invited her up to his room, where his suitemate Jim Leyland was waiting with his golf club. As usual, the Pirates manager was about to hit golf balls off his twenty-second-floor balcony, with Van Slyke ready to shag down below in the parking lot. Amy waved to her old friend, Slick, and couldn't wait to see Drabek, LaValliere, and, of course, Bonds later in the visit. When Leyland yelled, "Fore," and started rifling golf shots, no one laughed harder than Amy.

But much of that outward joy disappeared when Amy was away from Rich and alone with Peggy in their room. Rich's first impression was right on—the cancer and the chemo were ravaging her body. That weekend in Houston, for the first time, Amy was starting to see clumps of her hair fall out into the sink. She and Peggy had known this day was coming, but it was real now—and playing out in front of the team.

Peggy went to the hotel lobby to buy her a baseball cap, and the Pirates, of course, would have plenty to lend her as well. To take Amy's mind off her hair loss, Peggy suggested they all spend the day at the beach in Galveston, which was a novel idea until they returned to the hotel later that night. As they were about to valet their car, Amy noticed a group of teen girls dressed to the nines for their high school prom. She grew self-conscious about her hair, refusing to leave the car. Peggy told her to just take the garage elevator up instead. It was Amy's first sign of weakness, the first time cancer was winning.

All Amy wanted to do was go to the Pirates-Astros game the next night—with her cap on. But with her hair thinning out by the day and with her immune system compromised by the chemo, Peggy asked her not to go to the Astrodome. "And she just threw a fit," Peggy says. Amy had come specifically to see the Pirates, and she didn't care if she was at risk. She was going to that game, no questions asked, and she wasn't going to sit delicately in a sky suite or a booth or a bubble. She was going to hunker down with the crowd, shuck peanut shells, throw down a hot dog, yell at the umpires, and watch her dad coach third base for the first time.

She and Cindy ended up sitting next to Kristy Drabek and the Drabek kids, whom she used to babysit. It was like old times at the Green Room, and she barely paid any attention to her dad or the game. It was the stadium ambience that had lured her there; she'd just wanted a sliver of her old life back. Perhaps that's why her senses were heightened—because the imagery of that night stayed with her indefinitely.

After the game, she lingered by the clubhouse door to see Bonds, the other players, and, of course, Rich. When her dad emerged, she gave him another bear hug and excitedly described her night in the Astrodome stands.

"Oh, Dad, you should've seen this guy at the game," Amy said. "His beer belly was hanging out; his wife was throwing up—it was fun!"

"What?" Rich responded.

"They weren't even paying attention to their little kid, who was a brat," Amy went on. "He was running all over the place, giving the finger to his mother. And she was just laughing."

"Really?"

"Yeah," Amy continued. "Another guy booed the Pirates, and I got in his face. Told him to put a lid on it."

"Atta girl."

"Hey," Amy continued, "when we get back to the hotel, can we order a pizza in Jim's room?"

"Yeah, and we'll hit some golf balls again," Rich suggested.

"Yeah," she said, "I wanna see Jim hitting those golf balls."

Rich's admiration for his deteriorating daughter was never higher than at that moment. Two of her nine months to live were gone, but she was displaying no outward sense of depression or heartache. He still hadn't seen her cry one tear. Rich thought maybe Amy knew something he and the doctors didn't. Maybe she planned to beat this. Maybe the cancer wasn't winning.

When the weekend was over, she and Rich made tentative plans for their next visit. He would try to fly her up to Steubenville for a quick respite, or at the very least, he would see her when the Pirates returned to Houston in late July. In the interim, she promised to keep writing him, and he promised that the first-place Pirates would keep pushing for a World Series. "Deal," she said.

But the Braves, Expos, and Reds were lightweight opponents compared to a brain tumor. Amy's days consisted of chemo, radiation, and a twelfth-grade tutor at her home. She was unable to attend school because of the risk of contracting a cold or the flu, so she lived an isolated life at times—away from even Cindy.

One day in mid-May, suffering from cabin fever, Amy decided to leave the cul-de-sac for Cindy's house. She drove over in her Mitsubishi sedan and honked her horn. Out rushed Cindy for a look-see. They embraced, at which point Amy casually removed her baseball cap. "I'm bald," Amy announced matter-of-factly.

Since their last visit, Peggy had shaven Amy's head, and Cindy's initial reaction was, "We talked this week on the phone—why didn't you say anything?" Amy explained that her hair loss was inevitable and that Peggy took the razor to her as a preemptive strike. She said she didn't mind being bald; what she minded were the yahoos who kept thinking she was a boy.

She would wear a white Pirates cap or Gap hat wherever she went, and even though she also sported earrings, too often somebody would mistake her for a male. One day at a Shell station, she pumped her own gas and went to pay the bill. The clerk said, "Thank you, sir," which made her stark raving mad. She grabbed her breasts and said, "Would a 'sir' have these?" Then she stomped off.

The solution, according to her grandmother Ruth, was to wear a wig. In fact, Ruth said she could borrow hers. Amy wasn't the least bit vain, so she resisted it. "Bald is beautiful," she would say. Being bald also was the least of her concerns.

She wanted to give back to others in all of her round-headed glory; she wanted to do something noble and altruistic with her life. She signed up for Meals on Wheels, a volunteer job where she could deliver food to the less fortunate. It was a magnificent fit for her. All she'd have to do was make deliveries in her car. The hours were flexible and wouldn't be exhausting at all.

"She was like, 'Oh, I'm going to get to do something good with this wasted time of sitting around doing nothing,'" Cindy says. "She was so excited about it. But when she went to do orientation, they told her she couldn't do it because she would depress people. They were like, 'No, no thank you. We don't need that.'"

Anyone who'd spent a second around Amy knew she wasn't a downer. But this was the world she was living in now—judged by her baldness, the bags under her eyes, and her patchy skin.

She decided then to try her grandmother's wig. As sort of an experiment, she wore it out with Cindy for a night on the town in Fort Worth. Rich's buddy, Vince Genovese—the vacuum cleaner mogul—had sent his limo for them, and they had looked elegant in their party dresses, high heels, and, in Amy's case, blonde wig.

But in the middle of their gourmet dinner, Amy told Cindy, "This just doesn't feel right." She excused herself to the restroom and returned minus the wig—her head as shiny as a pool cue. "She thought people were looking at her more with the wig on," Cindy says. "Who knows? Maybe they were; maybe they weren't."

The bottom line was that Amy—in the midst of chemo, radiation, and a death sentence—was comfortable in her own wretched skin. She had decided to live in humor and peace rather than in pretentiousness and anguish.

"That amazed me," Rich says. "How do you do that? She wasn't mad at God. She wasn't mad at anybody. She knew she was going to die. She was just going, 'Well, whatever.' She'd go, 'Nine months? We'll see. I'll try to beat it. I think I can beat it.'"

By June, Amy had zero inhibitions left. She and the rest of her high school senior class were scheduled to graduate, but her doctors wouldn't allow her to walk. So she and Cindy had their own ceremony at the cul-de-sac, complete with caps, gowns, and a fake Merit Scholar rope around their collars. "Which was a hoot," Peggy says, 'because neither of them were on the honor roll. But, Cindy, God love her for just sliding in and making Amy a part of it, for making sure they had fun with it."

Fun was an understatement. Amy took pink lipstick that day and wrote "Class of '92" on her bald chemotherapy head. She and Cindy mugged for photos, wore the wig sideways on their heads, sang the alma mater, ate cake, and tossed their caps in the air. Amy was going to have this moment, like it or not—and definitely not with a straight face.

"Lipstick on her forehead? She was a clown that day," Rich says. "I called her, and although she didn't come out and say it, she was like, 'Yeah, I know I'm going to die, I'll be okay. How 'bout you, Dad? You gonna be okay?'"

The words on Sid Bream's T-shirt—*No Fear*—were definitely a mantra. She had an unspoken bucket list of things to do with her life or things to acquire, and one was to spend a twelve-hour day at the Six Flags Over Texas in Arlington. Peggy somehow let Amy talk her into it. Starting at 10 a.m. one day, Cindy and Amy went on every roller coaster or upside-down ride, at least twice. It was a kick—until Amy woke up the next morning with her forehead swollen five times its normal size.

"I called the oncologist, and I said, 'I'm bringing her in,'" Peggy says. "And so we got there, and they checked her out and said, 'It's okay.' But they said, 'Amy, no more roller coasters.'"

Most of her other wishes weren't off the table. She wanted the sweetest car she had ever seen in her life, a red Mazda Miata convertible. She dreamed of driving it with the top down, her bald head covered in a satin scarf. Peggy took note and left it at that. Amy's other immediate wish was to spend a weekend at her home away from home, Steubenville. Rich took care of this immediately.

It was just a quick weekend trip, a chance to spend quality time with

Roberta and Rich. But during those forty-eight hours, Roberta firmly believes she got to see Amy the supernatural.

Roberta had never been prone to hyperbole or bombast. But she swore that when Amy stepped out of a bedroom and into the morning light that first day, there was an opaque halo over Amy's head. She trembled and immediately called her two daughters, Tiffany and Leigh Anne.

"I saw an angel this morning," Roberta said.

"What are you talking about?" one of the girls responded.

"I don't know," Roberta answered. "But when Amy came out of her room, she looked angelic, as if there was a glow around her. Like in the movie *Ghost*."

True or not, otherworldly or not, Amy was continuing to inspire anyone she encountered. It was July now—nearly five of her nine months were gone—and Rich had yet to see Amy cry or shake a fist toward the heavens. "She acted like the tumor was her mascot," Rich says. "She'd say, 'Yeah, me and my tumor, we're going over to the store today.' Or, 'My tumor and I are gonna get some lunch and then run some errands.'"

Every moment that weekend and in every ensuing phone call or letter, Amy asked, "How are *you* doing?" rather than vice versa. She would ask about the team or about him—about coaching third base. Cancer was the obvious elephant in the room, but other than her cherubic face and hairless head, no one would have guessed it. Was she conning him?

During Pirates games when he was engrossed in his job, he wouldn't be mulling this over. But after the final out, win or lose, he'd race to call her, spend fifteen minutes catching up, hang up the phone, and become introspective. He had never been able to handle death—not Romey's especially. But somehow his eighteen-year-old terminally ill daughter seemed to have it mastered, seemed to have it in perspective.

"She had more fun after the diagnosis, she laughed more," Rich says. "Like before, if she got pissed off about something, she wouldn't talk to me. Or she wouldn't talk to somebody. But after she got the tumor, I never saw her angry. It was like a birthday party every single day for her. I don't know why. That's the magic of her.

"I got pictures of her smiles before and after, and it ain't even close. Before, she gave the old elementary, high school smile. After, she was grinning from ear to ear. Smiles that could've broken the camera. Ear to ear. But I can't answer why. I think part of it was she was the main focus of the family. And also whatever she said or did, it didn't matter. It didn't matter anymore. It was, 'Who cares? I'm gonna die. Who cares? Is someone going to get mad at me? I got nine months to live. What are ya gonna do? Get mad at me?'

"Maybe she went in her room at night and cried. But I never saw that. Maybe Cindy did; maybe her mom did. I only saw happy, happy, happy. I only saw, 'Oh, what the heck, let's go do it.' If I told her, 'Amy, before you go get your chemo, we're going to go skydiving,' she'd have been right there."

Peggy, Cindy, and Tim did see Amy in her rawer moments. She had wept right after her original diagnosis, and they'd seen stray tears or an occasional sulk after an excruciating chemo session. Their impression was that Amy kept all of that tucked away from Rich to please him, to unburden him. But Peggy and Cindy agreed that Amy never cried over her predicament, never doubled over, saying, "Why me?" Up until this point, they'd seen her sob over two things—when she couldn't go to Tim's activities or Little League games and when she couldn't spend her summer with the Pirates.

Those summers had been her oxygen for years, and when Tim got to go that July and she didn't, her tears flooded out. It was at its worst when she, Peggy, and Cindy drove Tim to the airport. But as they stood fidgeting at the gate, Amy gathered herself, kissed him good-bye, and told him to bring home an NL East pennant.

She couldn't help but be envious. For the first time ever, twelve-year-old Tim was going to be a batboy at Three Rivers Stadium in full Pirates regalia. "She'd have loved to be a bat boy," Tim says. So before he boarded the jet, Amy made Tim promise to sit or kneel by Jim Leyland in the third inning of every televised game. That way, she could see Tim up close, could say a telepathic hello to her little brother while he was gone.

When Tim arrived, he walked into a bustling Pirates clubhouse/ nuthouse. What a zoo! Van Slyke was still rolling his eyes at Bonds; Chico Lind was still sharpening his machetes; Rich was still holding kangaroo court—and the team still seemed indomitable. Other than a week at the end of May, the Bucs had been in first place every single day of the season, and it all began with their camaraderie. Other than Bonilla leaving for the Mets via free agency, the Pirates roster remained intact and unified, determined to avenge their NLCS loss to the Braves. Along the way, they were a sitcom.

About halfway through the season, pitching coach Ray Miller had bolted a small basketball hoop on a clubhouse wall—simply as a diversion. But before long, guys began playing one-on-one or two-on-two battle royales. Someone floated the idea of having a tournament, with Van Slyke serving as commissioner. Slick drew up a bracket, and for three hours before batting practice and for an hour afterward, the games took center stage. "Guys were sweating their butts off, cussing at one another," Rich says. "The game on the field that night actually became secondary."

But the more they played basketball, the better they played baseball. The team had an eleven-game winning streak starting in late July, and Rich—not to mention Jim Leyland—was convinced the hoop tournament had set their minds free. After two separate knock-down-drag-out tournaments, Leyland walked out waving his arms one day, and the players assumed he was calling the whole thing off. Instead, according to Rich, Leyland said, "You jerks are having all this fun, and you didn't even invite the skipper to play! That's horse manure!"

So Rich says Van Slyke promptly inserted Leyland into a bracket, where his first opponent was none other than Bonds. Leyland then emerged for his Bondsy matchup wearing baggy Chicago Bulls shorts to go with his knee-high white socks and Chuck Taylor sneakers. Poor Barry—he didn't have a chance. The entire squad was robustly rooting for the old school Leyland, who had an unexpectedly sweet shooting stroke and earned the upset win. "We were just as loose as we could be," Rich says.

But in that same vein, Leyland knew when to crack the whip. After a 15–0 home loss to Tom Glavine and the Braves in August, he told the team, "Hurry up and shower 'cause the cops are coming in to arrest you guys for impersonating major league players." Leyland knew none of this mattered—not the hoops tournament, not team chemistry, not the NL East title—unless they somehow reached the World Series.

Rich, on the other hand, needed the ups and downs of the season to escape Amy's tumor. If he'd let it, the stress of her nine-month battle would've rendered him useless. The demands of coaching third base conveniently took his mind off of Amy—at least from the first pitch of a game through the last.

Coaching third base was so consuming, so fast-paced, and so unforgiving that it mirrored the life of an air traffic controller. He could never exhale; there were no mental breaks. On the daily drives from Steubenville to Three Rivers Stadium, Tim would notice his dad practicing hand signals while steering the wheel with his knee. Rich also took copious notes on which outfielders had the strongest, most precise arms or which pitchers had the slickest pickoff moves toward second base. He knew Astros second baseman Craig Biggio would fake-talk to the second base umpire and then flash in for a pickoff throw. Rich kept all this information in a sacred black book—studying it, memorizing it. And then the games would start.

At first, there'd been a break-in period. He had to learn on the fly, or on the fly ball. One night against Atlanta, the Pirates had a runner on third with one out when someone clubbed a ball to the shallow right field corner. Braves outfielder David Justice raced a long way for it and appeared to stumble as he caught it. Rich sensed that Justice was falling down, so he had the runner tag up and chug for home. But Justice kept his footing and easily threw to the catcher for a double play.

Rich got the blame; the fans harangued him, wanted him strung up. Being a rookie, he naturally hung his head. But Leyland reminded him that you're not a real third base coach until you get someone gunned out at the plate. From then on, Rich settled in. He learned how to alternately speed up his signs and slow them down to keep the other team from decoding them. He learned that he had to constantly look at Leyland in the dugout for signs. He learned that Leyland's subtle sign to steal third base was putting his hand in the side of his pants. He even learned how to find Leyland in a crowded dugout by simply looking for the white puff of smoke from Leyland's cigarette.

"When a foul ball is hit, I've got to find my manager immediately," Rich says. "Maybe he wants a squeeze play. The game goes so fast. You've got hand signs to the man on second, hand signs to the man on first. Verbal signs to the guy on third. You get a headache. You need a Tylenol after every game. It's so fast."

Every day and every game, Rich learned a little bit more. He learned Bonds didn't want to be coached on third base. "I told him how many outs there were one time," says Rich, "and Barry said, 'I know how many (bleeping) outs there are.'" He learned to spit between his teeth, like all third base coaches do, and learned to talk and chew bubble gum at the same time. But most of all, he learned how to communicate with the Pirates runners at second base—the most critical, dire element of the job.

The runner at second base is in scoring position and needs to trust that he can take a sizable lead off the bag. But the runner can't always see an infielder secretly creeping up behind him for a pickoff play, which is where Rich came in. As third base coach, Rich was the baserunner's guide dog, so to speak. If he shouted, "Okay," that meant the runner could inch closer to third base. If the runner's lead was too lengthy or dangerous, he'd shout, "Hold." And if a pickoff play was in the works, he'd yell, "Back."

Those were Rich's three key words to the runner at second: *Okay. Hold. Back.* But there was one major problem: in the packed, cavernous big league stadiums, the runners couldn't always hear him.

So Rich came up with his best solution. He would bend his bow-legs, crouch into an athletic stance, cup his hands over his mouth for a megaphone effect, and shout one of those three words to the runner.

He did so much bellowing and hollering through cupped hands that he'd get a sore throat on a nightly basis. But it was the only way to get his message across. The crouching and hand cupping became synonymous with Rich. It was his quasi-batting stance.

Amy, back in Texas, was missing all of this nuance, not to mention the entire Pirates summer. She'd hear all the stories from Rich and Tim in their phone calls or letters. She'd hear how Tim, as batboy, went to fetch a bat during a game, came sprinting back to the dugout, and slipped—sliding straight under Leyland's legs on the bench. "You're safe!" Uncle Jim shouted.

She'd laugh and tell Tim how she'd always see him on TV during the third inning, photobombing Leyland. "Saw you! Saw you!" she'd marvel. But other times, she would turn melancholy, wishing she was in the Green Room at Three Rivers or in Steubenville with Tennis Shoe Ernie. Peggy could sense her wistfulness and had a bright idea straight out of Amy's bucket list: she bought her the red Miata.

Peggy had taken Amy with her to a dealership, where there it sat in broad daylight—a slightly dinged red Miata convertible at an affordable price. The dings had come from the heavens—i.e., a hailstorm—and the car salesman took one look at Amy's bald head and had his heart grow two sizes.

"I'll make this work," he told Peggy.

"It's her dream," Peggy answered.

Peggy ended up having to drive the car off the lot because Amy had no idea how to operate a stick shift. Peggy stopped in a church parking lot to tutor her, and, before long, Amy was gunning it past every cute boy on the road. She and Cindy would go on joyrides with the car's top down, Amy's bald head exposed to the wind and red-hot Texas heat. Who cared if she came home sunburned? Peggy just handed her a bandanna for the next joyride, and off Amy and Cindy would go again.

All the way around, Amy seemed nonplussed and, more often than not, upbeat. For the time being, the chemo and radiation were not as debilitating or tiring. Plus, the Miata was giving her an added boost.

John Cangelosi—her former Pirates crush who was now playing for the Rangers—met her and Cindy for lunch one day and marveled at her vigor. As she drove up in her racy Miata, bandanna flapping, Amy had a radiant smile on her face—as if this were all a temporary setback.

"I thought she was coming out of it at the time," Cangelosi says. "I thought she was going to beat it. I thought she was in remission when I saw her. Things were looking a little bit better."

On Sunday night, August 9, Rich seconded that notion. Amy had called him just after the team arrived in New York to begin a Monday series with the Mets—and he sensed an increased optimism in her voice. He'll never forget where he was. He was sitting on Jim Leyland's side of their adjoining hotel suite, when Amy flat-out told him she was kicking cancer's derriere.

"Dad, I'm doing good. We're gonna beat this thing. We're gonna lick it."

She mentioned a bone marrow transplant that might be in the works, a procedure that could alter her prognosis for the better. She said Rich's cousin Donna Jean was a potential match; it appeared that the proverbial arrow was now pointing up for Amy.

Leyland overheard much of the discussion and started waving for Rich to hand him the phone. "Amy, how ya doin', honey?" Leyland asked. "You're doing good? Can't wait to see you."

When Rich hung up, he wondered if he'd been hallucinating. Did Amy say *bone marrow*? The tumor might be null and void? Either he was too far removed from Texas or reality, but he allowed himself to buy into what Amy was prognosticating. "She talked me into believing that she was going to get through this," Rich says. "She talked me into it. I'm thinking, 'How did you get so strong when you've never been through something like this?' There was like, hope. There was some hope."

Leyland, that night in the New York hotel, had a brainstorm. Since Amy was feeling more energetic, he suggested they fly her in for a Pirates playoff game that October. "Let's make a memory for her," Leyland said. Rich's rule was that the kids could miss school only for the World Series.

But this was an extraordinary circumstance, and Rich was on board. He phoned Texas the next day to tell Amy the news. It would be up to her doctors whether she could travel.

By the end of September, the Pirates held a comfortable nine-game lead in the NL East standings and were about to get a rematch with the Braves in the NLCS. So the trip from Texas to Pittsburgh was a tentative go—as long as the logistics could be worked out. Amy's doctors had several requests. They wanted her to take a private plane to lessen the risk of catching a cold or the flu. They told her she needed to be back in forty-eight hours so she wouldn't miss any radiation treatments. They told her . . . to have the time of her life.

Rich and Peggy coordinated as best they could. The Pirates home playoff dates were Friday, October 9, for Game 3; Saturday, October 10, for Game 4; and Sunday, October 11, for Game 5—they could only pick one. Since Amy had treatments on Saturdays and Mondays, they chose Game 5 on Sunday, the 11th. She'd have her radiation that Saturday morning, the 10th; fly to Pittsburgh immediately afterward on Vince Genovese's private Learjet; and return Monday morning, the 12th. It would be a whirlwind.

Thankfully, Genovese's plane could fit six because Amy wasn't going anywhere without Peggy, Cindy, and Tim, who had returned to Texas at the end of August. They were all over the moon. They had never seen a playoff game firsthand, and as a bonus, Tim was going to be a playoff batboy. All Amy had to do was stay healthy enough to fly. "Because she was still sick," Cindy says. "She just happened to be happy and sick at the same time."

On the morning of October 10, Genovese's limo pulled up to the cul-de-sac. The sight of it had all of them squealing. For much of the summer, that limo had been somewhat at their beck and call, and Genovese hadn't wanted it any other way. Whenever Peggy was stuck in the hospital with Amy, Vince would instruct his limo driver to take Tim to school or have the limo pick Tim up after school and drop him off to where Peggy was. He was the only twelve-year-old around with his own limo waiting outside on the school curb. "I kind of got used to it—like, 'Oh, man, this is normal,'" Tim says. Other days, the limo would swoop by Cindy's house to take her to see Amy. It was almost their home away from home.

They all piled in for the ride to Amy's radiation treatment in Dallas. Amy apologized for the diversion, as was her way, but her session thankfully went off smoothly and on time. They were all set to head to the airport . . . when Peggy let out a gasp.

She had forgotten one of Amy's important refrigerated medications; it was a must-have. But the flight was scheduled to leave out of a private Fort Worth airport in an hour, and they didn't have enough time to swing back to the cul-de-sac. Tim started crying because he feared the trip was off. "It was hectic," Cindy says. "Everyone was freaking out." Peggy used the driver's car phone (cell phones weren't in everyone's side pocket yet in 1992). She called the hospital, where Amy's doctor arranged for the prescription to be filled in Pittsburgh. Thankfully, it turned out to be just a false alarm.

The Learjet was the next adventure. They wondered how a toilet worked at 30,000 feet and liked how the luxurious seats faced each other—as if they were sitting at a card table. There were shelves full of orange juice, soda, peanuts, and pretzels, as much as they could drink and eat. There was no flight attendant to police them. "We thought we were high class," Tim says.

They arrived in time to watch the tail end of Game 4 on TV, a disconcerting 6–4 loss to the Braves. Atlanta led the best-of-seven series 3-games-to-1, and when Rich caught up with them at their hotel afterward, it was a bittersweet moment. He was thrilled to see Amy and the whole group. Mike and Bubba were both present as well. But it was looking like another empty season, another year without a World Series.

Sunday's Game 5 was an obvious must-win, and Amy came prepared with her Buccos pom-poms. She had missed her Pittsburgh summer, so this one night at the stadium was going to be three months rolled into one. When she arrived at the ballpark, she made certain to stop by the Green Room, where she used to be teacher/den mother/babysitter. Little Scott Van Slyke and tiny Kyle Drabek, the two future major leaguers, had sprouted. She hugged everyone in her path, and everyone reciprocated—Barry Bonds included.

The cancer was in the back of everyone's minds—except *hers*. Cindy noticed this right away, that Amy was in such utter joy that she had checked her diagnosis at the door. She was as wide-eyed, joyful, and punchy as Cindy had ever seen. It was like their pseudo-graduation day. This was Amy's great escape from her death sentence: a playoff game, a chance to spend time with her dad and her brothers, a chance—albeit slim—to see her father inch one step closer to his World Series wish.

Amy and Cindy sat five rows behind home plate, the kind of box seats you get when you know someone. And, yes, they knew someone—the whole team. Many of the Pirates families were bunched near them, including Tom Leyland, the priest brother of Jim Leyland. For a split second, they thought they may need to tone down their banter since a priest was nearby. But on a crisp, brilliant night like this, that wasn't going to happen.

Right from the first inning of the game, the Pirates put Rich to work at third base. Gary Redus led off the game with a double, which meant Rich was crouching, cupping his hands, and hollering toward second base from the get-go. Before long, Bonds, Jeff King, and Lloyd McClendon followed with doubles of their own off Braves starter Steve Avery. Before the game, Leyland had reminded Rich that he needed to be ultra-aggressive against Atlanta's stellar pitching because scoring chances were generally rare. So with all these doubles, with all these runners standing on second base, with the Pirates raucous crowd making it impossible to hear, Rich more than ever crouched, cupped his hands, and shouted . . . crouched, cupped his hands, and shouted . . . crouched, cupped his hands, and shouted. Rinse and repeat.

Amy—who had her eyes trained on her dad—had never seen him like this before. She had never really *seen* him coach third base, period. In Houston, the last time she'd watched the team in person, she had paid virtually no attention to the field, having been more engrossed by the Astrodome's ambience or lack thereof. Plus, the Pirates hadn't scored a ton in Houston. But on this night, Rich was constantly cupping his hands, constantly waving in runs. Through six innings, it was 6–0 Bucs.

While it was all happening, Amy told Cindy, "Look at my dad! Look at my dad!" They laughed so heartily at his coaching stance that even Tom Leyland glanced over at them, wondering what the commotion was. "We were literally just two teenagers acting like fools," Cindy says. "We were acting like crazy people."

Amy being Amy, she began to tell jokes. "What is my dad doing over there? What is he cupping his hands and telling them? Is he asking them if they're hungry? Is he asking them what they should do after the game?"

"Is he asking them if they want Chinese food?" Cindy chimed in.

"Is he asking if they want pizza?" Amy countered.

"Is he asking for a ride home?" asked Cindy.

"Is he barking like a dog?" deadpanned Amy.

That's when Amy barked herself, like a Chihuahua. The two of them were giggling like hyenas—spouting out as many sophomoric one-liners as possible. "We just had tears streaming down our faces from the laughing," Cindy says. "Her dad is kind of bowlegged, and it was funny. It was just joy taking over, I guess."

The final score was Pirates 7, Braves 1. Atlanta still led the series, three games to two, with the next two games scheduled for Georgia, but there was a palpable confidence in the Pittsburgh clubhouse, according to Tim. He saw grown men hug like they'd never hugged before. He heard Chico Lind say, "Let's go do this." He heard Van Slyke say, "We got this; we still got a chance."

Rich exited the stadium with a discernible hop in his step. They all climbed into his car for the trip back to their hotel—Amy, Cindy, Mike, and Tim jammed in the backseat, Rich and Bubba in the front. Just a few minutes into the ride, Amy, sitting directly behind Rich, leaned forward to wrap her arms around her father's neck. Right next to his ear, she seemed to have something important to ask.

"Hey, Dad," Amy said, "when you get down in that stance and you cup your hands, what are you telling those guys at second—'the chicken runs at midnight' or what?"

There was a pause, ever so slightly, to register what she had just said. And then there was uncontrollable, high-octave, ear-piercing, mind-altering laughter. "I almost drove off the road," Rich says.

"What are you talking about, Amy?" asked Tim.

"I don't know—just 'the chicken runs at midnight,'" Amy said, still laughing.

"What?" said Rich. "The chicken runs at midnight? Really? Is that what you said? Where'd you come up with that one?"

"I don't know," Amy said, grinning. "It just came out."

The comment was nonsensical; that's the part that perplexed them. No one knew whether chickens ran at midnight or at noon, whether chickens even ran, jogged, or sprinted at all. No one knew whether chickens were nocturnal or morning animals. No one had ever given it even the slightest thought. Neither Amy nor anyone else had eaten chicken before the game—just hot dogs—and no one had had a conversation that day about poultry or fowl. The statement was so random, so original, so arcane, and so esoteric that it *had* to stick. It was an instant classic.

"All right then," Tim announced, "the chicken runs at midnight."

Back at the hotel, the kids darted in to see Peggy, who had stayed behind to watch the game on television. "Chicken runs at midnight, Mom," was Tim's greeting. Peggy was obviously stumped. They explained the story behind it, all of them laughing as hysterically as they had in the car. They still didn't know what it meant, but because it came from Amy—who was in the eighth of her nine months—it wasn't about to be forgotten.

That evening was one of the family's all-time highs. Rich and Peggy, divorced years before, were bonded and united, all because of Amy. Bubba and Mike, both of whom lived away from their sister in the Steubenville/Pittsburgh area, took advantage of the rare visit and hugged her repeatedly. Mike began to cry; he didn't want Amy, Cindy, Peggy, and Tim to fly back to Texas the next day.

"Who said we're leaving?" Amy said. "Cindy and I are driving to Atlanta for Game 6."

It was another of Amy's jokes, of course. Or was it? She and Cindy literally got on the hotel phone to dial the American Automobile Association. They wanted to find out how far the drive was from Arlington, Texas, to Atlanta. The answer was 800 miles, about twelve hours, though Amy figured she could floor the Miata and get there in ten. Peggy shook her head no—sorry to be playing the spoiler role. But Amy had another radiation appointment in Dallas that Monday; she'd have to watch Game 6 in the cul-de-sac living room.

Rich said his good-byes that night, because while Amy and crew would be flying to Fort Worth in the morning, he would be jetting to Atlanta with the team. On his way out the door, he gave Amy a robust bear hug and an "I love you." Then he sheepishly asked her, "The chicken runs at midnight?"

Two days later, Amy, Cindy, and Tim crowded around the TV for Game 6. A Bonds home run started an eight-run second inning off Tom Glavine, and the Pirates were on their way to another rout. Rich found himself thinking of Amy, thinking of "the chicken runs at midnight" every time he crouched and cupped his hands in the 13–4 Pirates victory. He was literally chuckling in the third base coaching box. The series was now tied three to three, with the winner-take-all Game 7 coming the following day. Amy mulled that over in her mind: win, and her dad was in a World Series. That she wanted to see.

About four hours before Game 7's first pitch, Amy badly wanted to hear her dad's voice. She knew he'd be a nervous wreck—even more than she already was—so she dialed Fulton County Stadium in Atlanta to be a diversion, intending to tell him, "We got this." When a switchboard operator named Nell answered, Amy asked for Rich Donnelly in the Pirates clubhouse. Nell told her the clubhouse wasn't open yet. Amy hung up disappointed.

But a second later, she decided she had a juicier idea. She'd leave a message for him, a message guaranteed to perk him up, guaranteed to blow his mind. "Let's get him," she told Cindy. She called back and told Nell to jot down and deliver the following note:

Dad,
    The chicken runs at midnight.

                                    Amy

Nell asked her to repeat that, told her it sounded a little peculiar and off. So Amy slowly said, "The chicken . . . runs . . . at . . . midnight. Make sure that's on the note."

"Okay," said Nell, "if that's what you want the message to be."

A few minutes later, one of the Pirates clubhouse kids ushered in a "While You Were Out" message to Rich. "Coach, we got this note from upstairs," the kid said. Rich figured it was a good luck note from someone, a generic "go get 'em" message. He took a quick glance and then broke out in hysterical laughter. Second baseman Chico Lind happened to be loping by just at that instant.

"Hey man, what's this?" Lind said in his Latin accent, jabbing a finger at the note.

"The chicken runs at midnight, man," Rich said with a crooked smile.

"Cheee-ken runs at meeednight! Let's go!" Lind chanted. "Cheeken runs at meeednight."

Lind then gallivanted all over the clubhouse, repeating the phrase. Bonds, Van Slyke, and LaValliere all looked at Lind like he was cuckoo. But the second baseman, who just liked the ring of it and had no idea what the phrase was about, wasn't done yet.

During the pregame introductions on NBC—with Amy, Cindy, and Tim riveted to their television in Texas—each Pirates starter jogged toward the third base line when his name was called. The first seven batters in the Pirates lineup just routinely slapped five with each other, grunting or barely saying a word out loud. But when Lind was announced, he traipsed toward his teammates, hand slapped each one of them, and instructed, "Cheeken runs at meeednight, let's go; Cheeken runs at meeednight, let's go."

The threesome on the cul-de-sac erupted from their seats. "We just went nuts," Cindy says. "Amy was like, 'Did you hear him? What did he say?' It kind of made her feel like maybe she was there."

What happened over the next few hours was seismic. The Pirates jumped ahead 1–0 in the first inning and were up 2–0 by the sixth. Drabek, who had pitched poorly in the series previously, was locked in. Amy, way too superstitious, wouldn't let anyone move or swap seats. Cindy and Tim begged to use the restroom, but she shouted out, "Nope. We can't jinx this."

They should've listened. In the eighth inning, still leading 2–zip, Amy, Cindy, and Tim started talking about the impending World Series. Rich had already promised they could all go. So to get a jump on the rest of the country, they started dialing the airlines to see what the airfare was to Pittsburgh . . . then Amtrak to see what a train ride would cost . . . then Greyhound to see what a bus ride would run. "We got way ahead of ourselves," Tim says.

Entering the ninth, the Pirates needed just three more outs to reach the Fall Classic. Rich was on the dugout's top step, the better to see every detail. But Drabek yielded a leadoff double and then watched Lind—a Gold Glove second baseman—mishandle a hard-hit ball. Up came who else but Sid Bream.

The trio in Texas moaned. They feared Mr. No Fear. But Bream walked to load the bases, prompting Leyland to remove Drabek from the game. In came reliever Stan Belinda, who gave up a fly ball sacrifice that scored a runner from third. It was now 2–1 Pittsburgh, with runners on second and third. Belinda then induced Atlanta's Brian Hunter to pop out. The Buccos were one out away, and Rich imagined Bob Prince's pulsating voice, imagined the boys back in Steubenville cheering, imagined cupping his hands in an actual World Series.

The batter was Francisco Cabrera—a reserve, a no-name. But he had a chance to be Bill Mazeroski. He crushed a ball foul early in his at-bat, which is when the Pirates soap opera reared its head. Van Slyke, the center fielder, waved his archenemy Bonds, the left fielder, closer to the plate—just in case Barry had to charge a ball and throw out the potential winning run. But eyewitnesses say Barry flipped him off and never moved an inch.

A minute later, Cabrera lined a hard ground ball to left field, where Bonds was still playing a hair too deep. David Justice scored to tie it at 2–2—and now here came Sid Bream chugging around third base. About to be a hero or a bum.

Bream was arguably one of the slowest men in baseball. But he had legs, and he had faith—and he relied on them both. The throw from Bonds was slightly off course, and Bream scored on an awkward hook slide. The Braves won 3–2.

Of all people, it had been Bream—one of the kindest, sweetest, sincerest men Amy had met in the game. But she hated him for that split second. It was probably the final Pirates game she would ever get to watch, the final time she'd ever get to admire her father in a black and gold baseball uniform. Deep down she knew it, even though no one else on the cul-de-sac was thinking it. So Amy, eighteen-year-old heartbroken Amy, crumpled into a ball on the floor in tears.

She wasn't sobbing over her cancer or over pain or her death sentence. What she was crying about was the World Series. How Rich had been denied once again. How she would never get to see one.

Letter from Amy

Dad,
    C.R.A.M.—with feeling.

                                    Love,
                                    Amy

Eighteen

The Ninth Month

R ich did an interview in the days following Sid Bream's slide. He was asked what his heartache felt like, and his unrehearsed answer was, "Like a death in the family."

If he could've hit rewind—knowing Amy's diagnosis—he would've used less flippant terminology. But after spending forty-eight hours with his daughter that previous weekend, the honest truth was that Rich thought Amy was halfway home, halfway to staving off the tumor.

It was the city of Pittsburgh—including the surrounding area of Steubenville—that was on more of a ventilator. After the ninth inning collapse in Atlanta, Rich says the whole tri-state area "almost shut down." The schools were half empty, and local newscasters were in tears on air.

On the team flight back from Georgia, Van Slyke dubbed it "The Trip to Nowhere"—considering they'd been just one out away from a trip to the World Series. "Nobody spoke, nobody ate," Rich says of the flight. "Complete silence for two hours. We all got off the plane and went straight to our cars. Nobody said good-bye to one another."

Roberta took the brunt of it at Rich's house. He wouldn't talk on the car ride home or use complete sentences once he got there. "Just little grunts and shoulder shrugs," he says. The day after the loss, he literally lay in bed from 5 a.m. to 6 or 7 p.m.

"Not hungry, not nothing," Rich says. "Was embarrassed to go out of the house. The lowest point in my baseball career."

Down at the Texas cul-de-sac, only one phrase was getting them through the day: *the chicken runs at midnight*. It had become as much a part of their vernacular as good morning and good night. Amy began signing many of her notes and letters with *C.R.A.M.* But out of all of them, Tim led the chorus. He would say "the chicken runs at midnight" as a substitute for "hello," "good-bye," "thank you," and "I'm hungry." Most of all, every time he'd hang up the phone with Rich or part ways with Amy, he'd say, "Love you . . . the chicken runs at midnight."

To the Donnellys, the phrase was appropriate for any and every situation. It became the family motto. "I started out saying it maybe ten times a day," Tim says. "Then even more. We still didn't know what it meant, but it meant a lot to us."

October soon crept into November, when every day seemed to bring a new development. In baseball, Barry Bonds was leaving the Pirates via free agency, either for the New York Yankees or the San Francisco Giants. In Steubenville, Rich was packing for a cruise to the Caribbean with Jim Leyland and other baseball luminaries such as Bob Feller and Mark (The Bird) Fidrych. In Arlington, Cindy had moved into her own studio apartment. And at Dallas Children's Hospital, Amy was about to undergo a third round of chemotherapy.

Rich had a false sense of security that everything was going to be okay with her, partly because Amy had seemed to respond adequately to the other two rounds of chemo. Plus, she seemed so vibrant in Pittsburgh. The truth was, she had fooled him. It was an act. Around her dad—whether on phone calls, in letters, or during the trip to Game 5— she made sure to exude normalcy. She never wanted to add misery to his day. But after the Game 7 loss, with no World Series to look forward to, her smiles were harder to come by, more forced. Rich, all the way back in Steubenville, had no idea.

Normally, Peggy would've been by Amy's side at the hospital 24/7, but, that November, Peggy had gone to back to work close to full-time, leaving Amy with her grandmother, Ruth, or a family friend. Then on a day near Thanksgiving when Peggy wasn't around, Amy suffered a grand mal seizure. The family friend who witnessed it frantically called Peggy to say she'd better get to the hospital. Amy was in her ninth month.

After Amy's seizure, Cindy and Tim began arriving every day in Vince Genovese's limo to see her. Tim brought Amy a soft, furry chicken doll, the kind of stuffed animal you snuggle. "Chicken runs at midnight," he told her. She winked back at him. But Cindy could tell something was off.

Amy was starting to have sores on her skin. Cindy heard it was a reaction to her newest medications, but the telltale warning sign was that doctors weren't allowing Amy to return to the cul-de-sac. As long as the seizures were reoccurring, she had to stay in the hospital. Ruth, whom Amy called "Gram," moved into Amy's hospital room full-time and witnessed Amy's next two horrible seizures. "My mom just screamed," Peggy says. "And we'd have to haul Gram out of the room because she just didn't do well with some of that stuff."

Amy's bone marrow transplant had fallen through, and Peggy says she complained that the newest experimental meds "felt like they were burning" her from the inside out. Cindy was like Amy's sister—she could read Amy's body language and facial expressions, could tell Amy was in anguish. And she knew it for sure in early December when Amy asked to speak to Rich immediately. "She couldn't even sit up to dial the phone, so I called him for her," Cindy says. "Then I handed her the phone."

According to Cindy, Amy's opening comment to her father was, "Dad, I'm not doing good. Can you please come?"

He told her no. He said he and Roberta were leaving in the next few days for their cruise with Jim Leyland, that it was too late to cancel or rearrange their plans. He mentioned he'd be back in about a week, that maybe he would come down for Christmas or she could shoot up to Steubenville.

Amy said, "Okay, Dad, chicken runs at midnight," and hung up. Then she bawled her eyes out.

Cindy was seething at Rich, but no one had told him about the seizures; no one had directly told him Amy was starting her decline.

Again, based on how she'd beamed at Game 5 in Pittsburgh—"the chicken runs at midnight" game—he was operating on the assumption that Amy was annihilating cancer. Even though she had said on the phone, "Dad, I'm not doing good," he thought it was a random, inconsequential setback. There was a word for his behavior: *denial*.

"This is terrible to say, but I thought everything was okay, that she was going to beat it and that dying wasn't even a question," Rich says. "It was like she just had the flu. I thought, *I'm up here; what can I do for her?* When I'd talk to her, she was bubbly; she was fine. Like she wasn't even that sick anymore. I thought, *She's going to kick it, and we're going to see her in the spring.* I didn't think it was serious anymore.

"If her doctor would have called and said, 'Rich, I need you to come within a week. Don't go on the cruise,' I'd have been there in a minute. If I would have thought she was in trouble, I'd never have gone. Never."

After Amy cried for a spell, she swore Cindy to secrecy. She didn't want to create drama with Peggy, didn't want her mother to know her dad had chosen Bob Feller and Bird Fidrych over his daughter. "And then she never talked about it again," Cindy says.

Either way, it was a clear example of Rich's detachment, his lack of overall awareness. He had little faith, and no apparent way of regaining it. "If faith was a hundred-yard football field, I was on my own thirty-yard line—and it was third and long," he says.

The physical pain Amy had was worsening by the day. She had difficulty swallowing food, or just didn't have an appetite at all. She wasn't smiling as much. In the third week of December 1992, Amy's doctor pulled Peggy aside to say, "We're going to let her go home for Christmas." Being a nurse, Peggy knew it was code for "she's going to die," knew it was the doctor's way of getting Amy home one final time. "But I just didn't want to believe it," Peggy says. "I just couldn't allow myself to think that."

No one called Rich to invite him to the cul-de-sac. It was Amy's time with just Peggy, Gram, Cindy, and, of course, Tim. They wanted her visit to be beyond special, and Tim kicked that off by trying to decorate the frame of the house with Christmas lights. He dug out every colored bulb, every blinker, every wreath, every plastic Santa they'd ever owned. All of it was going up there somewhere, disorganized as that may be, because this had to be the best Christmas ever.

"Me and my neighbor were up on the roof, laying down wreaths, putting, like, every light we had up there, trying to do it up like the Griswolds," Tim says.

Peggy picked up Amy at the hospital in the Miata, and as they drove into the cul-de-sac, Amy immediately started cracking up. Tim's Christmas lights were hung crooked, the wreaths arranged indiscriminately. "It looked awful," Tim says. "I just remember her and Mom laughing at the shoddy job we did."

But it was also the thought that counted, and Amy told her little brother thank you. Still, her energy was low, and that altered some of Peggy's holiday plans. She had bought two tickets to a local theatre production of *Cats*, the musical Amy had always hoped to see. But as much as Amy wanted to get gussied up, enjoy a night out on the town, and listen to that music, she couldn't summon the strength. Cindy went with her mom, Brenda, instead.

The upside of the visit was the unfiltered conversations they all had. They reminisced about Amy's makeshift classroom, which was still fully intact in the garage. Some of her "students" were in high school now; Amy wondered aloud if they had straight A's. She also had private chats with Cindy, and in a moment of introspection, she looked deep into her best friend's eyes and said, "Do you think Timmy will be okay? Do you think my mom will hang in there?" She didn't mention Rich.

Amy also brought up something precious to her: the younger cancer patients at the hospital. She couldn't help but notice them—these kids with bald heads who'd lost their childhoods to an insidious disease. She noticed how they would be carted around the cancer ward in a red wagon twice a day so they could see the sights, particularly the Dallas skyline, through a large bay window. Oftentimes, the kids would have to wait in line or be turned away completely because there was only one available wagon. That broke Amy's heart. She told Peggy in a somber chat that Christmas that when she was gone, she hoped people would send money for new red wagons in lieu of flowers.

They all exchanged presents, of course, and Amy's favorite gift, hands down, was a music box that played songs from *Cats*. "She went crazy," Peggy says. Rich telephoned later in the day to wish Amy a Merry Christmas, and no one led him to believe she was declining at all. Her health seemed to be status quo, and he honestly assumed he'd see her again at spring training.

A couple of days later, Peggy drove her back to Children's Hospital in the Miata. The convertible always lifted Amy's spirits too, which was the whole idea. Gram came in a separate car, while the ever-reliable Cindy stayed with Tim. They all hoped for the best, but around New Year's Day, the situation turned dire. Amy slipped into a coma.

The family shifted into emergency mode. Gram announced she'd stay by Amy's side 24/7 so Peggy could spend a few hours at work each day. Cindy volunteered to move into their house and take care of Tim. Rich was a whole other story.

Peggy didn't want to be the one to break the news to Rich, because every time she had called him with updates in the past, he'd tell her, "You're making it sound worse than it really is." He felt that way because whenever he'd eventually talk to Amy, she'd tell him, "Oh, I'm fine, Dad. I'm good. I'm getting better"—even though it was all a front.

So this time, Peggy had the doctor call Rich for her. The conversation was one-sided, brutal, and direct.

"Rich, Amy's not doing well. She's lapsed into a coma, and you'd better get here."

Rich hung up, sat down on his bed, and started crying. "It finally hit me," he says. Roberta booked him a flight, and within hours, he was on his way to Texas. He blamed himself for letting baseball and Lucy get between him and Amy. His guilt was off the charts. He was convinced it was all too late to fix. When he entered the ICU at Children's Hospital and saw his daughter lying in bed unresponsively, he felt two feet tall.

Before long, he cornered Amy's doctor to ask for the truth. The only glimmer of hope remained a bone marrow transplant, with Rich's cousin Donna Jean a potential match. Otherwise, all Rich could do was sit by Amy's bed and wait patiently—the one thing he was worst at.

He paced . . . he sat down . . . he paced . . . he watched her heart rate . . . he paced . . . he watched her oxygenation levels. He was going stir-crazy—until a nurse told him Amy could hear anything Rich said.

He was incredulous over that, but the nurse insisted that coma patients can hear rather well in their altered consciousness. The nurse then put a sign on Amy that read, "If you don't want me to hear what you're saying, you'd better whisper." It sounded precisely like something Amy would write—just the right dose of attitude—and it got Rich and Peggy thinking.

Peggy brought in a set of headphones so Amy could listen to the *Cats* show tunes. It was a smart idea; they'd just run the music on a loop four or five hours each day. Peggy would stare at her much of the time, hoping the show tunes would snap her out of the coma. "What I saw was a hint of a smile on her face," Peggy says, "as if she were saying, 'Mom, it's going to be okay.'"

Although Amy never spoke, at some point in the day, Rich and Peggy would have a conversation with her, like this one.

PEGGY: "Amy, I brought your father coffee today—and he
     spilled it all over himself."
RICH: "Well, I didn't want coffee, Peggy; I wanted a donut."
PEGGY: "You didn't say that."
RICH: "See, Amy, your mom never listens to me."

They'd all laugh and think Amy was laughing inside.

Gram would be sitting with them—she refused to leave as well—so there would eventually be one big conversation, like a fireside chat, by Amy's bed each day. Then before Rich left her room at night to sleep in a hospital bunk bed, he would say the magic words: "Good night, Ames. Love you. The chicken runs at midnight."

This went on for much of January—show tunes, conversations, and the family motto. Rich just refused to climb up out of his chair. He had basically been an absentee dad for eighteen years, so this was his skewed and hopeless way of making up for it. "After everything I did to her, she accepted me back—and because she did that, I wasn't leaving her side," Rich says. "I almost thought it was sacrilegious to leave the hospital."

His good friend in the area, the former Dallas Mavericks guard Brad Davis, invited him to an NBA game, telling Rich he needed fresh air. Rich refused at first, but then he began mulling it over out loud in his daughter's ICU room. "Should I go, Amy?" he asked. He closed his eyes and imagined her response, which he says went something like this: "If you don't go to that game, I'm going to go ahead and die. What are you lying around in here for?"

So Rich went that night, though it hardly freed his mind. In the ensuing days, he and Peggy made certain that Tim—now in seventh grade—came by for his own visits. The poor kid was overwhelmed, but he, too, knew what to say when it was time to leave: "Amy, it's Tim. Love you. Chicken runs at midnight. I hope you get better."

Amy was now on her eleventh of nine months. To Rich, in his warped baseball frame of mind, that was an extra-innings victory of sorts. He marveled at how brave and resilient his daughter was. Still a hair in denial, he kept waiting for a bone marrow transplant that would never come. "I kept thinking they're going to put it in her, and she's going to just magically awaken," he says. But by the third week of January, Rich and Peggy were summoned into a private room for a meeting.

The doctors informed them that Amy's kidneys and liver were deteriorating and that her other organs would soon follow. The doctors spelled out their options. They could keep Amy on a ventilator and reinsert a chest tube. But before the docs could say another word, Peggy waved them off. "I said, 'That's it, no more, stop,'" Peggy says. "I said, 'I don't want you to do anything else to her. Let her go.'"

One of the doctors said, "Peggy, there's always a chance." But Peggy only grew angrier. A year of heartache had boiled over. "I was pissed," she says, "because there wasn't anything else to do." Rich yielded to Peggy on this one. For the longest time, Peggy had rooted for the same miracles as Rich, had hoped Amy would just open her eyes one day and say, "Let's go to Six Flags." But when Peggy told the doctors, "I don't want her to suffer anymore," Rich realized it was no use.

In the early morning of January 28, 1993, they were going to unplug Amy from the ventilator. A doctor found Rich and told him it was time to say good-bye. He walked in, slow and unsteady, without a game plan or speech. All he could think of were the words *thank you.* "I must have said thank you a hundred times," Rich says. "Just thank you for everything, just thank you for everything she'd done for us. I just told her I loved her so much. I didn't really say, 'When you're gone, I'll remember you.' I didn't say that. Didn't say anything about dying. I was at a loss."

The good-bye lasted all of three or four minutes—because he had nothing left emotionally. He pivoted, found the door, looked back one more time, and said, "Love you . . . the chicken runs at midnight." It felt like the right thing to say.

Rich sat in the waiting room, this time waiting for death. A little later, a doctor nodded his way. He knew what that meant. He returned to his hospital bunk bed, in the private room reserved for parents with terminally ill children. There was a pay phone on the wall, similar to the one at Xavier's Brockman Hall, the one where he bared his soul to Peggy twenty-five years before. This time he called Roberta and said simply, "She's at peace now. She won't have to suffer anymore."

He and Roberta talked about life, about Rich's life. He felt so irrelevant, that everything he'd done with his career—being drafted, coaching in the big leagues, becoming a Pittsburgh Pirate—was insignificant. He vowed never to get mad at his boys for petty things again, no more ripping up Bubba's term papers or badgering Tim for striking out or pulling out his belt to whip Mike. Maybe he'd be able to live up to that vow, maybe he wouldn't. Maybe he'd get back to church, maybe he wouldn't. But everything was different.

He went to help clean out Amy's hospital room, including the dresser drawers, and he found an envelope addressed to him, another one of Amy's patented letters. Feeling queasy, he opened it. There was a check for $400 inside—money she'd made from all those years working at Chuck E. Cheese's and so on. Her accompanying note was succinct.

Dear Dad,

You know that red wagon? It's the one the terminally ill kids get to ride. It's their big thrill of the day because they never get out of here to go home. They never get to go anyplace.

So, Dad, do me a favor. When I'm gone, take this check and buy each one of those kids a wagon. So they won't have to wait anymore. Because there's only one right now. I know you are the right person to ask. I know that you are a man who can get things done.

Love,

Amy

Rich broke down again, right then and there. That was his remarkable Amy in a nutshell—thinking of kids first, putting herself last . . . right down to the final days of her life. How many more of these letters would he find lying around?

He and Peggy decided they wanted to tell Cindy in person that Amy was gone. They owed her that much. So they piled into a car along with Peggy's mom and headed to Cindy's apartment. Along the way, Ruth began to eyeball Rich, not in a pleasant way. It was bad enough that

Rich had cheated on her daughter Peggy, but Ruth felt he had always neglected her granddaughter Amy to boot. So Ruth let Rich have it.

"Do you have any idea how much Amy loved you, what you meant to her?" Ruth said, seething.

Rich answered, "Yes." But he was being a phony. He had been blind when it came to Amy.

"I lied—I didn't know," he says. "I didn't see it. I didn't pick it up. I just didn't, and it's terrible that I didn't. Everybody has some regrets on what they could've changed in their life. And I just didn't see it. Everything was going too fast for me in my life to stop and see it. I didn't.

"Amy's life, it was like a blur. All those years, seventeen to eighteen years with Amy, a blur. Half the time I wasn't even there, and the other half I was an idiot. Like, wow . . . That was just a short drive from Dallas to Arlington, but it was also the longest drive of my life."

As they pulled up to Cindy's, they passed Moore Memorial Gardens, the cemetery they had chosen for Amy. By chance, Cindy's apartment overlooked the graveyard, which gave all of them some peace—Cindy would be able to keep an eye on her. Peggy knocked on Cindy's door, and at first there was no answer. She was sleeping. The previous night, Cindy had stayed late in the ICU with Amy until Peggy shooed her home at about 2 a.m. Now they were waking her up to say it was all over.

Cindy started weeping, and Peggy was hesitant to leave her alone in the apartment. They were about to pick up Tim at school, and Peggy pleaded with Cindy to go with them. But Cindy preferred to meet them later at the cul-de-sac. When they left, she says she got in the shower and had another godawful cry.

Tim had already been paged out of class that morning and was camped in the principal's office when his parents arrived. He was still a prepubescent, and he didn't know how he was supposed to feel or react. All he knew was that his sister, his second mom, his teacher—all wrapped up in one—wasn't going to be around anymore. On the car ride home, he just sat in the backseat mumbling "the chicken runs at midnight . . . the chicken runs at midnight . . . the chicken runs at midnight."

It took Rich three days to arrange the funeral, and his last bit of business was to choose a tombstone and epitaph. Cindy had temporarily moved into Amy's room, so she was there to help Rich and Peggy pick an inscription at the cemetery. She knew her friend would've rejected anything along the lines of *Our Beloved Amy*—"Oh, she would've shot us down with lightning bolts," Cindy says—so they settled simply on

Amy Elizabeth Donnelly
April 16, 1974—Jan. 28, 1993

Amid a winter downpour, the three of them drove away from the graveyard in a somber mood—until Rich suddenly slammed on the brakes, nearly hydroplaning his car. "I've got it! I've got the inscription!" he announced.

He told them what he was thinking, and they all laughed and high-fived. Rich then did a U-turn back to Moore Memorial Gardens, where a funeral adviser named Laura Bell was still finishing up their paperwork.

"We've changed our minds," Rich said. "We want something else on our daughter's headstone."

"What would you like?" she asked.

"We want the words, 'THE CHICKEN RUNS AT MIDNIGHT.'"

"That's kind of strange, isn't it?" she responded. "What does that mean?"

"It's what we want," Rich said. "It's what my daughter would want. That's Amy—she was different; she always wanted to be different. Either you put 'the chicken runs at midnight' or we're outta here."

Laura Bell acquiesced—no further questions asked—and Rich drove back convinced he'd done right by Amy. "All I know is that there we were in a funeral home, and it should've been super depressing," Cindy says. "But after that, we were laughing so hard. We were really giggling. We thought it was the greatest idea."

The funeral was held the next day in a local Catholic church. It had been a while since Rich had been in one. He arrived early to meet the

priest, and already sitting in a pew was none other than former Rangers
manager Bobby Valentine, who had fired Rich about eight years before.
Valentine had never met Amy, but a baseball man had lost his daughter,
and baseball men tend to have other baseball men's backs. Valentine
offered his condolences, and Rich began to realize the kind of sacred
day this would be.

Next to the casket was a family portrait of Amy and her three brothers. She was front and center in the blown-up photo—Queen Elizabeth
to the hilt. Rich told Bubba, Mike, and Tim not to leave Peggy's side all
day, and Roberta sat near Peggy as well. In walked the former Pirates
player John Cangelosi, the one who had been Amy's crush. Sid Bream
sent Rich a sympathy card. Amy's former soccer teammates from the
Twisters showed up. Even Jerome Donnelly, Rich's own abusive father,
was there to lend support. Not only that, but for the first time in Rich's
forty-seven years on earth, Jerome hugged him. Amy had made it
all happen.

Rich found himself kneeling in church that day, not quite a believer
again but willing to give it a momentary try. Rich asked the same questions he asked when Romey died young—*Why is this happening?*—but
ended up just as confused as ever.

He still didn't know what to make of what he considered another
cruel, confusing move by God. He still didn't know what to do with
death.

Letter to Amy

Amy,

I took your check, and I bought more red wagons.
The hospital has them. You should've seen the kids'
faces. Then again, maybe you did.

Amazing, huh?

Love you . . . the chicken
runs at midnight,

Dad

Nineteen

"Half of Me Is Gone"

A my was in the air, 24/7. Whether Rich was on his way to a game of racquetball or the grocery store, he would strike up a conversation with her. "People would see me going down the street, and I'd be talking to myself," Rich says. "But I'd really be talking to her."

It could be about anything. It could be about the red wagons or Barry Bonds signing with the Giants or Bubba's season at Robert Morris. It could be about Cindy having a boyfriend or about the 1993 Pirates or about the pickle juice he'd just spilled on his shirt.

"I'd go, 'Amy' or 'Ames'—I'd say, 'What about that one?'" Rich says. "She always loved it when I messed up. If I dropped slop all over myself or had peanut butter all over my face, she just loved it. So if I'd have a stain on my shirt, I'd say, 'How 'bout that one, Amy? Are you kiddin' me?'"

A few weeks after Amy died, her tombstone with its inscription still hadn't arrived. Cindy would keep checking the cemetery, and one night on her way back to her apartment, there it was. She called the Donnellys, and Tim begged her to pick him up. He couldn't wait until morning. So, in the pitch-black, Cindy and Tim were in the graveyard with a flashlight examining it. Just as they had requested, it read:

AMY ELIZABETH DONNELLY
April 16, 1974—Jan. 28, 1993
THE CHICKEN RUNS AT MIDNIGHT

It was so glorious, so perfect, that they went back the next day in broad daylight. They would read it, reread it, and reread it again. Cindy, whose apartment was just a hundred feet up an adjacent hill, made daily pilgrimages there herself, just to pull weeds or wipe the tombstone clean. Amy used to do that years before when she'd visit the gravesites of those random little girls. Thinking back, Peggy and Cindy couldn't help but believe that was a sign. Perhaps Amy sensed she would be one of those little girls herself.

It was a raw, introspective time for everyone. Just three weeks after Amy's passing, Rich was back in spring training for another Pirates season—although these weren't Amy's same Pirates. Not only had Barry Bonds departed via free agency, but Doug Drabek had bolted for the Astros and Chico Lind (along with his machetes) had been dealt to Kansas City. Mike LaValliere was released later, in April. Amy would've only had Andy Van Slyke's kids left to babysit.

The returning players made a beeline for Rich that spring to pat him on the back and offer their condolences. Jim Leyland and the other coaches—Rich's buddy Milt May in particular—kept their distance until Rich let them know he was ready to freely talk about it. In Rich's life, baseball men had often led him astray. But it was also all true about baseball men having each other's backs. "They were there for me," Rich says. "I didn't know what to do, didn't know how to act."

He was comforted most by a black address book he kept in his locker. Inside that book, folded neatly and preserved inside a protective flap, was the "chicken runs at midnight" message Amy had left him in Atlanta before Game 7. More than a memento or the family motto written down, the note was Rich's manifesto. "It never left my side," he says. "It was a constant reminder to straighten up. A constant reminder of her. Everything she did. But mostly a reminder to straighten up."

Now he knew what his mother meant when she said after Romey died, "When you lose a child, half of you is just gone." Half of Rich was gone now too. He had many sleepless nights those first few months— blaming himself for Amy's death, having one-way conversations with

God. He would've had to be a full-time believer to have a two-way conversation, but he wasn't there yet, wasn't sure he'd ever get there. He'd say to God, "This is self-inflicted, isn't it? This is what I get for acting like I did, isn't it? You were trying to get my attention and it wasn't working—so you punished me. You punished me with something that would grab me."

He spent the 1993 baseball season with remorse on his mind. Forget the Pirates win-loss record; that wasn't going to be pretty. What mattered more to Rich was whether he could change his priorities. How he could've chosen a Caribbean cruise over Amy was mind-numbing. But he'd done that. How he could've been in denial over Amy's "9 months to live" prognosis was mind-boggling. But he'd done that, as well.

Rich looked in the mirror every day from then on out . . . and saw Amy. They had the same facial expressions, at times the same temper. As a kid, he had punched out his doctor for wanting to give him a shot, and, as a kid, Amy had kicked her ballet teacher in the shins. They were twins. He was her. But Amy had changed during her eleven-month battle. She'd calmed herself down, smiled from ear to ear, trusted God and put herself last. Could he?

The first tests came in that 1993 season. The team was in Montreal one night, and a team employee—who will remain nameless—told Rich he had met two "hot" girls and asked Rich whether he wanted to be part of a double-date. "In my old days, I would've said, 'Sure, yeah, let's go, send her up,'" Rich says. "But I said, 'There ain't no way.' I went back to my room, ordered a pizza and watched the horse races."

Rich was so thrilled with himself that he kept it going. Jim Leyland loved to frequent karaoke bars; the manager would sing an Irish tune and then harmlessly toss back a beer or two. "He'd say, 'Come on, go with me,'" Rich says. "And I wouldn't go. He'd get mad at me. 'Come on!' he'd say. But I knew what was going to happen; we'd be out till four in the morning. And I didn't want to do that. You go out till four in the morning, and you'll start drinking. Something'll happen . . . I'm proud that I ignored it."

Rich tried his best to lose himself in the note he carried around from Amy—and in the season. The latter was difficult because 1993 was an ugly year. The team spent exactly one day in first place, April 9, and they were in a tailspin from there on out. Even the masterful Leyland couldn't make up for the squad's lack of pitching. At times, Rich got pretty lonely over at third base. But whenever there was a runner on second and he'd start crouching and cupping his hands, Amy would enter his consciousness.

That became the best part of Rich's season and ensuing seasons—seeing a runner in scoring position. It was cathartic on two levels: one, because it meant the Pirates were preparing to score, and, two, it got him reminiscing about Amy. The more she entered his mind, the better. Rich remembers bumping into Bonds that year in San Francisco and Barry telling him how sorry he was about Amy's death, that if he ever needed anything to let him know. Rich knew right then and there why Amy fell for Bondsy; he wasn't the heartless, selfish teammate everyone made him out to be.

The worst part of the 1993 season was the World Series being a pipe dream again. After three consecutive playoff years, the Pirates finished in fifth place at 75–87. The organization was in a rebuild and, with their low budget, certainly wouldn't pursue free agents. Rich's dream of a Fall Classic no longer seemed realistic, and he knew it. It depressed him. He also knew Leyland wouldn't tolerate fifth place. If the team's outlook didn't improve, there was no telling whether Leyland would want to stay a Pirate.

Down in Texas, Peggy and Cindy weren't only reminiscing about Amy; they felt her presence. About six months after she died, the two of them finally found the mental fortitude to sort through Amy's bedroom. As Cindy was thumbing through a magazine on Amy's desk, a Post-it note fell out. It had Amy's handwriting on it, as well as a drawing. Cindy peered closer. It read, "the chicken runs at midnight"—right next to a smiley face. "It was like she was saying, 'I'm okay, I'm here,'" Cindy says.

In response, Cindy decided to write letters back to Amy—although she stopped short of mailing them to God. "They were mostly negative, like 'This sucks' and 'I wish you were here' kind of thing," Cindy says. "They were more about Timmy, like, you know, 'He's a good kid and I still make him kiss me on the cheek in front of his friends.' You know, just silly things, like an 'I'm watching out for him' kind of thing."

The point is, everybody was still in an interactive relationship with Amy. Bubba and Mike found old letters she'd written them, letters that were signed C.R.A.M. Tim wrote Amy's initials on the brim of his baseball cap. Cindy drove the red Miata. But Peggy's discovery on Mother's Day 1994 topped them all.

Peggy had been in the process of renovating her kitchen and around that time, she asked workers to move some boxes temporarily into the garage—Amy's old classroom. On that Mother's Day, Peggy went out there to get ice from the ice maker and noticed something otherworldly—one of Amy's old pink ballet slippers on top of a box. She nearly fell over.

"Just one slipper, and we didn't know where it came from," Peggy says. "I knew it right then—she was definitely watching me. There's no question. I'd never had the sense of the presence of someone like I did with her."

Other times, when Peggy was feeling depressed and would be curled up on the couch, she'd hear Amy's voice saying, "Lying there isn't going to do any good, Mom. Get up and go. Enough of this crap." It was so Amy, and so true. Peggy told people that Amy was the woman Peggy always wanted to be. All of them were still learning from her, whether it was Peggy, the boys, Cindy, or Rich.

As 1993 morphed into 1994, Rich still was resisting the temptations of baseball, the temptations of the road. But he was also still having unfulfilled chats with God. His visits to church were random, and, heaven forbid, he wasn't about to go pray during the baseball season. He still saw that as being taboo.

But on the eve of the '94 season in San Francisco, Jim Leyland called Rich out of the blue on a Sunday morning. It was Easter, and Leyland wanted someone to go with him to church. Rich knew that Leyland was Catholic—that he was a Notre Dame fanatic as well—but the manager had never invited Rich to Mass before. It all struck Rich as odd. He thought baseball men didn't pray around other baseball men. He had thought this ever since his Billy Martin days.

Leyland, though, emphatically told Rich, "We're going to church—it's Easter." They hailed a cab, and although they caught only the last part of the Easter service, it was a breakthrough of sorts for Rich. He and Leyland had kneeled and prayed together—and he'd managed to keep his job.

"I felt like, 'Hey, it's okay now,'" Rich says. "It's okay to go to church. It's okay to be a man about your faith. That was a key moment for me, to where I could say, 'Hey, no one's going to make fun of me anymore. I don't care. I'm going to go to church.' If Jim Leyland can go to church—he's my boss—I can go to church, and it's okay if one of my players is there. Grow up. Be a man. If you want to go to church, you don't have to yell down in the lobby that you're going to church. But when someone asks where you're going, tell 'em that's where you're going."

The Pirates kept losing in both '94 and '95, but in terms of personal growth, Rich felt he was on the verge of winning. One of his racquetball friends, Ron Meyer, was a talk-show host on the Global Catholic Radio Network. He invited Rich to tell his listeners about Amy. Rich shared how Amy had been happier and more spiritual in her final eleven months than in her previous seventeen years. He explained how the phrase "the chicken runs at midnight" was a mystery, that Amy had just randomly blurted it out, that no one in his family knew what it meant. But he said he chose it as her epitaph because it was the essence of Amy's spirit, an amusing reminder of her strength and courage. The feedback from the interview was all positive.

Before long, Rich received an invitation to speak at a men's conference at Seton Hall University. Apparently, someone had heard the Meyer interview and wanted more. In front of thousands of people, he told the story of his uneven faith. How he'd once been the "greatest

Catholic of all of them." How he had been the kind of kid who would hold Mass in his basement by himself with a piece of Italian bread. How he bet his childhood friend Emory Knowles that he'd never curse in his life—a wager he undoubtedly lost. How baseball had gotten him off course. How he'd lost his faith. How he'd thought he was "too good" for church. How infidelity had cost him his family. How it was sad that the "only thing that got my attention was the death of my daughter." How he was perhaps back to being himself because of Amy. How the phrase "the chicken runs at midnight" would always move him.

Soon, with the help of an organization called Catholic Athletes for Christ, he was speaking everywhere from Detroit to Seattle to Chicago to New York to Houston. In fact, the Houston speech was witnessed by a Catholic cardinal who called Rich later to offer congratulations. The cardinal told Rich that a janitor at the church who was an atheist had heard Rich's talk and asked to be baptized. "I'm thinking, *Okay, I can pay back*," Rich says. "I cannot take back what I've done, but I can go forward and help. And that gave me a sense of satisfaction that all this happened for that purpose."

He was helping others, but he also needed to help himself. He would speak of his renewed faith, but he still privately felt he had one foot in the door of the church and one foot out. For instance, when he checked into hotels on the road, he immediately asked the concierge to point him in the direction of the nearest Catholic place of worship. But sometimes he would go there, and sometimes he wouldn't.

"Well, I was struggling, because the bad part of my life was actually fun," Rich says. "I guess the best way I can describe it is, you can't be a part-time Christian. I was part-time. I was working part-time. I was half-assed. It was a convenient faith, I call it. I did it if it was convenient. If it wasn't convenient, I didn't do it. I wasn't all-in. I was like, 'Uh, I had a lot of fun doing it the other way. Boy, I don't know.'"

He had certainly evolved. When Jerome died on July 17, 1995, Rich didn't dance on his father's grave; he wept. He and Jerome had reconciled to a degree after Amy's death, and Jerome's funeral was another dark day, another visit to a cemetery that conjured up memories of both Romey and Amy. His empathy toward Jerome confirmed what Rich thought—that he had turned a corner spiritually. But there was still an anger inside of him, an impatience, a feeling he still wasn't what he aspired to be.

"I was pretty sure I was doing the right thing, but I wasn't really sure," Rich says. "See, I left that window open. Like if I got tempted real good, maybe I would do something bad. In other words, if a beautiful girl had come up to me, I might have given in and gone with her."

As a matter of fact, that exact scenario played out. Lucy, the hygienist/waitress Rich had fled years before, contacted him and was looking for a reunion. Rich steered clear. He was facing tests everywhere he looked.

Then in the midst of this internal struggle—trying to make sense of the connection between God, Amy's death, and himself—Rich's dream died. Jim Leyland removed him from third base.

Gene Lamont, Leyland's original third base coach with the Pirates, had been fired by the White Sox and was available for hire heading into the 1996 season. It's not that Leyland was unhappy with Rich's performance at third; at least that's not how he explained it to Rich. Leyland just considered Lamont the premier third base coach in the game and couldn't pass him up. So Leyland made Rich his bench coach for 1996.

"I didn't talk to Jim for three days," Rich says. "He knew I was avoiding him, and he sent a message to Milt May that I either straighten up or I'd be gone. Because I was pissed off."

Rich's self-esteem and professional identity were wrapped up in coaching third base. There would never have been a "chicken runs at midnight" if he had been a bench coach. The job was a natural high, and its key benefit at that point was that it reminded him of his daughter. Without that job, there'd be no possibility of waving in the winning run of a World Series Game 7, no more crouching and cupping his hands . . . crouching and cupping his hands. No more reminders of Amy on the baseball field.

It was like another death.

Letter to Amy

Amy,

    I'm sorry. I can't yell 'the chicken runs at midnight' to the runners at second base anymore.

    It's just a fact of life.

Love you, C.R.A.M.

Dad

Twenty

Chicken Man

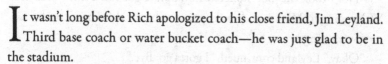

It wasn't long before Rich apologized to his close friend, Jim Leyland. Third base coach or water bucket coach—he was just glad to be in the stadium.

It was simply the end of Rich's most cherished coaching stint, and it took him a few days to adjust his mindset. Once he did, Rich assured Leyland he'd always have his back. "One thing that Rich has always been is loyal," Leyland says. "I never worried about him wanting my job or anything like that. He was so supportive."

But fairly soon, even Leyland didn't want his own job. The Pirates had become a hot mess, finishing in last place three of the first four years after Bonds left—including an eighty-nine-loss season in 1996. Worse yet, the team's new owner Kevin McClatchy was hemorrhaging money. There was faint chatter that the ball club could move out of Pittsburgh. Leyland was under contract, but appeared to be looking for an escape.

The franchise that had long coveted Jim Leyland most was the Florida Marlins. Leyland had previously played golf with Marlins owner Wayne Huizinga and gone out of his way to publicly praise Huizinga's morality. Normally, a manager wouldn't comment on another team's owner, so something seemed fishy—pardon the pun.

But Leyland's real connection in Florida was with the Marlins general manager Dave Dombrowski, who had been an executive with the White Sox in the 1980s when Leyland was their third base coach. Dombrowski had promised to build a win-now veteran club via free agency—zeroing in on Bobby Bonilla and Moisés Alou, to name two—which was just the way Leyland liked it. After the rebuild in Pittsburgh, Leyland was done with low-budget rookies. Florida was an obvious match.

Just a few days following the 1996 season, Rich was in his Steubenville basement, sitting in his easy chair. The phone rang. It was Leyland.

"You packed yet?" Leyland asked.

"Packed? Packed where? What are you talking about?"

"We're going to Florida."

"When?" Rich asked. "I can't go to Florida. I've got plans this week."

"No! I took the job," hollered Leyland. "I got you a three-year deal. We're going to Miami, and you're going to be my third base coach."

(Screaming.)

"Okay," Leyland continued, "I gotta go. Bye."

(More screaming.)

Still hyperventilating a minute later, Rich put two and two together. Gene Lamont had just been named Leyland's replacement in Pittsburgh, which opened up the Marlins' third base coaching spot. Rich immediately told Roberta—who had come rushing in thinking Rich won the lottery—to sell the house, that they were moving to Florida, that he was back in the third base coaching business. In a lot of ways, they *had* won the lottery.

On their flight down to the Sunshine State, Rich prayed they'd find a house near a church. He knew it needed to be "convenient," that if it weren't, he'd never attend. A few weeks later, Roberta told Rich to meet her at a prospective home she liked. As he pulled into the driveway, he saw a steeple two blocks away—within walking distance. Better yet, it was a Catholic church. They bought the house; there would be no excuses now.

When the season started, Rich was encouraged by the Marlins roster. He saw familiar faces, such as Bobby Bonilla and John Cangelosi. He saw superstar faces, such as pitcher Kevin Brown, Gary Sheffield, and Moisés Alou. He saw peach-fuzzed faces, such as shortstop Edgar

Renteria, twenty; first baseman Jeff Conine, twenty-one; and second baseman Luis Castillo, twenty-one. It was up to the fifty-two-year-old Leyland to meld them.

The first time Rich stepped back into the third base box, he thought of Amy and C.R.A.M. He felt as if he was in his rightful place, with a team that had World Series aspirations. The only issue was that their old nemesis, the Atlanta Braves, was in the same division, the NL East. In other words, the road to the World Series would likely go through Atlanta. For motivation and to get his spine tingling, Rich would often pull out the message Amy left him in Atlanta in 1992, the "While You Were Out" note. It was still pressed neatly inside his black address book. Georgia and Amy were always on his mind.

On the first day of summer, June 20, the Marlins were twenty games over .500 and only two and a half games behind Atlanta. If nothing else, they were in position to reach the playoffs as a wild card team. There was no shame in that. As usual, Tim—now a high school junior—was watching the standings from a distance, back at the cul-de-sac in Texas. He asked his dad if he could fly to Florida for the summer, and Rich said yes. Mike, who was a placekicker at University of the Cumberlands in Kentucky, would occasionally be visiting as well.

The two boys were older now and seasoned in the ways of a baseball clubhouse. Rather than exclusively serving as batboys, they were assistant clubhouse attendants who would run errands for players. They'd hustle out to Alou's BMW for a pair of shoes he'd left behind or fetch a pizza for Bonilla. Cangelosi was their pal from the old days who used to hit them ground balls—and still volunteered to do so for Tim. "All the players knew who they were," Rich says. "They were part of the Marlins family the same as they were in Pittsburgh."

By mid-July, the Braves had incrementally extended their division lead to six games, and Leyland was tiring of some of his team's mental mistakes, particularly at second base. The starter there, Castillo, had made a team-high nine errors in half a season, and, as talented as the kid was, he seemed in over his head. Leyland wanted a dependable veteran at second—this was no time for a youth movement. As the trade deadline approached, he and Dombrowski discussed their needs, and number one was second base.

According to Rich, Leyland was holding court with the coaches one day and moaned, "I just wanna go find a second baseman who can catch the ball, throw it to first, and not make mistakes." Bruce Kimm, who had been on Leyland's staff in Pittsburgh, brought up the name of an obscure Colorado Rockies minor leaguer he'd seen in a fall league—which wasn't exactly what Leyland had in mind.

"I've seen this kid who's now at Triple-A Colorado Springs," Kimm said. "Jim, you'll love him 'cause he's from your favorite school, Notre Dame."

"Notre Dame, really? What's his name?"

"Johnny Counsell, I think," Kimm said. "I don't know. Craig Counsell, maybe."

"What position?" Leyland asked.

"Left-handed hitting second baseman," Kimm answered.

"Well," groaned Leyland, "if he's so good, how come he ain't in the big leagues?"

The answer, which neither Leyland nor Kimm knew at the time, was fate and injuries. Craig Counsell had been an eleventh-round draft pick out of Notre Dame in 1992 after batting .339 with twelve homers as a Fighting Irish senior. But he was skinny, had no meat on his bones, and broke his ankle and then his foot by simply fouling balls off on himself. When healthy in 1995—which is when Kimm saw him—the Rockies thought enough of Counsell to give him a three-game audition in the big leagues. He went 0-for-3. He then broke his leg on another foul ball in 1996, missing nearly the entire season. He seemed destined to be a Triple-A lifer.

But in the first half of the 1997 Triple-A season, at age twenty-six, Counsell was batting .335 with about a fifty-game errorless streak at second base. Word had gotten around. All Kimm told Leyland was that the Rockies big league second baseman Eric Young was blocking Counsell's path to the majors—and that maybe he should mention Counsell's name to Dombrowski.

Dombrowski put one of his scouts on the case, Dick Egan, and a couple of days later, Rich remembers hearing Egan's scouting report on Counsell: slight build, not overly fast, fundamentally sound, mature, a winner, pretty solid, not elite. The "fundamentally sound," "mature" and 'a winner" comments resonated with Dombrowski, who says Counsell became their main second base priority. With all the Marlins weapons, they just wanted reliability—someone to be a role player. "We didn't need another all-star," Dombrowski says. So, on July 27, 1997, when the Rockies asked for just journeyman pitcher Mark Hutton in return, Counsell became a Marlin.

It was an unorthodox trade. Usually at the trade deadline, contending teams use minor leaguers to acquire veterans, but this was the polar opposite—Florida had traded a veteran for a no-name. Leyland thought he was done with low-budget rookies. Rich remembers Leyland telling Kimm, "If this guy can't play, you're fired."

Counsell walked into the Florida clubhouse on July 28, looking all of eighteen years old. Tim and Mike thought he might be the newest clubhouse attendant, certainly not a prized second baseman. Leyland, who can come across gruff at first sight, waved Counsell over to his office and said, "Tell me about yourself." Counsell, unable to tell a lie, was blunt.

"It's not always going to look pretty," Counsell said, "but I'll get the job done for you."

A wary Leyland told Counsell to meet him at the batting cage. On his way there, Leyland—unimpressed with Counsell's physique—stuck his head in the coach's room and grumbled, "I ain't gonna put him in the lineup today. This guy might just be a utility guy. But let's check him out."

The cage only exacerbated matters. Counsell's batting stance was an anomaly. With his front foot planted open, he would hold the bat completely vertical, his back elbow up even with his eyebrows. As he awaited the pitch, he'd flap his arms as if he was about to take off in flight. It was Counsell's timing mechanism, his overexaggerated strategy of staying on top of the baseball. But Leyland's eyes bugged out. Now he knew what Counsell meant when he mentioned it wouldn't look pretty. "What the heck is this?" Rich remembers Leyland asking.

The results weren't any spicier. Counsell swung at ten pitches and, according to Rich, popped up eight or nine of them. "We traded for this guy?" Leyland ranted.

The manager then asked Rich to hit Counsell some ground balls at second. "Move him around a little bit," Leyland requested. So Rich hammered grounders ten feet to Counsell's left and then ten feet to Counsell's right. The kid was late to most of them. "What the heck did we do?" Rich remembers Leyland griping. "This kid can't play a lick. I wouldn't sign this guy out of a tryout camp."

Leyland glared over at Kimm, who drawled, "He'll be all right." But Leyland wouldn't let Counsell sniff the field that night, using the veteran Kurt Abbott instead. The next day, Counsell showed up early for extra hitting. Leyland moseyed on over to watch and again witnessed Counsell mostly hit pop-ups or ground balls.

"So after two rounds," Counsell remembers, "Leyland says to me, 'Hey, don't ever come out here again. If I have to watch you hit, you're never going to play.'"

But just to spite Kimm and everyone else, Leyland wrote Counsell into the lineup that night. "You wanted him, you got him. He's starting today," Leyland told Kimm.

"Well, you don't have to start him," Kimm answered.

"Well, he's startin'," Leyland snapped. "But I'm battin' him eighth. I don't want to see too much of him, so I'm battin' him down at the end."

Counsell trotted out there and did what he'd always done at every level—he competed. He had his first major league hit and turned a double play into a Marlins victory over the Reds. Two games later, Leyland reinserted him against the rival Braves to see if it was a fluke. But Counsell had another hit and turned a key ninth inning double play to seal a 1–0 victory.

"I told ya," Kimm gloated to Leyland. "I told ya he can play."

"We'll see how good he is," Leyland shot back. "We get Maddux tomorrow."

Twenty-four hours later, Leyland started him against the future Hall of Famer Greg Maddux. Counsell flailed at Maddux's pitches and went 0-for-2 with an error. Leyland scolded Kimm again. The manager was going to give the kid one more shot in the series finale against the Braves on August 3. All Counsell did was go 1-for-3 again in an 8–4 victory. "Jim started scratchin' his head," Rich says.

The whole clubhouse was picking up on Counsell's vibe. The team won eight of its first nine games after the trade—and the one they lost was on Counsell's day off. Nothing fazed the kid. He wasn't intimidated by the Sheffields, the Browns, and the Bonillas. He acted like he'd been there before. And in a poignant sort of way, he had been.

He was the son of former Twins minor leaguer John Counsell, who had gone on to work as video coordinator and community relations director for Craig's hometown Milwaukee Brewers. John would bring his young son to the clubhouse, where Craig learned how to blend in, how to be seen and not heard. "He was a classic one-word, two-word, three-word answer guy," John says of Craig, "but huge at soaking up information."

Craig was in the clubhouse during the 1982 Brewers World Series run and studied how the players conducted themselves. He tagged along on community service appearances, where he'd get to spend quality time at the houses of the Brewers' two star players, Paul Molitor and Robin Yount.

"So we're coming home from an event one day, and we drop a player off," John Counsell remembers. "Craig's twelve years old. I said, 'I've never asked you who your favorite players are.' He goes, 'You'll be mad at me.' I say, 'What do you mean I'll be mad at you?' He said, 'My favorite are Paul and Robin, and you probably think I like 'em because they're the most popular players." I said, 'Well, why do you like 'em?' And Craig goes, 'Because they're the same at home as they are at the ballpark.'"

That self-awareness side of Counsell is why he became one of Leyland's favorite players. And it's also why he caught the eyes of young Tim and Mike Donnelly—because he would've fit in with them at the cul-de-sac. Counsell looked about their age and was about as bony as they were as well. They figured if he could make it to the big leagues, so could they. "It gave me hope," Tim says. "I said, 'Man, I've got a shot to get to the majors.'" But most of all, Counsell was the nicest, sincerest, most unassuming player they'd come across . . . since Sid Bream.

In fact, the day the boys knew Counsell was special was the day he showed up at the Marlins stadium driving a black faded, dinged-up 1991 Nissan Altima—a four-door family car. It belonged to his sister, Jennifer, who was living abroad in Australia temporarily. The first time Counsell tried pulling it into the team parking lot—amid all of the BMW, Mercedes, and Lamborghini luxury cars—he was denied entry.

"Where're you goin'?" said the parking lot's security guard.

"I'm a player," Counsell said.

"Yeah, you wish," said the guard.

For ten minutes, Counsell tried arguing his way in—although arguing wasn't his forte. Eventually, a clubhouse attendant came out to rescue him, and from then on, Tim and Mike were sold on Counsell. He was everyman; he was Bream. Then when he let them hang out at his locker, when he hit them fly balls and ground balls before home games, Counsell became their No. 1.

"I might have talked to his boys more than I talked to Rich," Counsell says. "They were just good kids hanging out with their dad like I had hung out with my dad. They were baseball kids. I felt I'd lived a similar life for sure. So I think I respected that—that they were just there because they wanted to share time with their dad more than anything."

Tim and Mike admired how "normal" Counsell was, how unpretentious. Counsell earned a minimum rookie salary and stayed at a local AmeriSuites motel for $40 a night. Tim particularly considered him his role model. One day, Counsell—who liked the way Tim fielded a baseball—asked him if he wanted to play for Notre Dame someday. Tim answered, 'Heck, yeah." If he could've, Tim would've followed Counsell around all day—particularly to the batting cage.

There was something fascinating about the way Counsell hit a baseball. The upright stance, the flapping of his forearms and elbows, the toothpick legs. Tim couldn't put his finger on it at first, but Counsell reminded him of something.

Then one afternoon, Counsell needed someone to throw him batting practice. So Tim went to find Rich.

"Dad, the Chicken wants to take some batting practice," Tim said.

"Who?"

"The Chicken—Craig Counsell," Tim said.

At that point, Tim explained that Counsell had the body of a chicken, the biceps of a chicken, the gait of a chicken, and the batting stance of a chicken. But the flapping of his arms was the clincher. The boys wouldn't dare say it around Counsell—"We weren't going to go up to him and say, 'What's up, Chicken?'" Tim says—but they clearly meant it as a term of endearment. To Tim and Mike, Counsell was the "Chicken Man" or "the Chicken," forever after.

"We were on the turnpike driving home one night in Florida," Rich says. "They're in the backseat, and I'm talking to the boys the way I used to talk to Amy. I said, 'Guys, who's your favorite player?' And they go, 'The Chicken—we love the Chicken.'"

Rich was amused by it all, but his mind was basically elsewhere. He was still semi-tortured inside, still beating himself up over his role in Amy's death. Perhaps he always would. He felt God had punished him for his infidelities and his deficiencies as a parent. "God has a way of sending you a message," Rich says. "You think you get away with something, think you're free and clear—but you're not. If you hurt people, you're going to be hurt back. I felt guilty. I felt like Amy's death was my punishment." Coaching third base was a convenient three-hour escape every day—his respite—but he knew he needed to get to church more, to make peace with himself and with God once and for all.

On a road trip at the end of August, he set his alarm early to attend a Sunday Mass. It was 6:30 a.m., and the hotel lobby was deserted as he began his three-block walk to the church—not a player or fellow coach in sight. He settled into a pew and suddenly recognized the person seated directly in front of him. It was Craig Counsell.

When Counsell saw Rich, they nodded at each other and smiled. After the service, they walked back to the hotel together, never once discussing their faith or Counsell's secret nickname, the Chicken. The truth was, Counsell was somewhat like Rich—he wasn't constantly in church, but found himself drawn there at times. Counsell considered himself "a little more than an Easter-Christmas Catholic, but not much." Like most young boys, he had struggled with the meaning of religion and was in church that Sunday to continue his education.

"I probably questioned it more than I believed in it, to tell you the truth," Counsell says. "As a kid, I remember asking a priest, 'I don't understand this Father-Son-Holy Ghost thing. Explain it to me. I don't understand the Holy Ghost. You've got to explain it to me.' I never got a good answer. It was about faith, that's for sure."

Rich was twenty-four years older than Counsell, old enough to be his father, but their conversation on the way back to the hotel was easy, free-flowing. They connected. Counsell began talking about that day's game and asked Rich what he knew about the opposing pitcher. Rich was impressed by the kid's attention to detail. At the time, Counsell was batting a whopping .352. Had he played a full season, he would've been a leading candidate for Rookie of the Year. Rich patted him on the back as they parted ways and remembers thinking, *What a wonderful kid this guy is! Now I know why my kids are attracted to him.* He also found it intriguing that of all the Marlins on the trip—staff, trainers, coaches, players—only two had made it to Mass that morning:

Him and the Chicken.

Letter to Amy

Amy,

I wish you were here to see this.
I'd have a ticket for you in the front row.
C.R.A.M.

Love,

Dad

Twenty-One

World Series

Once September rolled around, the Marlins seemed a virtual lock for the National League wild card spot. The playoffs were nearing, and it was time for Jim Leyland to use his genius. Having played an entire summer in the oppressive Florida heat, Leyland's first move was to shift batting practice inside at least five days a week—to preserve the players' endurance and energy. It was World Series or bust.

On the day they clinched the wild card in Montreal, Leyland waved the whole team over for a chat. "I want only one thing from you guys," the manager droned. "Win the number of games that's on my back." Leyland turned around to expose his uniform number and then walked away.

"Jim wore No. 11," Rich says. "And eleven was the exact number of games you had to win to win it all. The players erupted."

The team opened the first round in San Francisco against who else but Barry Bonds and the Giants. Tim badly wanted to go on the trip, and Rich—knowing how precious playoff games were—let him miss a couple days of school to fly out. Too old to be a batboy, Tim sat on the bench in his No. 45 Donnelly uniform. He didn't dare talk to his father, who was crouching and cupping his hands at third base, crouching and cupping his hands. But after the Marlins took Games 1 and 2 on the road, Tim and his dad embraced. Rich told him he was sorry he couldn't come back to Florida for Game 3.

Just as Rich was mentioning this, the Marlins owner Wayne Huizinga happened to be striding by and overheard. "Where are you going?" Huizinga said to Tim. "Back to Texas? No way. You're good luck. You're getting on our plane back to Miami."

Rich called Peggy for approval, and she gave Tim the green light. He was the only kid or family member to fly on the team charter, and he predictably found a seat near Craig Counsell. Tim was on the bench again for Game 3 when the Marlins clinched the best-of-five series in Florida—Counsell blasting a key RBI double. Their next opponent, as if it had been ordained, was the Atlanta Braves.

Just entering Atlanta–Fulton County Stadium for the NLCS gave Rich and Tim an eerie sensation. It was the site of Sid Bream's slide, although Bream was long gone by now, having retired in 1994. Somehow that was a relief—one less old nemesis to worry about.

Just the sight of Braves pitchers Greg Maddux, John Smoltz, and Tom Glavine was unnerving enough. But the Marlins had fared well against Atlanta during the regular season, winning eight of twelve. And it turned out that Florida had arguably better pitching. Kevin Brown won Game 1, and Livan Hernández won Game 3. Counsell was on fire, leading the team with a .429 batting average. After Hernández won Game 5, Brown sent the Marlins to the World Series by winning Game 6 on Atlanta's turf.

At the final out, Rich remembers gasping, and later, the sting of cheap champagne in his eyes. He had never in his life laughed for an hour straight, but that's how he celebrated the World Series berth, the dream of his lifetime. Eventually, Milt May, the team's batting coach who'd been on those old Pirates staffs with him, came hopping over. May's wife, Brenda, had been close with Amy, but Milt had not once brought up her death these entire four years. He had decided he would give Rich his space. But on this night, in Sid Bream's old stadium, May put his arm around Rich and whispered, "I know how much this means to you and Amy."

Rich broke down. Amy hadn't lived to see her dad in a World Series, and he'd thought he wouldn't live to see it either. His whole life flashed before his eyes—the stickball games in the alleys of Steubenville, the Jell-O-powder slides in his kitchen, the workouts with Romey, the burned-down stadium of Greenville, the war of words with Ted Williams. And, of course, Amy . . . Queen Elizabeth.

"I just thought to myself, *Amy, we're goin'. We're actually goin' to the World Series*," Rich says. Meantime, Tim—wearing his own Donnelly uniform—had identical thoughts. As he embraced Rich, he told him, "Dad, Amy would've loved this. She's looking down on us right now. I know it. I know it."

By this time, Tim hadn't been to school for about two weeks, and no chance he was missing the World Series—not over Wayne Huizinga's dead body. The Marlins were about to take on the American League Champion Cleveland Indians, who were even more loaded offensively than the Braves. They had Manny Ramirez, Jim Thome, Sandy Alomar Jr., Matt Williams, and another former Atlanta nemesis, David Justice. On paper, they were probably the more lethal team.

The series was a yo-yo. The Marlins would win a game; the Indians would win a game—rinse and repeat. Leyland refused to let his team panic or give in. After the Indians routed the Marlins in Game 4, 10–3, to even the series at 2–2, Leyland told his players, "Muhammad Ali was the greatest of all time, but he didn't win every round." The team let out a collective whoop. They were in this for the long haul.

Rich was experiencing every emotion under the sun, or lights. The Indians manager, Mike Hargrove, was one of his dearest friends, having played for Rich in the minor leagues. Grover, as he was known, was even godfather to Rich's son, Mike, and also his namesake. But now Rich and Grover had to act like mortal enemies.

Rich suddenly knew why they called it the "World Series"—because the whole world was tuned in. After one of the games, Tiger Woods asked him for his autograph. Gloria Estefan was singing the national anthem. Exactly twenty-three family members and friends were staying at his house, some sleeping on couch cushions. Rich even flew Tim's high school principal down for part of the series as a thank-you for letting Tim miss twenty-eight days of school.

Rich had been daydreaming about a World Series since he was five, so he took time to smell the roses, or the infield grass. Whenever the Marlins took the field, he'd look around and think, *Two backup catchers from Ohio (him and Jim Leyland), a pitcher from Cuba (Livan Hernández), a shortstop from Columbia (Edgar Renteria), a second baseman from Notre Dame (Craig Counsell), and a reliever from the Dominican Republic (Félix Heredia). Ain't baseball great?*

But it all had to end sometime, and when the Indians forced a seventh, winner-take-all game in Florida, it wasn't entertainment anymore; it was irregular heartbeats. In the Marlins clubhouse before the game, Leyland's pep talk was, "Boys, I've run out of things to say, but I do know one thing—when you come back through those doors, you'll be World Champions." They were all on the verge of a breakdown.

Rich had tried to calm himself by going to the racetrack on the day of the game with Yankees coach Don Zimmer. It was the Steubenville in him—nothing like a bet to take your mind off things. Zimmer asked him who the Marlins' starting pitcher was going to be, and Rich said, "Al Leiter." "Ooooooooooh," Zimmer said.

Leiter pitched well enough to not be the "goat." He struck out seven, and through six innings, allowed only two runs. It wasn't his fault the Marlins had zero. The Marlins had only nine outs left, and, back in their clubhouse, Tim was pacing, shaking like a leaf. He had been gracious enough to give up his uniform and his seat in the dugout to his brother Mike, who because of football hadn't been able to attend the previous six games. But it was lonely in the locker room—just him and the clubhouse attendant—and Tim kept fidgeting, sighing. He'd been a Marlins good-luck charm. He thought that if only he could go to the field, maybe in some inexplicable way his presence would kick-start a rally.

The clubhouse attendant, Mike Wallace, noticed Tim's desperation and said, "Go put a jersey on and get your ass out there." Only batboy uniforms were available—all of them with the No. 97 on them—and Tim was dressed in a matter of seconds. There were two entrances to the first base dugout, one near the bat rack where Leyland sat sucking down cigarettes and one near the camera well, closer to the right field bullpen. Tim, trying to be discreet, snuck in by the cameras, as far away from Leyland as possible. He then settled in, hoping for fireworks.

Right away, Bonilla blasted a leadoff home run in the seventh inning, slicing the Indians' lead to 2–1. Tim felt like a rabbit's foot. The energy in the dugout was escalating, and he crept up the dugout steps to gain a better vantage point. He gazed over at the bullpen to watch relievers Dennis Cook and Antonio Alfonseca warm up, and their pitches seemed to all be electric. The pop of the catchers' gloves sounded like gunshots. Pure adrenaline can do that.

Entering the bottom of the ninth inning, the Marlins still trailed, 2–1. They only had three outs to live. Moisés Alou led off with a single against Indians closer José Mesa, and after Bonilla struck out on an elevated 3-and-2 pitch, up came catcher Charles Johnson. C. J., as he was known, was a .250 hitter who generally pulled the ball to left field. But he guessed right on Mesa's 1–2 fastball—when normally he'd have gotten something off-speed—and drilled a base hit to right. Hargrove had been the one to call for that fastball and immediately assumed Rich had stolen his sign. He and the entire Indians bench started chirping and cussing at Rich.

Alou had advanced to third on Johnson's hit, which brought up Craig Counsell with one out. His only mission was to get the tying run in, although a ground ball could be disastrous. "I remember going up there saying, literally, 'We could lose here if I hit into a double play,'" Counsell says. "And José Mesa had a real good sinker. But I also said, 'I'm hitting in the bottom of the ninth in the seventh game of the World Series. I'm swinging the bat. I'm not taking pitches.'"

In the dugout, Tim was inching further up the steps. But in the stands, Counsell's father, John, took a superstitious walk from his seat over the third base dugout toward the right field foul pole. He was convinced his son always hit better when he hid behind that pole. So that's where he stood for the at-bat, one eye open and one eye closed.

The Cleveland outfield was supposed to be shaded toward left field because the left-handed Counsell rarely pulled fly balls deep to right and because Hargrove wanted to pitch Counsell away. But two inexplicable things happened to the Indians—one fortuitous and one not so much. The first anomaly was that Indians right fielder Manny Ramirez, after chasing down Johnson's base hit down the right field line, stayed to yell at some Marlins fans heckling him in the right field corner. He was supposed to shift back toward center field for the Counsell at-bat, but instead he hugged the right field line. The Indians dugout frantically waved towels, imploring him to move toward right center, but either he ignored them or didn't see them.

The second mishap was Mesa throwing an 0-and-1 pitch down-and-in—the one spot Hargrove wanted to stay away from. Counsell's eyes lit up at Mesa's mistake—and he powered the ball far to straightaway right field, directly in front of his father. He thought he had perhaps one-hopped the outfield wall, that both Alou and Johnson would score to win the World Series. But Ramirez was where he wasn't supposed to be: under the ball. He caught it on the warning track, and only Alou was able to score on the sacrifice fly. The fact that Ramirez was out of position turned out to be a lucky stroke for Cleveland. But at the very least, Counsell had taken care of business. The game was tied, 2–2. John Counsell returned to his seat.

It was only the third Game 7 in World Series history to go into extra innings, and every pitch from then on meant heart palpitations. The Marlins reliever in the tenth inning, closer Robb Nen, had rarely thrown 100 mph before, but Tim swears he did that night. Then when the game droned on into the top of the eleventh inning, Tim thought Marlins reliever Jay Powell hit 100 mph as well. "I don't know if the guys were just juiced that night or what," Tim says. "But every strike, guys were yelling, 'Yeah!' And every ball, they were like, 'Ah, shoot.'"

Entering the bottom of the eleventh, the game was nearly four hours old. The Indians Game 3 starter, Charles Nagy, had replaced Mesa, and Bobby Bonilla opened the eleventh with a single. Reserve catcher Gregg Zaun then popped up a sacrifice bunt attempt for the first out, with Bonilla barely sliding safely back into first base. Up again walked Craig Counsell.

His father took another stroll to the right field foul pole, again hiding behind it, again hoping for karma. With the count 1-and-2, Counsell reached hastily for a middle-away pitch, rolling it over toward second baseman Tony Fernández. Counsell's first fear was that he'd hit into a routine, inning-ending double play. Fernández was a four-time Gold Glove fielder, as slick as they come. But whether it was the baseball gods or Fernández's nonchalance, the ball skipped under his glove into right field, an error.

Bonilla was the potential winning run on third base, with Counsell on first—one out. Rich's childhood dream had never been to score the winning run of a World Series Game 7; it'd been to *wave in* the winning run. He was just odd that way, but here was his chance. While Nagy was intentionally walking the ensuing batter, Jim Eisenreich, to load the bases, Rich remembers his heart rate escalating. The Indians third baseman Matt Williams walked over toward him to say, "I can't breathe, can you?" Rich answered, "No," and tried spitting through his teeth. "Nothing came out," Rich remembers. "Nothing but air."

The next batter, center fielder Devon White, hit a ground ball toward Fernández, who, instead of trying to end the inning with a double play, threw home to catcher Sandy Alomar for the force-out. Everyone moved up a base, which meant Craig Counsell stood on third next to Rich.

Tim was thrilled at the thought of his favorite player perhaps scoring the biggest run of his life. He was quite conscious that everyone could be mobbing Counsell in a minute. But Rich wasn't thinking that far ahead. It barely even registered with Rich that it was Counsell.

Rich's job was to instruct the runner at third, whoever that might be. Third base was the gateway to victory, to euphoria, to understanding, to heaven. But third base could also break their spirit if they let it. People have died at third—not in the literal sense, of course. But they've died just the same, whether they're baserunners in extra innings, like Craig Counsell, or middle-aged men who have been stopped short of finding peace . . . like Rich.

So Rich leaned in and told Counsell to be wary of the short backstop at Pro Player Stadium, that sometimes wild pitches or passed balls bounce right back to the catcher for easy outs at the plate. He also warned Counsell not to run carelessly into an out, knowing that the entire city of Miami would have both their heads if he did. They were in this together. Rich was his partner in crime, his wingman, his sage counselor, an adviser whose sole purpose was to wave Counsell in as soon as it was safe or apropos. In other words, he was Counsell's life coach.

The batter, with two outs, was Edgar Renteria, twenty-one years old, his whole baseball life ahead of him. Rich was fifty-one, his whole baseball life the curse of him. Either Rich's narrative was going to change or it wasn't, and this time, on an eleventh inning 0-and-1 slider from Nagy, Renteria sent a line drive up the middle.

The ball was tipped negligibly by Nagy's glove, sailing over second base and safely into center field. There were no words between Rich and Counsell, no direct order to run. Counsell just instinctively raced toward home, his hands held high over his head, and diligently stepped on the plate. He can't remember his thoughts as he leaped into the air toward his teammates, other than just a global feeling of bliss. "It's joy is what it is," he says. "It's just pure joy."

Rich's arms were extended in the air too as he paraded toward the group hug with Counsell at home plate. From there, he practically levitated to the simultaneous hugfest with Renteria near first base. "I jumped higher than I've ever jumped in my life, and I can't jump," Rich says. "You lose control of your whole being. It's an out-of-body experience."

He wanted to find Jim Leyland, his fellow coaches, Roberta, Tim, Mike—every one of his loved ones inside that stadium. But Tim, as he raced frantically out of the first base dugout, wanted only to find his father . . . to tell him about the miracle.

Tim had watched Renteria's at-bat from the far end of the dugout, facing the batter's box at a forty-five-degree angle. In his sight line, right above Renteria's head, was an electronic, digital scoreboard. On display was the score, the inning, the number of outs, the number of balls, the number of strikes . . . and the time of day.

Tim instantly put two and two together. His eyes, as if guided by the heavens, couldn't have been in a more strategic spot. Just as he had seen his friend Craig Counsell land on home plate, he had seen the scoreboard directly overhead. "Almost simultaneously," Tim says.

His face became ashen then, his mouth agape, tears filling up his eyes. He was wailing, for a completely different reason than the other 67,000 witnesses. He searched for his dad in the Counsell dogpile. Nothing. He searched for his dad in the Renteria dogpile. Nothing. Then, halfway between first and second base, Tim and Rich found each other's eyes.

"Dad! Dad! Look!"

"What do you mean, look?"

"Dad, behind you! Look at the clock!"

Rich wheeled around and saw the time: it was just past midnight.

"Dad! The chicken ran at midnight!" said Tim, screaming, weeping, hyperventilating. "Craig Counsell, the Chicken, scored the winning run at midnight!"

Rich Donnelly just about fainted.

Letter to Amy

Ames,
    It's me and Tim.
    You're here. You are here. YOU ARE HERE.

HOME

Twenty-Two

Did God Run
the Bases?

Rich and Tim embraced in the tightest, most comforting, most earnest hug of their lives. It was almost 12:10 a.m. before they let go. When they finally separated—mayhem all around them—Rich felt light-headed, limp. "Amy did this," he half whispered. "How could she say something five years before that made no sense? And then everything I ever wanted in my life in professional ball happened. It happened just the way she said it."

He could not stop the sobbing. These weren't tears of joy; these were tears of a miracle. These were outlier tears, especially for a middle-aged man who didn't entirely believe, who only halfheartedly had faith, who thought miracles in the Bible were lies. Rich looked up at the heavens and decided God was real, that Amy was on his shoulder, that he was right to put "The Chicken Runs at Midnight" on her tombstone, that he knew what it meant now, that in his opinion she had made his World Series dream come true and saved his soul all in one midnight trip around the bases.

He felt free, devoid of any weight or burden. He saw Jim Leyland running a lap around the field, gesturing thank-yous to the fans. So Rich followed his boss through the outfield grass, gesturing a thank-you to Amy up above.

The celebration eventually shifted to the clubhouse, where a large contingent of family members and media had congregated. There was no wiggle room at all. It was such a zoo that pitcher Alex Fernandez shouted, "Guys, into the trainer's room! Players and coaches only! Players and coaches only!"

There had been chatter for months that no matter how the team fared in the postseason, the owner Wayne Huizinga was going to break up the team, trade its parts bit by bit, let free agents walk. In a lot of ways, that made the title bittersweet. So Fernandez directed everyone into that training room for an "auld lang syne," to have every player and coach, one by one, deliver a testimonial.

Rich was afraid to enter, afraid to look these men in the eye, afraid of the new raw emotions, afraid to bare his soul, afraid they'd scoff at his miracle. He walked in out of pure obligation, but he lay low in the far reaches of the room.

"They were asking each player to get up and talk or say something funny," Rich says. "And I'm over in a corner, bawling my eyes out. I sort of hid behind the training table, and I said to myself, *Please, Alex, don't call me. Don't call me up. Don't. I'm embarrassed.* Nobody knew about this. Nobody knew about 'the chicken runs at midnight,' about what had happened. So I'm saying, *Please don't call on me. Please, Lord, don't let them call on me. Because I'll break up, and I don't want to break up in front of the team. I wanna be a man. I don't want to ruin it for everybody. I don't want to bring everybody down.*"

He slumped and hid himself skillfully enough that Fernandez either didn't see him or sensed he should spare him. Rich tried listening to the speeches of Kevin Brown, Bobby Bonilla, and Gary Sheffield, but they didn't resonate. What resonated, as he continued to bawl in the back of that room, was Amy's message on the note inside his black address book, the one from Atlanta five years before. He wanted the testimonials to end, wanted everyone out of that clubhouse—so he could have a private moment with that "While You Were Out" note, his last little physical piece of Amy.

By nearly 4 a.m., he got his wish. Tim and Mike were waiting by the clubhouse door as Rich, all alone by his locker, pulled out the note from Atlanta. He read it five times, ten times, twenty times—and imagined a phone call from Florida to heaven. "I wanna call you, Amy, so bad," he whispered. "And I wanna tell you that the chicken *did* run at midnight . . . *It did*."

He and the boys were home by dawn, but Rich couldn't comfortably sleep, not for twenty-four, forty-eight, or even seventy-two hours. He'd nod off temporarily, but then would be jolted awake by the magnitude of Counsell's "chicken run," by how mystical life truly was. As he lay there with insomnia, particularly the day after Game 7, he had the distinct feeling he'd been cleansed.

"It was like somebody just washed my body inside and pulled everything out of it," Rich says. "It was like I took a bath inside. I was still dirty going into Game 7, and it just washed everything out—all the crying did. I cried more that night than I did when Amy died. I couldn't stop. That's why when I was in that trainer's room, I was hiding. I was crying not because she died, but because of the message I felt she was trying to send me. When I found out that the chicken ran at midnight, it was like a flushing of my body."

There was so much to process in the ensuing days. Rich found himself piecing together the events of the previous weeks and months, events that at first seemed coincidental, but now felt to him like the intricate work of a higher power. For instance, how did Tim, in the most frenzied baseball moment of their lives, happen to connect "chicken" and "midnight" as Counsell was crossing the plate? Other than being perfectly positioned to see Counsell and the digital clock, how was he able to instantly grasp and then verbalize the correlation? Did God choose Tim as the messenger because Amy was his second mom? Was God trying to reach Rich through Tim? Why was Tim so fascinated by C.R.A.M. to begin with? Why was he the one kid who would say it ten, fifteen times a day while Amy was dying? Because God and Amy knew this eleventh inning moment was coming his way?

Tim marveled at all of this as well. He thought perhaps the C.R.A.M. seed had been planted in his head when the Marlins clinched the Braves series ten days prior. The final out that night had come close to midnight, which had prompted Tim to think of Amy and her epitaph. "I was sure Amy would've been proud of beating the Braves," Tim says. "And she and 'the chicken runs at midnight' kind of reentered my mind when we won that series. But I never thought about Craig Counsell playing the role of the chicken. Never."

Rich felt there were still more so-called coincidences that must have been preordained. What if the Marlins hadn't traded for Counsell? Was God responsible for that? Did God plant the trade in Bruce Kimm, Dave Dombrowski, and Dick Egan's collective minds? Did God dream up Counsell's ridiculous batting stance? If his stance had been normal and mundane, Counsell would have never become the chicken—so was God the one urging him to flap his skinny arms? Was it God who nicknamed him "the Chicken" through Tim? Was it God's idea to use Counsell as a conduit when he saw him in church that one day with Rich? Was that when God decided that the chicken named Counsell should actually run at midnight?

All of this crossed Rich's mind day and night. He wondered whether God—or maybe even Amy herself—orchestrated Game 7. In the ninth inning, when the Marlins trailed by a run, was it God or Amy who planted Manny Ramirez down the right field line rather than in right center? If Ramirez had followed orders, Counsell's game-tying sacrifice fly would've been a game-winning double instead. It would've all ended closer to eleven o'clock than midnight. "Exactly!" said Rich. "Counsell couldn't *knock in* the winning run—he had to *score* it! Destiny!"

In the eleventh inning, was it God or Amy who caused Tony Fernández—an all-world defender—to botch a slow-rolling ground ball? Just so Counsell could find his way on base? Was it God or Amy who made sure Counsell wound up on third, next to her dad?

Rich believed all of the above, believed none of it was a coincidence. For instance, Counsell scored the winning run at precisely 12:06 a.m.

But his actual at-bat against Charles Nagy began at the stroke of midnight. NBC, which was broadcasting the game nationally, even showed the exact time on the digital clock after Nagy's third pitch to Counsell: 12:01 a.m.

So, in total, Craig Counsell took a six-minute journey—from 12 a.m. to 12:06—around the bases. The Chicken definitely *ran at midnight*. Rich decided you couldn't make this stuff up, and it changed his life.

He would walk down the street and seem to hear harps in his head. "Is that the Tabernacle Choir?" he'd ask himself and Amy. He had spoken to Amy all the time after she died. But this was new—rarified and different. Now, in October 1997, Rich was in his first *two-way* conversation with Amy, with God.

By having the Chicken run at midnight, Amy had answered Rich with something more than words: a miracle. That's what he considered the winning run of the World Series to be—divine intervention. He thought back to the car ride after Game 5 of the 1992 NLCS. Amy assured everybody she had no idea why, in the backseat of Rich's car, she had blurted out, "The chicken runs at midnight." "It just came out," she said. But Rich believed now that it was a premonition, that it was clairvoyance. He was certain it hadn't just indiscriminately been spoken, that Amy knew exactly what C.R.A.M meant the whole time. *Maybe*, he thought, *that's why she was so upbeat during her last eleven months, that she knew she wasn't really going away after she died. She was going to be right there hovering over the ballpark every night, hovering over the third base coaching box, waiting to speak to me through Craig Counsell.*

"I got scared, actually scared," Rich says. "You hear all this stuff about how when people die they come back. They're with you. They don't haunt you, but they're there. I started to go, 'Wait. Wait a minute. Is this happening to me with Amy? She's here?' I mean, I'm not a miracle believer. I've read about miracles in the Bible. I've read about the parting of the Red Sea; I've read about the Ten Commandments, I've read about our Lord changing water into wine, about the loaves and the fish.

And that's what this felt like. It was like this moment should be in the Bible. 'The chicken runs at midnight' should be in the Bible."

He spent Christmas and then New Year's Day 1998 enjoying these fresh, wondrous two-way conversations with his daughter. He'd enter restaurants by himself, convinced he should ask the waitress for a table for two—for him and Amy. A World Series game had brought her back to him, to the point that he said, "Amy was completely in my life. She wasn't a person who had lived and died. She'd been born a second time."

He sensed Amy's forgiveness. All those times she'd asked him to play Whiffle ball in the backyard or basketball in the driveway, all those times he'd ignored her or worked out with Bubba instead or treated her like a mascot—he felt she was telling him, "It's okay." Cheating on Peggy, deserting the family, skewering Amy's heart—he felt she was telling him, "No worries." Taking the cruise with Jim Leyland even though she'd asked him to quickly come see her —he felt she was telling him, "You're off the hook." He says it was an indescribable feeling to have a clean slate on every level with Amy. But now he felt he needed to make peace . . . with everybody else.

He could hear her telling him he had work to do. He heard her say, in another two-way conversation, "Okay, you've got one more chance here to make amends and straighten yourself out—for good. What you did was terrible, but this is your reprieve."

So Rich began to call all the people he had wronged in his immediate family, a long list. He started with Peggy, telling her he was an "idiot" to treat her so thoughtlessly, that he'd "really messed up" as a husband, a father, and a man.

"Can you forgive me?" he asked.

"I already have," Peggy said. "You did the best you could. But you have to forgive yourself. That's the tough part."

He asked if he could speak to Tim, who happened to be home that night with Peggy. Tim was a strapping high school baseball player by this point, no longer the impressionable prepubescent who tagged along with Amy and Cindy. When he picked up the phone and said hello, Rich could hear the testosterone in his voice. Tim was a man.

"Can you forgive me, Tim?" Rich asked.

Other than Rich, no one had lived and breathed "the chicken runs at midnight" more than Tim. He was having his own conversations with Amy, though he was naive in terms of their gravity. He would just tell her C.R.A.M., and thank her for letting him see the stadium clock as Craig Counsell was scoring. It hadn't changed Tim, though, because Tim didn't need changing like Rich did.

Rich needed all the mercy he could get. He told Tim he was sorry, that he hadn't always been the best father, that he was way too domineering, that he felt bad about his role in the divorce, that he wished he had never yelled at him over the phone for striking out—because he used to hate it when Jerome did that.

Tim was stunned to hear all of this, though it was true he'd been scared of his dad over the years. One time at Three Rivers Stadium, before batting practice, Tim had playfully tried hitting a ball over the fence with a fungo bat. Instead, the ball hit Pirates coach Terry Collins, who'd been jogging along the warning track. Tim was so afraid Rich would whip him that he raced into the stands and hid in the upper deck for several innings of the game.

"In the past, my dad didn't want to forgive," Tim says. "If something happened, he'd give us the silent treatment, if anything, and it was kind of up to us to call him and get back in his good graces."

On the phone call, Tim gathered himself and, like Peggy, told his dad, "I've already forgiven you." The divorce was what hurt Tim the most, but time—along with "the chicken runs at midnight"—had healed the wound as far as he was concerned. He and Rich spent the next several minutes talking about Tim's grades, his high school team, and the 1998 Marlins season. "After that, I think he was a lot easier to talk to about just life in general and any problems I had," Tim says. "I could talk to him like a dad instead of more of a general, you know?"

Rich made all the family calls he could. Then after consulting with

Amy, he had to figure out how to handle the rest of the world. Because the chicken running at midnight in a World Series Game 7—on the biggest stage possible—was too enormous to keep to himself. He couldn't just internalize this. Maybe it couldn't be written into the Bible, but it *could* be written. It could help someone, somewhere, sometime.

He finally knew what to do with what he thought was a cruel, confusing move by God. He finally knew what to do with death.

Rich would tell a story.

Letter to Amy

Amy,
   This is your fault. You're going to make me go around the country in the middle of winter telling this story and telling people about you.
   Can't wait, Ames.

Twenty-Three

Spreading the Gospel

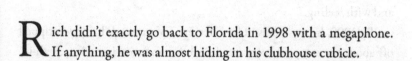

R ich didn't exactly go back to Florida in 1998 with a megaphone. If anything, he was almost hiding in his clubhouse cubicle.

He still had the same reticence he felt in the training room the night of the World Series win—afraid he'd melt down if he shared his story with the players. It was still too raw, too mystical, too personal. He told only one person in the organization: Jim Leyland. He told that guy everything.

Tim rarely visited during the season—he was a senior in high school chasing his own baseball career—but when he did, it was hard to act natural around the Chicken. Craig Counsell wasn't just a second baseman with an eccentric batting stance anymore; he was a mythical figure within the Donnelly family, a cult hero, a conduit of Amy's. But he was also a major league player, and Tim thought Counsell would be insulted if he were to hear about this nickname.

"That's another reason we kept the story private," Tim says. "I didn't want him to know I was calling him the 'Chicken Man.'"

It's not as if the story was a total secret. Rich had a friend in the local Miami media who had written an abridged version of C.R.A.M., although this was long before social media or a wide-ranging internet. The article had no chance of being retweeted or posted on Facebook pages. In other words, it came and went, like the wind.

The only reason John Cangelosi approached Tim with a furrowed

269

brow that season was, he says, because he had personally witnessed the post-midnight embrace between Tim and Rich, smack in the middle of the infield. Cangelosi says he overheard a hair of their conversation, but out of respect for their privacy hadn't delved into it further. But in the summer of 1998, he had a question for Tim.

"The rooster crows at midnight—what was that all about?" Cangelosi asked.

Tim tried his best to translate "rooster" into "chicken" for Cangelosi. But it was clear the story was going to keep circulating, and Rich decided he wanted to stay ahead of it, wanted to make sure it was told accurately and with feeling.

By 1999, he was ready. The Lifetime TV network had been tipped off about the story and contacted Rich for an interview. He was all-in, and the eight-minute piece was naturally a tearjerker. Several wives of big league players stumbled upon it. They told their husbands, and over the course of the next year, Craig Counsell began to hear chatter—either from players or fans who'd seen the TV piece—about him inspiring the Donnelly family, about him being some sort of chicken.

By then, neither Craig nor Rich was with the Marlins. Counsell had moved on to the Arizona Diamondbacks, while Rich had followed Jim Leyland to Colorado to become the third base coach for the Rockies. But Counsell wanted clarification, and during spring training 2000, he left word with the Rockies clubhouse to have Rich call the D-Backs clubhouse in Tucson.

Rich phoned back before dawn one morning, knowing that Counsell was always early to the facility during spring training. It was still dark outside when Counsell picked up, all alone in the D-Backs trainer's office.

According to Rich, Counsell casually asked how Tim and Mike were doing. Then he just came out and said, "I keep hearing I'm the chicken. What's this chicken?" Rich apologized for not telling him sooner and then took Counsell through Amy's apparent NLCS premonition of 1992 and then the midnight journey of 1997. Counsell got chills.

There was a discernible pause, but then overwhelming gratitude on Counsell's part. He found himself asking Rich, "Wait a second—why did we never talk about this in Florida?" But Counsell realized quickly that this was a personal story, that it was a story about family and about baseball, that it had probably been better off kept private. "This isn't about winning the World Series," Counsell would say later. "It's that Rich felt like he got another day with his daughter. In some magical way, Rich got that."

He thanked Rich for the call, hung up the phone, and closed the trainer's office door to be by himself. Craig needed time to process it all. He wanted to tell everybody and nobody. He wasn't sure he could do the story justice—so he just sat in the office with, if nothing else, reinforced faith. During his whole career in the big leagues, his nickname had been "Rudy"—because he was a Notre Dame underdog, just like the walk-on in the football movie *Rudy*. But he was now wrapping his arms around the nickname "the Chicken" and completely on board with it.

"I've always felt like this: it wasn't really me in the story," Counsell says. "I was just this character in the story almost. But I'm blessed to be in it. I'm just a small part in it. I'm just the guy with the goofy batting stance who got a nickname from Tim and Mike Donnelly. And if it wasn't for that crazy batting stance—some weird ideas in my head about how to hit—I wouldn't be the Chicken. So I'll take being the Chicken all day long."

Emboldened by the Lifetime piece and by Counsell's heartfelt approval, Rich began to spread the story, speaking to Catholic groups, not to mention high school and university groups. He would start by turning off the lights and popping in a VHS tape of the Lifetime feature. When he'd flip the lights back on, there wouldn't be a dry eye in the place. Then he'd express, especially to the men in the room, how he was turning his wrongs into rights. And how they all should learn from his past.

I was Amy's hero—and I didn't see it. She'd come sit with me in my Barcalounger. She just liked being with me. She'd say, 'Dad, let's go out back. Can you pitch to me?' And I'd say, 'I'll be out in a minute. I'm watching this game.' But if my boys asked me, I'd go out right away.

It's the regret I carry with me all the time. How stupid could I be? How selfish could I be? That meant the world to her to go play with her dad. So I beg all of you, if your daughter asks you to play anything, even tiddlywinks, go with her. If you have a daughter, don't be like me.

Every one of his speeches would end that way, with fathers in the crowd bawling, rushing home to their daughters. But the narrative got even better when Rich left Colorado in 2003 to become the third base coach for the Brewers. The Milwaukee shortstop was none other than Craig Counsell. Rich and the Chicken had been reunited. "He's part of our family," Rich would say. "He's like my son"—and more articles were written, more speaking engagements arranged.

In 2006, Rich became the third base coach for the Dodgers, and he was asked by manager Grady Little to share his story with the entire team, to a herd of hardened men. By the end, after Rich had pleaded with them to celebrate their daughters, the whole room applauded. Sandy Alomar Jr., who had been the Indians catcher the night of Craig Counsell's midnight run of 1997, happened to be in the audience that day as a first-year Dodger. And he walked up to Rich half grinning, half relieved.

"So the Chicken got us," Alomar said. "Why didn't you tell me we had no chance to win that night? Why didn't you tell me, Chicken Man? The Chicken story has to be told. We had no chance to win. If we'd known, we wouldn't have even played the seven games. We would've just given you guys the trophy."

Rich and the former Indians player embraced, with Alomar calling him "Chicken Man" the rest of their time in LA together. Via word of mouth, the story began to spread all over Major League Baseball. Soon hundreds of ballplayers knew of Amy Donnelly. Nomar Garciaparra,

Omar Vizquel, Jayson Werth, Brad Penny, Denny Neagle, Jack Wilson, Dioner Navarro, and Anibal Sanchez—to name eight—swore by the story, particularly Sanchez. The former Marlins pitcher had lost his firstborn, a son, to the dengue virus and was close to quitting baseball. But once he heard Rich's "the chicken runs at midnight" story, he was revived. A mutual friend connected him with Rich, and Sanchez thanked Rich personally, calling him his "hero."

By 2008, Rich was on the move again, hired once more by his childhood team, the Pirates, to be a minor league coordinator. He volunteered to give his Chicken speech to the organization's minor league coaches and staff, and just like in LA, many of the men broke down. Someone printed up "The Chicken Runs at Midnight" T-shirts and passed them out to the players. One of the minor league pitching coaches, a hulking former big leaguer named Brad Holman, had two daughters and couldn't get C.R.A.M. out of his mind. Since Holman's hobby was songwriting, he asked Rich if he could put the story to lyrics. Rich consented, and soon there was a "The Chicken Runs at Midnight" song. It began this way:

> *There was a coach up in the big leagues, not a worry in the world.*
> *He took life for granted until a phone call of a girl.*
> *She said, "Daddy, I'm sorry, I have to tell you something's wrong.*
> *The doctor says I have a tumor and I might not live too long."*
> *She went to watch them in the playoffs, and he was coaching on*
> *   third base,*
> *Yelling something to the runner with his hands around his face.*
> *And his team won the game that night and on the way home in*
> *   the car,*
> *She said, "What did you say to him when you were yelling*
> *   from afar?"*
> *CHORUS: "'The chicken runs at midnight,' is that what you*
> *   told him, Dad?"*
> *He said, "Honey, that is silly; what made you think of that?"*

The chicken runs at midnight—the imagination of a girl.
It probably should have been forgotten, but instead they're sacred
words.

Rich played the Holman CD probably fifty times the first night, gratified that he was paying Amy's story forward, just the way she'd asked him to in their two-way conversations. The good karma was following him around. He received a random call in early 2010 from John Canuso, the founder of the first-ever Ronald McDonald House, whose own daughter, Babe, had died as the result of leukemia. Canuso wanted to orchestrate an annual 12 a.m. 3K race in his hometown of Haddonfield, New Jersey, to benefit ill or challenged children in the area. But Canuso also wanted Rich to be the face of the event and name it, "The Chicken Runs at Midnight."

"How many runners you gonna have?" asked Rich when he arrived in Haddonfield for the race. "About forty?"

"No," said Canuso, "more like 2,500."

"How much money you going to raise?" Rich asked.

"I don't know—$4,000 or 5,000?" Canuso guessed.

The next morning, Rich and Canuso met for breakfast.

"How'd you do last night?" Rich asked. "Did you get your $5,000?"

"No, we didn't," Canuso said. "We raised $105,000."

Rich flew back home glowing, certain once and for all that he'd changed people's lives for the better. He felt he'd changed his as well, that he was walking the earth the way Amy would have walked it. He and Roberta had settled back into their life in Steubenville, where he could still see Tennis Shoe Ernie cleaning windows on the side of the main road, where he could still play racquetball every day with five-time world champion Sudsy Monchik, where the nuns were assuredly still playing college football parlays.

It was just a simple, contented life in the tri-state area . . . until Rich went in for a routine colonoscopy.

He woke up with cancer.

Letter to Amy

Amy,

Could you pester God for me? Could you pester him to let me exist?

I don't need no baseball, no racquetball, no golf, no Big Red [Steubenville High School] games, no visits to the Spot bar. I just want that one thing.

Just let me live a little longer so I can see my grandkids grow up.

Thanks, Ames.

Twenty-Four

How to Live and How to Die

E veryone says Roberta's not emotional, that she cries about once every thirty years. But on the day they found a tumor in Rich's colon, she made up for lost time.

When his anesthesia wore off that day—December 16, 2010—he saw Roberta's tormented face. He asked her what was wrong, and she tearfully told him they found a mass in his colon the size of a grapefruit.

The doctor happened to be one of his childhood pals from Steubenville, Dave Medich—they used to play roughneck football together in Rich's backyard—so Rich wasn't afraid to ask him straight out if he was going to die. Medich gave him a non-denial denial: "It's cancerous, Rich, and we've got to get it out."

When Medich left, Rich did what came naturally: he imagined a conversation with Amy. He says he asked his daughter for help, but what he heard back—over and over deep in his soul—was, "I've already taught you what to do."

From that moment on, Rich never once said, "Why me?" He never once punched his pillow or felt sorry for himself or yelled terse words toward the heavens. "No, I didn't," he says. "I told Roberta, 'Don't worry. Don't you worry. Whatever it is, I can handle this. I'll fight this till the end.'

"I turned into Amy. If I'd have had long blond hair, I'd have been Amy. I turned into Amy right there in the room. I know I did."

The next few months were painful and exhausting. Rich underwent surgery two days after Christmas 2010 and needed his two-way conversations with Amy to keep him sane, to keep him optimistic, to preserve his faith. Dr. Medich had to remove half of Rich's colon just to extract the hefty tumor and then re-attach it. The operation was taxing. Rich ended up losing forty pounds—shrinking from 200 pounds to 160—and had to stay twenty-four hours a day in a chair, because lying prone would cause his midsection and abdomen to pull. "For six weeks I felt like I had a tool box in my stomach," Rich says.

Bubba came to visit one day, and it lasted all of three minutes. At the time, Rich was downstairs in the basement, seated in his easy chair, and poor Bubba did a triple-take. "I was so thin, I was probably a cross between Ichabod Crane and Barney Fife," Rich says. "My broad shoulders—they looked like they were hanging on a hanger."

Bubba managed a weak, "How ya doin', Dad?"—then teared up and headed for the door. "He just walked out," Rich says. "Didn't say goodbye, didn't hug me or nothing. And I know what he was thinking: *That ain't my dad.* When I saw my own dad at the nursing home before he died, I had the same feeling—*That's not my dad.*"

But Rich wasn't truly alone in that basement; he had Amy. He sensed her by his side, could hear her pep talks loud and clear. When Amy was fighting her own cancer battle, she'd been worried about everyone but herself. The day she told Rich about her tumor, she'd said, "Dad, I'm sorry." Weeks before she died, she cared more about kids in red wagons than her red Miata. Sitting in his easy chair, too weak to eat, Rich flashed back to all of that.

"I just felt that no matter what happened to me the rest of my life, it wasn't anything near what she had gone through," Rich says. "I felt like, *Are you kidding me? Are you complaining about this? Look what she went through.* She had gone through the ultimate—and the ultimate means you're going to die, for sure. She went through the ultimate pain without being depressed. She went through the ultimate—there's nothing more ultimate than death. And she went through that at her age and cared about everybody else.

"So I said, 'I'm gonna try. I don't think I can match her. But I'm going to for sure try to be like her and not complain. Just be thankful for all the years that I've had. Just like she was.'"

Six months following the operation, Rich was back coaching in the Mets organization. God—he was convinced it was at Amy's prodding—had answered his prayers for health, and had given him baseball back to boot. Through an organization called "Catholic Athletes for Christ," he began delivering his "the chicken runs at midnight" speeches again all over the country. But this time, he had an ending, a punch line, a message that made his audience want to faint or praise God. At the least, it gave all of them goose bumps. In his speeches before the 1997 World Series, "the chicken runs at midnight" was just an amusing comment by a dying, altruistic teenager. But after the 1997 World Series, the phrase became a sign from heaven, a reason to believe, a teenager's prophecy that came true, a message from God that our loved ones are always with us from above.

Rich's journey was even more poignant now. He'd talk about how two of the most iconic playoff series in major league history—the 1992 NLCS and the 1997 Fall Classic—had connected life's dots for him. He'd tell audiences that the ultimate test for a person is when things go south. He'd say, "Amy's last eleven months were the key to this whole thing. Her last eleven months were more powerful than her first seventeen years."

Then with the audience in the palm of his hands, he'd wrap a bow around his speech by pausing, softening his voice, and saying, "My daughter wanted to be a teacher, and everyone thinks it's a shame she never got there. But Amy *was* a teacher—she taught me how to live . . . and she taught me how to die."

There'd be tears and then heartfelt applause. Every one of these speeches was a way to keep Amy alive, all over the country and the world.

Rich ended up being inducted into the Sports Faith International Hall of Fame that year, along with the late Steelers owner Art Rooney. After all his indiscretions, that was the other miracle. Rich had made the wrong Hall of Fame—not baseball's, but faith's. Or maybe he'd made the right one.

Roberta framed Amy's "While You Were Out" message from Atlanta and hung it beside the door leading to their Steubenville garage. She knew it helped to keep her husband on the straight and narrow, knew it needed to be the narrative in Rich's mind as he began each day. Rich would read it on his way out, say a word or two to Amy, and live the next twenty-four hours with a purpose. Then he'd do it all over again.

He prayed for entry back into the major leagues, and he's convinced that God—again at Amy's prodding—made it happen. In 2014, one of his former players with the Buccos, Lloyd McClendon, was named manager of the Seattle Mariners. He called Rich and invited him to be his third base coach. Rich let out a whoop and a thank you to the heavens. That made it forty-four years in professional baseball and fourteen in the third base coaching box—his home away from home.

On his first trip into Texas that year to play the Rangers, he and McClendon shared a cab to the new ballpark in Arlington on Randol Mill Road. Rich was unusually subdued on the ride, and McClendon had a feeling why. When the cab arrived at the field, McClendon turned to Rich and said, "You want me to come with you?"

Rich's answer was, "No, I think I'm better off alone." McClendon then climbed out of the cab so Rich could head to Amy's grave.

The cemetery was on the same street as the ballpark, Randol Mill Road—not a coincidence, according to Rich. Without baseball, there never would've been a "chicken runs at midnight." Without him coaching third or without the Craig Counsell trade, Amy's ending would've been different—and probably hollow. As much as baseball tore Rich and Amy—and the entire Donnelly family—apart, it had later brought them together tenfold. So, of course, the Rangers built their new stadium on the same street as Amy's cemetery. Baseball seemed to be in charge here.

When Rich arrived at Moore Memorial Gardens, he began looking for the oak tree next to the man-made lake. That had long been his landmark for finding Amy's headstone. The problem was, the graveyard had tripled in size since 1993. Fifteen more oak trees had been planted, and hundreds more tombstones had been laid down. Rich couldn't locate Amy.

He went to the cemetery's main office to ask a woman at the desk for help and bluntly said, "My daughter's buried here, and I can't seem to find where she is."

"What's her name?"

"Amy Donnelly. But there's also something strange written on it."

"Don't tell me. 'The chicken runs at midnight,'" the woman said. "You're her dad?"

"Yeah, I am."

"Do you know how many people come to see her here?" the woman went on. "Thousands. Thousands. Thousands come to visit and take a look."

He got his own chills at that moment—"the chicken runs at midnight" chills. Rich had done it—he'd saved others' lives and his own life, no question about it. He figured the rest of his days he could handle anything, which came in handy later that year when he was diagnosed with cancer again.

This time, it was prostate cancer, his second tumor in four years. His doctors told him he had three choices: remove the prostate, get radiation for thirty-five straight days, or have radioactive seeds inserted to destroy the cancerous cells over time. He chose the seeds and ended up treating the ordeal as if it was nothing, simply a blip. Another person might have panicked over a second bout of cancer, might have surmised that cancer was going to kill them. But Rich sensed Amy in his ear again, telling him that she had his back, telling him, "Dad, I got this."

She was his partner in crime, his wingman, his sage counselor. In other words, Amy was Rich's life coach. He was stuck on third base, a middle-aged man who for his whole life had been stopped short of finding peace. Third base was his gateway to victory, to euphoria, to understanding, to heaven. He didn't want to end up stranded there. People have died at third—not in the literal sense, of course, but they've died there just the same.

So Amy turned the tables—Rich says she morphed into his third base coach. He says he heard her advising him, heard her say, "I know how to give you peace, Dad. Listen to me good. Go . . . Go back to how you were as a young kid; go back to where you were happiest. Go back to your special place. Go back to where you were an altar boy in Steubenville, where you said the Serenity Prayer every night from your knees. Go back to your roots. Go back to church. Continue to be a good husband and father. You messed up, but you're forgiven now, Dad. You're forgiven. Just don't you dare do it again."

Then Amy crouched, cupped her hands, and waved her father home.

Afterword

Ever since I began sharing my "chicken runs at midnight" story, I've met a thousand Amys. It never fails. I'll be in a church hall, a conference room, or a university auditorium, and a woman will shake my hand and say, "You know, my name is Amy too." It warms my heart every time.

I can't get enough of my own Amy, which is why I'm thrilled about this book. When Craig Counsell, the Chicken, scored the winning run at midnight in Game 7 of the 1997 World Series, my family and I kept it quiet at first. We just didn't think anybody would be interested. And then I started thinking about how Amy had spent her last eleven months. She knew she was going to have to go through chemo. She knew she was going to be stuck in a hospital. She knew she was going to suffer. She knew she was going to die. And yet her biggest concern was everybody else—making sure that sick children got wagon rides, worrying how her mom and little brother were coping, doing things for others. Who does that?

So I said, "You know what? I don't know the results of my life yet. I don't know if I'm going to die in eleven months. I might die tomorrow, or I might die in ten or twenty years. So if she could help people from her sickbed, the least I can do is help people from my healthy bed, so to speak. The least I can do is tell this miracle story—as a testament to her."

And this book is the whole story. Nothing was held back. People probably didn't know that at one time Amy hated her dad. Just about a handful of years before her death, she wanted nothing to do with me. They don't know that. They don't know that her dad broke up a perfect family. My dream was to reach the big leagues, marry a beautiful girl, and have adorable kids. Well, I had four wonderful kids and a nice three-bedroom house with a two-car garage. Everything I dreamed of had happened. It happened. And then I tore it apart. I screwed it up. It wasn't Peggy's fault. She's amazing. It wasn't anything she did; it wasn't the kids. It was me. All of the selfish things I did. I'm the one who tore it apart. All these people who meet me—they think, *Oh, you're so wonderful.* If they knew the half of what I've done, they wouldn't say that. So this book has exposed me—but in a good way.

It taught me how to walk with God, how to be a better father, husband, friend, coach, and sportsman. That's why I've told the "chicken runs at midnight" story thousands of times to anyone who will listen. I do it because it changed my heart and my mind, and I hope it changes your heart and the heart of somebody you know or love.

This story has made heroes out of people in the same way that Amy was a hero, and I can vouch for that, because I've seen it with my own eyes. Let me give you an example. I adopted my second wife Roberta's two daughters, Tiffany and Leighanne, when they were young, which means they heard all about Amy and the chicken runs at midnight. Well, on the night of October 1, 2017—twenty years after Craig Counsell scored his winning run—Tiffany and Leighanne attended the Route 91 Harvest music festival on the Las Vegas Strip. A gunman suddenly opened fire, and my two daughters thought they were goners.

As they fell into a panic, a woman in front of Leighanne was shot in the face. Instead of staying down in the fetal position, Leighanne got up, removed her blouse, and used it as a tourniquet to control the woman's bleeding. With bullets still coming, Leighanne then lay gently over the woman to protect her, shouting to Tiffany, "We are not leaving this girl behind!"

A minute later, another woman sitting near Tiffany was shot in the stomach. Like her sister, Tiffany made a tourniquet and used her body to shield the victim. She screamed back at Leighanne, "We are not leaving these girls. If we die, we die!"

But they didn't die—that's the point—and when I heard their story that night, I thought of Amy of course. The girls were heroes, just like her, and had been inspired by C.R.A.M.—there was no doubt in their minds and in my mind. It turned out that "the chicken runs at midnight" had saved more lives.

And I'm not done. On January 7, 2018, my son Mike, who was in the dogpile with Counsell on the night Craig scored the Game 7 winning run in 1997, was killed trying to save another person's life.

Mike was a troubled soul, and I blame myself for that. After I broke apart our family, I wasn't there for him, wasn't around enough to make sure he stayed on the straight and narrow. After being a placekicker for University of the Cumberlands in Kentucky, he fell on hard times. He was arrested multiple times and served time in jail. But this past fall, he was out of prison and turning his life around. He had kept old letters from Amy, and they seemed to help energize him. He saw one she mailed to him way back in October 1992, just a few days after she'd first said, "The chicken runs at midnight." Here she was, dying at the time, but she still wrote this letter:

Mike—

Hey! This past weekend was great! You look great! I was so glad we got to see each other. Oh well. We will be up for hopefully one of your games and one of Bubba's. We are going to see if we can get to both of y'all's games in the same weekend. Keep kicking, 'cause you're going to be a pro, and I want a huge house on the lake and I'm sure Dad and Mom and the other two will put their orders in soon!

With all my love,

Amy!

Mike treasured that old letter, and his brother Tim remembers seeing Mike over Christmas 2017 and thinking he was finally pulling it together. Then on that ill-fated night—January 7, 2018—Mike was driving down a three-lane Dallas, Texas, highway. He saw a stranded car blocking two of the lanes. There'd been an accident, and a man and a woman were trying to push the car to the side of the road. He pulled over to help and told the woman that he'd take over for her. Just then, there was a flash of light. Another car was barreling in their direction at a high speed. Mike, with one arm, grabbed the woman's shirt and yanked her out of the way so she wouldn't be hit. But in the process of saving her life, he lost his. He was run over by the car and died instantly.

He wasn't just a good Samaritan; my son was a martyr. He died for someone else—for a woman who was raising twins. He got her out of the way and jumped in front of the car, and I truly believe he was taught to be selfless by Amy—by Amy's strength and by Amy's story. I believe that the miracle in 1997 had led him to save a life in 2018, to be a hero just like Amy. Oh, and I should mention that he died just before midnight.

When I flew to Texas for Mike's funeral, I lost it. It had been twenty-five years. Amy died in January 1993, but it felt like I'd been at that same cemetery ten minutes ago signing a paper and getting ready to bury her. I'm thinking, *You're in the exact same place; the only difference is your other kids are grown up now.* Bubba was there, with his two daughters. Tim was there with his baby. Last time I'd been in that cemetery, Bubba was in college and Tim was twelve or thirteen years old. So I sat in the parking lot, thinking, *Who would have ever thought I'd be back in that building again to bury another child?* It was a tough day.

It was a very cold morning, about ten degrees outside, but the first thing I did at the cemetery was walk to Amy's grave. I stood over it and had a talk with her. I said, "Amy, can you believe this? Can you believe we're back here?" I stood there for twenty minutes, freezing, but I didn't care. I just felt I was with her. I was talking to her right there. We used to kid about Mike's head being big, and I told her, "Can you believe they even have a casket to fit his big head into?" Because that's the way she would talk. She would say, "They probably don't have one big enough for you, Bucket Head." So I was at her grave crying, laughing. Amy was comforting me again, just as if she was there.

I went back to our house on the cul-de-sac after Mike's funeral and wandered into the backyard. I hadn't been there since Amy's funeral, and I stood by a fence and looked out and remembered the kids running through here. I remember the day we played hide-and-seek and I jumped over the fence and hooked my pants on the fence, and there I was, hanging on the fence, upside down, and Amy came around the corner saying, 'You're it; you're it. We found you.' And I just cried my eyes out.

I've talked to her a lot since Mike died. If she'd been around, she'd have made sure everyone had enough to eat at the house. Or she'd have said, "Hey, we're going to clean the garage. If you're not going to help, get the heck out of the way." She'd have been wonderful. She'd have said, "Dad, he's finally at peace. It's okay." I felt she was there, putting her arms around me. When I was at the graveyard, that's what I felt. She was there with Bubba and Tim, hugging me, saying, "Dad, it'll be okay."

If my faith was at 100 percent before—and it was—it's even more now. The woman whose life my son saved just found out she's pregnant with a boy, and she says she'll be naming him Mike. The saga just keeps growing.

I believe in the magic of "the chicken runs at midnight," and I hope you will spread that magic with me. I pray that everyone who reads this book will pass it on. I want to show people how a seventeen-year-old girl with eleven months to live was happy. I honestly can't find a picture of her not smiling after she got cancer, after she got the tumor. I can find plenty before where she wasn't. But after? It's like a miracle. She did not frown. She did not waver. She left a legacy.

So I will crisscross this country getting the message out. Whether it's in your town or my town, please come up and say hello. Please come up and tell me you learned just one-tenth of what I learned.

Even better if your name is Amy.

Rich Donnelly, Steubenville, Ohio

Acknowledgments

T*he Chicken Runs at Midnight* isn't just a book title or a mantra; it's a way of life. People gravitate toward its message—one of hope—and they rally around it, just like they've rallied around me during this project. I want to thank my wife, Robin, and my one-in-a-million children, Cole and Riley, for their sacrifice and smiles as I chased this tale. I bow down with gratitude to my parents, Patricia and Edward, as well as to my brother, Robert, and my sisters Jennifer Friend-Kerr and Amy Roberts (of course I have a sister named Amy).

I thank my agent Andrew Blauner, for believing in me and this book when no one else did. I am grateful for Matt Baugher of HarperCollins Christian Publishing and his dogged belief that Zondervan and *The Chicken Runs at Midnight* were a match. I was lucky to have Zondervan's wise John Sloan—in his swan song—providing me with sage editing advice. Other editors and staffers Carolyn McCready, Dirk Buursma, Kim Tanner, Betsy Fata, Beth Silfin, Kait Lamphere, Curt Diepenhorst, and the indefatigable Brandon Henderson were trustworthy advisers and beyond impressive.

Bruce Nicki and James Sheets of VSI media were swift and precise with their interview transcriptions. I also want to acknowledge the salt-of-the earth Jeff Ausiello, who helped me first bring this story to life for ESPN, and also others in Bristol such as Tim Kurkjian, Jon Fish, Robert Labay, Victor Vitarelli, Craig Lazarus, Denny Wolfe, and John Skipper.

I want to thank my friends Tom Wald, Gary Pener, Johnny Sweet, Grant Halverson, and Jeff Freedman for their unwavering support.

More than anything, this book would not have happened without Cindy Sample, Peggy Donnelly, Tim Donnelly, Bubba Donnelly, Roberta Donnelly, Patti Katic, Marlene Stanko, and the late great Mike Donnelly. Their endless graciousness, cooperation, and enthusiastic storytelling were the core of this project. I am grateful for the insight provided by Jim Leyland, Mike Hargrove, John Cangelosi, Anibal Sanchez, Brad Holman, Donnie Teramana, Dewey Guida, Gary Kessler, Jerry Barilla, John Counsell, and, most of all, Craig Counsell, who besides having great timing is the baseball man everyone should admire and emulate.

Finally, the most heartfelt thank you—along with a standing ovation—goes to Rich Donnelly, God's third base coach, who opened up his life, his pain, his awakening, and his hometown of Steubenville, Ohio, to make this book a reality. His ability to recall the letters he received from Amy is priceless, and he is an inspiration to us all, particularly in the way he has coped with both life and death.

And then there's . . . Amy Donnelly. I feel like I knew her. And after reading this, I hope you do too.

C.R.A.M.
Tom Friend, April 2018